The International Collection

Canadian Living

The International Collection

Home-Cooked Meals From Around the World

BY THE CANADIAN LIVING TEST KITCHEN

Transcontinental Books

{editor's note}

Canadian cooking has been largely built upon a foundation of recipes that were brought to this country by immigrants. While much of what is considered "Canadian food" originated in the British Isles, France and eastern Europe, our cuisine now gets inspiration from across the globe. Asian, African, Middle Eastern, Latin American and countless other cooking styles have become integral parts of the beautiful mosaic that makes up Canada's culinary culture.

Canadians are special because we hang on to our cultural diversity. In fact, The Canadian Living Test Kitchen consists mainly of first- and second-generation Canadians. My own father, a proud Canadian, was born and raised in Scotland and still has an accent despite living here for decades. Being proud of our varied ethnicities doesn't take away from our patriotism. If anything, our "glowing hearts" are big enough to hold affection for all that we are – and all that Canada represents.

Another thing we all agree on: We don't want complicated recipes that require multiple trips to specialty stores and hours of prep time – especially when we could just as easily get authentic ethnic food at a restaurant. That's why we in The Test Kitchen have risen to the challenge. This book is a delicious collection of easy-to-prepare, Tested-Till-Perfect dishes – from appetizers to desserts – that have origins around the world and use common staples. And for those recipes with authentic ingredients, we've provided everyday supermarket substitutions.

These recipes represent the new Canadian food. Enjoy. And cook them with pride.

—Annabelle Waugh, food director

Opposite: Baked Fennel Parmesan (page 139). Page 2: Mini Alfajores (page 273)

TRANSCONTINENTAL BOOKS

1100 René-Lévesque Boulevard West
24th Floor
Montreal, Que. H3B 4X9
Tel: 514-340-3587
Toll-free: 1-866-800-2500
canadianliving.com

Bibliothèque et Archives nationales du Québec
and Library and Archives Canada
cataloguing in publication

Main entry under title :
The international collection : home-cooked meals
from around the world
"Canadian living".
Includes index.
ISBN 978-0-9813938-5-8
1. Cooking, International. I. Canadian Living Test
Kitchen. II. Title: Canadian living.
TX725.A1I57 2011   641.59   C2011-941063-X

Project editor: Christina Anson Mine
Copy editor: Jill Buchner
Indexer: Gillian Watts
Art direction and design: Chris Bond
Front cover design: Michael Erb

Printed in Canada
© Transcontinental Books, 2011
Legal deposit – 3rd quarter 2011
National Library of Quebec
National Library of Canada
ISBN 978-0-9813938-5-8

We acknowledge the financial support of
our publishing activity by the Government
of Canada through the Canada Book Fund.

For information on special rates for
corporate libraries and wholesale purchases,
please call 1-866-800-2500.

{contents}

Rosemary Shrimp in Sherry (page 16),
Sesame Roasted Eggplant Purée (page 18)
and Clams in Garlic and White Wine (page 17)

{appetizers}

Italian The tighter and more compact the artichoke, the fresher it is. To eat one, pull off each leaf, dip it in butter and pull it between your teeth to release the tender bottom, then discard the tough leaf. Once the leaves are gone, cut up the heart, which is known as the jewel in the crown.

Steamed Artichokes With Lemon Pesto Butter

1 **lemon,** halved

6 **large artichokes** (about 2½ lb/1.125 kg)

LEMON PESTO BUTTER:
¾ cup **butter,** softened

¼ cup chopped **fresh basil**

3 tbsp grated **Parmesan cheese**

1 tsp grated **lemon zest**

1 tbsp **lemon juice**

Pinch each **salt** and **pepper**

1 clove **garlic,** minced

Rubbing all cuts with lemon as you work, trim artichoke stems to level. Using serrated knife, cut off top third of each artichoke. With scissors, snip off thorny tips of remaining leaves. Open centre leaves slightly. Using teaspoon, scrape out tiny centre leaves and hairy choke beneath. Set artichokes aside.

LEMON PESTO BUTTER: In food processor, blend together butter, basil, Parmesan cheese, lemon zest, lemon juice, salt and pepper until smooth. Stir in garlic. Spoon 2 tbsp into centre of each artichoke; set remaining butter mixture aside. *(Make-ahead: Cover and refrigerate artichokes and butter separately for up to 24 hours.)*

Place steamer basket in wok or shallow pan; add enough water to come 1 inch (2.5 cm) under basket. Cover and bring to boil; reduce heat to medium-high. Stand artichokes in basket; cover and steam until outer leaf is easily pulled off, about 35 minutes.

Microwave remaining butter mixture until melted. Place in centre of platter for dipping; surround with artichokes.

Makes 6 servings. PER SERVING: about 260 cal, 4 g pro, 24 g total fat (15 g sat. fat), 10 g carb, 3 g fibre, 75 mg chol, 369 mg sodium. % RDI: 8% calcium, 9% iron, 24% vit A, 17% vit C, 20% folate.

Italian This recipe shows how elegant and flavourful a dish can be with just a few honest, high-quality ingredients. Use a vegetable peeler to shave the Parmesan into pretty curls.

Beef Carpaccio With Arugula

In spice grinder or in mortar with pestle, coarsely crush together mustard seeds, peppercorns and fennel seeds.

Spread spice mixture on waxed paper; roll beef in mixture to coat. In large heavy skillet, heat 1 tbsp of the oil over medium-high heat until ripples form on surface; sear beef all over just until spices are browned, about 45 seconds per side. Refrigerate beef until cold. Wrap tightly in plastic wrap and freeze until firm, about 2½ hours.

Using sharp carving knife, slice beef as thinly as possible. Divide arugula among 8 plates; top with beef. Sprinkle with capers, Parmesan cheese and salt; drizzle with remaining oil. Serve with lemon wedges to squeeze over top.

Makes 8 servings. PER SERVING: about 266 cal, 18 g pro, 20 g total fat (5 g sat. fat), 3 g carb, 1 g fibre, 40 mg chol, 471 mg sodium. % RDI: 20% calcium, 21% iron, 14% vit A, 15% vit C, 27% folate.

2 tsp **mustard seeds**

2 tsp **black peppercorns**

1½ tsp **fennel seeds**

1 lb (450 g) **beef tenderloin premium oven roast**

½ cup **extra-virgin olive oil**

8 cups **baby arugula**

2 tbsp **capers,** drained and rinsed

3 oz (85 g) **Parmesan cheese,** shaved

1 tsp **sea salt** or salt

Lemon wedges

{appetizers}

Italian Nothing is more rewarding than making your own dough for this crescent-shaped ravioli-style pasta. You'll usually find this type of pasta appetizer only in restaurants, but it's a sumptuous start to a home-cooked feast.

Squash Agnolotti With Sage and Walnuts

1 small **butternut squash** (about 2 lb/900 g), halved

½ cup **smooth ricotta cheese**

¼ cup grated **Parmesan cheese**

1 tsp **salt**

½ tsp **pepper**

¼ tsp **grated nutmeg**

⅓ cup **butter**

24 **fresh sage leaves**

¼ cup chopped **walnut halves**, toasted

PASTA:
2 cups **all-purpose flour**

3 **eggs**

½ tsp **salt**

In greased baking dish, roast squash, cut side down, in 425°F (220°C) oven until tender, about 45 minutes. Meanwhile, drain ricotta in fine sieve for 30 minutes. Peel and mash squash; measure 2 cups into bowl. Mix in ricotta, Parmesan cheese, ¾ tsp of the salt, ¼ tsp of the pepper and nutmeg. *(Make-ahead: Cover and refrigerate for up to 24 hours.)*

PASTA: Mound flour on work surface; make well in centre. Add eggs and salt to well; **beat** with fork, working around well and gradually incorporating most of the flour into egg mixture, to form ragged dough. Knead for 10 minutes, working in enough of the remaining flour to make smooth dough. Wrap and let rest for 20 minutes.

Divide into thirds; wrap 2 pieces separately. On floured surface, roll out remaining piece into 5-inch (12 cm) long strip; dust with flour. Feed through widest setting of pasta machine until edges form smooth line, folding dough in half and lightly flouring after each pass. Set machine to next narrowest setting; **roll** dough through once without folding. Repeat rolling dough through until next-to-finest setting is reached, cutting dough in half if awkward. Flour dough; run through finest setting.

Using 3-inch (8 cm) round cutter and 1 length of dough at a time, cut out rounds; set aside in single layer. Place 1½ tsp squash mixture off-centre on each round; brush edge with water. Fold in half; **pinch** edge to seal. Place on cornmeal-dusted baking sheets. Repeat with remaining dough and filling. *(Make-ahead: Cover with damp towel; refrigerate for up to 3 hours.)*

In large pot of boiling salted water, cook agnolotti until tender but firm, about 6 minutes.

Meanwhile, in skillet, melt butter over medium heat; fry sage leaves and remaining salt and pepper until fragrant, 2 minutes. Pour into warmed pasta serving bowl. Drain agnolotti and add to bowl; toss with walnuts.

Makes 8 servings. PER SERVING: about 253 cal, 8 g pro, 15 g total fat (7 g sat. fat), 22 g carb, 2 g fibre, 93 mg chol, 669 mg sodium. % RDI: 11% calcium, 12% iron, 51% vit A, 13% vit C, 22% folate.

~ *beat* ~

~ *roll* ~

~ *pinch* ~

Spanish Shrimp scented with rosemary and sherry are irresistible – and ready in a flash. Serve with Clams in Garlic and White Wine (opposite), Sesame Roasted Eggplant Purée (page 18) and a crisp white wine for a relaxed Spanish tapas menu.

Rosemary Shrimp in Sherry

2 tbsp **extra-virgin olive oil**

2 cloves **garlic,** minced

1 lb (450 g) **raw colossal shrimp** (size 12 to 15), peeled and deveined (tails intact)

1 tbsp **fresh rosemary leaves**

¼ cup **dry sherry** or semidry sherry

½ tsp each **salt** and **pepper**

¼ tsp **hot pepper sauce**

In large skillet, heat oil over medium-high heat; sauté garlic until light golden and fragrant, about 10 seconds.

Add shrimp and rosemary; sauté just until shrimp are pink, about 1 minute. Add sherry, salt, pepper and hot pepper sauce; sauté until liquid is reduced by half, about 3 minutes.

Makes 4 servings. PER SERVING: about 168 cal, 17 g pro, 8 g total fat (1 g sat. fat), 2 g carb, trace fibre, 129 mg chol, 417 mg sodium. % RDI: 5% calcium, 16% iron, 4% vit A, 3% vit C, 3% folate.

Spanish Clams are a favourite dish along Spain's sunny coasts. Ladle these clams into small bowls and offer plenty of crusty bread to soak up the delicious broth.

Clams in Garlic and White Wine

Cut prosciutto into strips. In large skillet, heat oil over medium heat; fry prosciutto until crisp, about 2 minutes. Using slotted spoon, transfer to paper towel–lined plate to drain.

Add garlic, half of the parsley and the hot pepper flakes to pan; fry for 1 minute. Add wine; bring to boil over medium-high heat. Add clams; cover and steam until clams open, about 5 minutes. Discard any that do not open.

Sprinkle with prosciutto and remaining parsley.

Makes 6 to 8 servings. PER EACH OF 8 SERVINGS: about 42 cal, 3 g pro, 2 g total fat (trace sat. fat), 2 g carb, trace fibre, 7 mg chol, 34 mg sodium. % RDI: 2% calcium, 19% iron, 3% vit A, 10% vit C, 3% folate.

2 thin slices **prosciutto** or serrano ham

1 tbsp **extra-virgin olive oil** or butter

6 cloves **garlic,** minced

⅓ cup chopped **fresh flat-leaf parsley**

¼ tsp **hot pepper flakes**

½ cup **dry white wine**

2 lb (900 g) **littleneck clams** or Manila clams

Mediterranean Baking or grilling eggplant gives it a wonderfully smoky flavour and velvety texture. Serve this purée on a platter with flatbreads and crusty bread.

Sesame Roasted Eggplant Purée

1 large **eggplant** (1 lb/450 g)

1 **sweet red pepper**

4 cloves **garlic,** peeled

2 tbsp **extra-virgin olive oil**

2 tbsp chopped **fresh cilantro**

2 tbsp **tahini**

1 tbsp **sherry vinegar**

¾ tsp each **salt** and **pepper**

½ tsp toasted **sesame seeds**

Place eggplant and red pepper on foil-lined rimmed baking sheet; pierce eggplant all over with fork. Place garlic on separate square of foil; drizzle with 1 tsp of the oil. Wrap foil up around garlic; add to baking sheet. Bake in 400°F (200°C) oven until eggplant and pepper skins are blackened and eggplant and garlic are soft, about 45 minutes. Let cool.

Cut eggplant in half; scrape flesh into food processor, discarding skin. Peel and seed pepper; add to food processor along with roasted garlic, 1 tbsp of the remaining oil, the cilantro, tahini, vinegar, salt and pepper. Purée until smooth. *(Make-ahead: Cover and refrigerate for up to 24 hours.)*

Spoon into shallow serving dish. Drizzle with remaining oil; sprinkle with sesame seeds.

Makes 2 cups. PER 1 TBSP: about 19 cal, trace pro, 1 g total fat (trace sat. fat), 1 g carb, trace fibre, 0 mg chol, 54 mg sodium. % RDI: 1% iron, 1% vit A, 10% vit C, 1% folate.

TIP | ROUND OUT YOUR TAPAS MENU WITH STORE-BOUGHT STAPLES. TRY A MIX OF OLIVES, CHEESES, SLICED CURED MEATS OR SAUSAGE, NUTS AND ROASTED OR MARINATED VEGETABLES. IF YOU CAN'T FIND SPANISH VERSIONS, USE OTHER MEDITERRANEAN TIDBITS INSTEAD.

SPICE BLENDS

Every cuisine has its unique spice blends, which give local foods their characteristic flavours. Here are a few to make and keep on hand in your international pantry. Store them in an airtight container in a cool, dark place for a month or two.

CHINESE FIVE-SPICE POWDER

• Mix together equal parts cinnamon, ground cloves, ground Szechuan or black peppercorns, ground fennel seeds and ground star anise. Some blends contain ground ginger instead of Szechuan pepper; experiment to find your favourite combination.

HERBES DE PROVENCE

• Mix together ¼ cup each dried marjoram or oregano, dried thyme and dried savory; 1 tsp each dried basil and rosemary; and ½ tsp dried sage. **Makes 1 cup.**

MALAY-STYLE CURRY POWDER

• In skillet, toast spices separately as follows over medium-low heat, shaking pan, until slightly darkened and fragrant.

5 to 6 minutes: 3 tbsp coriander seeds

2 to 3 minutes: 1½ tsp whole cloves, 1 tsp white peppercorns, ½ tsp black peppercorns, 2 sticks cinnamon and half whole nutmeg, broken in pieces

1 to 2 minutes: 2 tbsp fennel seeds, 4 tsp cumin seeds and 2 tsp aniseed

30 seconds: 1 tsp fenugreek seeds

10 seconds or until a shade darker: 7 tsp turmeric and 2 tsp cayenne pepper

• In clean coffee grinder, grind toasted spices (except turmeric and cayenne), ½ tsp black cardamom seeds and 6 whole green cardamom pods until in fine powder. Strain through fine sieve into bowl. Return any coarse bits to grinder and grind until fine; add to bowl. Mix in turmeric and cayenne. Let cool completely. **Makes ½ cup.**

GARAM MASALA

• Lightly crush 2 tsp green cardamom pods. Reserve seeds; discard pods. Break half cinnamon stick into pieces. In skillet over medium heat, toast cardamom seeds, cinnamon, 4 tsp each cumin seeds and coriander seeds, 2 tsp black peppercorns, and 1½ tsp whole cloves, stirring, until slightly darkened and fragrant, 1 to 2 minutes. Let cool. In clean coffee grinder, grind to powder. **Makes ⅓ cup.**

ZAHTAR

• With fingers, crush 1¼ tsp dried thyme until powdery. In small skillet over medium heat, toast thyme, ¾ tsp ground sumac (or 2 tsp grated lemon zest), ½ tsp sesame seeds and pinch salt until fragrant, about 3 minutes. **Makes 2 tsp.**

Greek These rolls, called dolmades in Greece, are a bit fiddly to make, but their sunny cinnamon, mint and lemon flavours are the reward for all that hard work.

Stuffed Vine Leaves

⅓ cup **extra-virgin olive oil**

3 **green onions,** thinly sliced

2 cloves **garlic,** minced

1 small **onion,** minced

⅔ cup **short-grain rice**

2 tbsp **dried currants**

2 tbsp **pine nuts**

2 tbsp **lemon juice**

½ tsp **salt**

¼ tsp **cinnamon**

1 cup **boiling water**

1 tbsp each chopped **fresh dill** and **fresh mint**

1 jar (500 mL) **preserved grape leaves**

In skillet, heat half of the oil over medium heat; fry green onions, garlic and onion, stirring occasionally, until softened, about 5 minutes. Stir in rice, currants, pine nuts, lemon juice, salt and cinnamon; pour in boiling water and bring to boil. Cover and reduce heat to low; simmer until rice is slightly softened, about 10 minutes. Stir in dill and mint; let cool.

Meanwhile, drain and separate grape leaves. In large bowl, cover 32 of the larger most-intact leaves with boiling water; soak for 10 minutes. Drain and chill in cold water; drain and pat dry.

Place each leaf, shiny side down, on work surface. Spoon 1 tbsp of the rice mixture in centre near stem end; fold sides over and roll up neatly. Place, leaf-tip side down, in clean skillet.

Drizzle with remaining oil; add enough water to come two-thirds up sides of rolls. Cover with a few of the remaining leaves.

Cover pan and bring to boil; reduce heat and simmer gently until rice is tender and almost no liquid remains, about 35 minutes. Uncover; let cool. *(Make-ahead: Refrigerate in airtight container for up to 2 days.)*

Makes 32 pieces. PER PIECE: about 44 cal, 1 g pro, 3 g total fat (trace sat. fat), 5 g carb, 1 g fibre, 0 mg chol, 151 mg sodium. % RDI: 1% calcium, 2% iron, 2% vit C, 2% folate.

Middle Eastern Hummus is usually made with chickpeas, but there are versions made with other pulses. Drizzle this golden dip with a little extra-virgin olive oil, if desired. Serve it with celery, carrots and toasted pita wedges.

Lentil Hummus

In large pot of boiling salted water, cover and simmer lentils until tender yet still retaining their shape, about 10 minutes. Drain; let cool to room temperature.

In food processor, purée together lentils, tahini, lemon juice, oil, salt and pepper until smooth. Stir in parsley and garlic. Transfer to small serving bowl. *(Make-ahead: Cover and refrigerate for up to 24 hours.)*

Makes 2¼ cups. PER 1 TBSP: about 34 cal, 2 g pro, 2 g total fat (trace sat. fat), 3 g carb, 1 g fibre, 0 mg chol, 37 mg sodium. % RDI: 4% iron, 2% vit C, 14% folate.

1 cup **dried red lentils**

¼ cup **tahini**

3 tbsp **lemon juice**

3 tbsp **extra-virgin olive oil**

½ tsp each **salt** and **pepper**

¼ cup minced **fresh parsley**

2 cloves **garlic,** minced

TIP | TAHINI, A MIDDLE EASTERN STAPLE, IS SIMPLY A PASTE MADE BY GRINDING SESAME SEEDS. IT'S WIDELY AVAILABLE IN SUPERMARKETS.

Greek One sheet of phyllo makes a soft, slightly crisp wrapper for these triangular cheese-filled pastries. For a crunchy version, use two sheets, brushing with butter between layers. Serve with the Greek licorice-flavoured liqueur called ouzo.

Tyropitakia

FILLING: In bowl, beat together feta, ricotta and Romano cheeses, eggs, pepper, cinnamon and nutmeg until fairly smooth with some larger chunks. Stir in walnuts, green onions, parsley and dill. *(Make-ahead: Cover and refrigerate for up to 24 hours.)*

Place 1 sheet of the phyllo on work surface, covering remainder with damp towel to prevent drying out. Brush lightly with some of the butter; cut lengthwise into 4 equal strips.

Spoon about 1 tbsp of the filling about ½ inch (1 cm) from end of each strip. Fold 1 corner of phyllo over filling so bottom edge meets side edge to form triangle; fold up triangle. Continue folding triangle sideways and upward to end of strip, without wrapping too tightly. Repeat with remaining phyllo and filling.

Place triangles on parchment paper–lined rimless baking sheets; brush with some of the remaining butter. *(Make-ahead: Cover with plastic wrap; refrigerate for up to 24 hours. Or freeze until firm; layer between waxed paper in airtight container and freeze for up to 2 weeks. Bake from frozen, increasing baking time by 5 minutes.)*

Bake in top and bottom thirds of 400°F (200°C) oven until golden, about 15 minutes.

Makes 36 pieces. PER PIECE: about 77 cal, 3 g pro, 6 g total fat (3 g sat. fat), 4 g carb, trace fibre, 24 mg chol, 127 mg sodium. % RDI: 5% calcium, 3% iron, 4% vit A, 2% vit C, 5% folate.

TIP | PHYLLO SHEETS THAT ARE DRY, CRUMBLY OR BADLY TORN ARE TOUGH TO WORK WITH AND CAN LET FILLING SEEP OUT DURING BAKING. IF OUTER SHEETS ARE TOO TORN TO USE, DISCARD THEM AND TAKE NEW SHEETS FARTHER DOWN IN THE STACK.

9 sheets **phyllo pastry**

⅓ cup **butter,** melted, or extra-virgin olive oil

FILLING:

1¼ cups crumbled **feta cheese** (about 6 oz/170 g)

¾ cup **ricotta cheese**

½ cup finely grated **Romano cheese** or shredded Asiago cheese

2 **eggs**

½ tsp **pepper**

¼ tsp **cinnamon**

Pinch **nutmeg**

½ cup chopped **walnuts**

2 **green onions,** minced

3 tbsp chopped **fresh parsley**

3 tbsp chopped **fresh dill**

Russian These small baked pastries – here with two simple, traditional fillings – are served as hearty appetizers, as snacks with tea or as partners for soup. They're wrapped in convenient store-bought butter puff pastry, but you can use homemade puff pastry or your favourite flaky pie pastry instead.

Piroshki

1 pkg (1 lb/450 g) **butter puff pastry**

1 **egg yolk**

1 tbsp **milk**

Salmon Filling or Cabbage Filling (recipes, below right)

Unroll pastry; using 3-inch (8 cm) round cutter, cut out circles, rerolling scraps. Whisk egg yolk with milk; brush some lightly over edge of each circle. Place scant 1 tbsp filling in centre of each; fold over dough and pinch edge lightly to seal.

Place on parchment paper–lined baking sheet; brush lightly with some of remaining egg mixture. Prick each top once with fork. Bake in 400°F (200°C) oven until golden, about 25 minutes.

Makes 24 pieces. PER PIECE (WITH SALMON FILLING): about 101 cal, 3 g pro, 6 g total fat (3 g sat. fat), 8 g carb, 1 g fibre, 30 mg chol, 95 mg sodium, 39 mg potassium. % RDI: 5% iron, 3% vit A, 2% vit C, 2% folate.

TIP | IF YOUR PASTRY IS A LITTLE STICKY, INVERT IT ONTO A LIGHTLY FLOURED SURFACE AND PEEL OFF THE PAPER.

Salmon Filling

Mix together 4 oz (115 g) skinless salmon fillet, finely diced; 1 hard-cooked egg, finely chopped; 2 tbsp finely chopped fresh parsley; ¼ tsp salt; and pinch pepper. In small skillet, melt 1 tbsp butter over medium heat. Fry 2 tbsp finely diced onion until softened, 3 to 4 minutes. Let cool slightly; mix into salmon mixture. **Makes about 1¼ cups, or enough for 24 piroshki.**

Cabbage Filling

In small saucepan, melt 2 tbsp butter over medium heat. Fry half small onion, finely diced, and 1 small clove garlic, minced, for 2 minutes. Add 2 cups finely chopped cabbage (white inner leaves only), and ¼ tsp each salt and pepper. Cook, stirring often and reducing heat if cabbage is browning, until cabbage is tender and no liquid remains, about 10 minutes. **Makes about 1¼ cups, or enough for 24 piroshki.**

Turkish Dip croûtes or crunchy fresh vegetables into this tangy, piquant spread known as muhammara in Turkish. It's also lovely as a condiment alongside roast pork, lamb or chicken thighs.

Roasted Pepper Pomegranate Dip

1 cup chopped **roasted red pepper**

½ cup toasted chopped **walnuts**

½ cup toasted **fresh bread crumbs**

1 **jalapeño pepper,** seeded and minced

1 tbsp **pomegranate molasses** (see page 264)

½ tsp **ground cumin**

½ tsp each **salt** and **pepper**

2 tbsp **extra-virgin olive oil**

2 cloves **garlic,** minced

2 tbsp minced **fresh parsley**

In food processor or blender, purée together red pepper, walnuts, bread crumbs, jalapeño pepper, pomegranate molasses, cumin, salt and pepper until smooth. With machine running, add oil in thin steady stream. Stir in garlic. *(Make-ahead: Refrigerate in airtight container for up to 2 days.)*

Stir in parsley just before serving.

Makes 1 cup. PER 1 TBSP: about 52 cal, 1 g pro, 4 g total fat (trace sat. fat), 3 g carb, 1 g fibre, 0 mg chol, 110 mg sodium. % RDI: 1% calcium, 2% iron, 5% vit A, 37% vit C, 4% folate.

Middle Eastern Strips of juicy, well-spiced chicken served with a velvety sauce are an irresistible treat all over the Middle East. Soak the wooden skewers in water for at least 30 minutes to prevent scorching.

Sumac Chicken Skewers With Lemon Yogurt Sauce

LEMON YOGURT SAUCE: Line sieve with double thickness cheesecloth; set over bowl. Spoon in yogurt; cover and let drain in refrigerator for 1 hour to make about ½ cup. *(Make-ahead: Refrigerate for up to 24 hours.)* In bowl, whisk together yogurt, parsley, lemon zest, lemon juice, salt and pepper. *(Make-ahead: Cover and refrigerate for up to 2 days.)*

In separate bowl, whisk together oil, sumac, parsley, garlic and cayenne. Cut chicken crosswise into ¼-inch (5 mm) thick strips; add to oil mixture and toss to coat. Thread 1 strip onto each of about twenty 6- or 8-inch (15 or 20 cm) soaked wooden skewers. *(Make-ahead: Cover and refrigerate for up to 8 hours.)*

Place on greased foil-lined rimmed baking sheet. Broil 6 inches (15 cm) from heat until no longer pink inside, about 5 minutes. Sprinkle with salt. Serve with lemon yogurt sauce.

Makes 20 pieces. PER PIECE: about 44 cal, 4 g pro, 2 g total fat (1 g sat. fat), 1 g carb, 0 g fibre, 12 mg chol, 73 mg sodium. % RDI: 2% calcium, 1% iron, 2% vit A, 2% vit C, 1% folate.

TIP | SUMAC, A TART SEASONING USED AS FAR BACK AS ROMAN TIMES, IS AVAILABLE IN MIDDLE EASTERN AND SPECIALTY MARKETS. IF YOU CAN'T FIND IT, SUBSTITUTE 1 TSP EACH GRATED LEMON ZEST AND SWEET PAPRIKA.

2 tbsp **extra-virgin olive oil**

1 tbsp **ground sumac**

1 tbsp chopped **fresh parsley**

2 cloves **garlic,** minced

Pinch **cayenne pepper**

12 oz (340 g) **boneless skinless chicken breasts**

¼ tsp **salt**

LEMON YOGURT SAUCE:

1 cup **Balkan-style plain yogurt**

1 tbsp chopped **fresh parsley**

½ tsp grated **lemon zest**

1 tsp **lemon juice**

¼ tsp each **salt** and **pepper**

Indian Spring roll wrappers are an easy substitute for pastry around these tasty snacks. And the Coriander Chutney (below) is a must to put over top. To get the perfect texture for the garlic and ginger, use a fine grater or rasp.

Spiced Lamb Samosas

1 tbsp **vegetable oil**

1 small **sweet onion** (12 oz/340 g), diced

1 lb (450 g) **ground lamb**

3 tbsp minced **hot green peppers,** seeded if desired

2 cloves **garlic,** finely grated

1 tbsp finely grated **fresh ginger**

1¼ tsp **garam masala** (recipe, page 19)

¾ tsp **ground cumin**

¾ tsp **ground coriander**

¾ tsp **salt**

¼ tsp **ground allspice**

¼ tsp **cinnamon**

⅓ cup **green peas**

¼ cup chopped **fresh cilantro**

¼ cup chopped **green onion**

16 square (8-inch/20 cm) sheets thawed **frozen spring roll wrappers**

1 **egg yolk**

Vegetable oil for frying

In large nonstick skillet, heat oil over medium-low heat; fry onion, stirring, until translucent, about 15 minutes. Remove from pan; set aside.

In same pan, sauté lamb over medium-high heat until no longer pink, 5 minutes. Spoon off 2 tbsp fat. Add hot peppers, garlic and ginger; cook over medium heat, stirring often, for 3 minutes. Stir in garam masala, cumin, coriander, salt, allspice and cinnamon; cook for 3 minutes. Stir in peas and reserved onion. Stir in cilantro and green onion.

Cut spring roll sheets in half. Mix egg yolk with 1 tsp water. One at a time, lightly brush some over edges of pastry. Spoon 2 tbsp of the filling about ½ inch (1 cm) from end. Fold 1 corner of wrapper over filling so bottom edge meets side edge to form triangle. Fold up triangle. Continue folding triangle sideways and upward to end of wrapper; fold flap over to adhere. Repeat with remaining wrappers, yolk mixture and filling. *(Make-ahead: Freeze on baking sheet until firm. Transfer to airtight containers and freeze for up to 1 month. Cook from frozen.)*

In deep fryer or large saucepan, heat about 1½ inches (4 cm) oil until deep-fry thermometer registers 350°F (180°C). Deep-fry samosas, in batches and turning once, until golden and heated through, 4 minutes. Using slotted spoon, remove and drain on paper towel–lined tray.

Makes 32 pieces. PER PIECE: about 79 cal, 3 g pro, 5 g total fat (2 g sat. fat), 5 g carb, trace fibre, 16 mg chol, 94 mg sodium, 56 mg potassium. % RDI: 1% calcium, 3% iron, 2% vit A, 5% vit C, 3% folate.

Coriander Chutney

In food processor, purée together 4 cups fresh cilantro leaves; ¼ cup water; half green finger hot pepper, seeded; 4 tsp lemon juice; and ¼ tsp salt until smooth. *(Make-ahead: Refrigerate in airtight container for up to 4 hours.)* **Makes about 1 cup.**

Indian Pappadams, an Indian cracker bread, are available in mini size, and in a variety of flavours, in Indian grocery stores and some supermarkets. If you can't locate them, serve the salad on toasted pita wedges, rice crackers or melba toasts.

Chicken Tikka Salad on Pappadams

In saucepan of simmering water, cover and poach chicken until no longer pink inside, about 12 minutes. Drain; let cool. Finely chop.

In bowl, whisk together yogurt, almond butter, mayonnaise, lemon juice, cumin, coriander, salt, turmeric, ginger and cayenne pepper; stir in chicken, apple, green onion and currants. *(Make-ahead: Cover and refrigerate for up to 24 hours.)*

Mound heaping 1 tsp onto each pappadam; garnish with cilantro leaves.

Makes 50 pieces. PER PIECE: about 20 cal, 2 g pro, 1 g total fat (trace sat. fat), 2 g carb, trace fibre, 4 mg chol, 39 mg sodium. % RDI: 1% calcium, 1% iron.

TIP | IF YOU HAVE LEFTOVER COOKED CHICKEN OR TURKEY, YOU CAN USE 2½ CUPS DICED INSTEAD OF COOKING THE CHICKEN BREASTS.

2 **boneless skinless chicken breasts**

⅓ cup **Balkan-style plain yogurt**

2 tbsp **almond butter** or cashew butter (or 1 tbsp natural peanut butter)

2 tbsp **light mayonnaise**

1 tbsp **lemon juice**

1 tsp **ground cumin**

1 tsp **ground coriander**

½ tsp **salt**

½ tsp **turmeric**

Pinch **ground ginger**

Pinch **cayenne pepper**

½ cup finely chopped cored **Granny Smith apple**

¼ cup finely chopped **green onion**

¼ cup **dried currants** or chopped raisins

50 **mini pappadams**

Fresh cilantro leaves or fresh mint leaves

French Serve small slices of this rich duck and pork pâté with Dijon mustard and pickles as an appetizer or as part of a buffet. Serve large slices with a crisp, lightly dressed green salad as a plated appetizer. The pastry makes it a bit more involved than other pâtés, but it's well worth the effort.

Pâté en Croûte

1 boneless **pork loin centre chop** (about 6 oz/170 g)

2 **boneless skinless duck breasts** (about 8 oz/225 g each)

3 tbsp **brandy**

1 tbsp chopped **fresh thyme**

¾ tsp **pepper**

Pinch **ground allspice**

2 tbsp **unsalted butter**

1 **onion,** finely diced

4 oz (115 g) **duck liver,** or pork or chicken liver, finely chopped

2 **bay leaves**

¾ tsp **salt**

¼ tsp **nutmeg**

¼ cup **dry white wine**

1½ lb (675 g) **pork belly**

2 **eggs**

¼ cup **whipping cream**

1 **egg yolk**

PASTRY:

2⅔ cups **all-purpose flour**

½ tsp **salt**

⅔ cup cold **unsalted butter,** cubed

2 **egg yolks**

¼ cup **sour cream**

¼ cup **cold water**

PASTRY: In bowl, whisk flour with salt. Using pastry blender, cut in butter until in fine crumbs. Whisk yolks, sour cream and water; drizzle over flour, tossing with fork and pressing to form ragged dough. Halve; press into squares. Wrap; refrigerate for 30 minutes or up to 24 hours.

Thinly slice pork and 1 of the duck breasts across the grain; place in bowl. Stir in brandy, 2 tsp of the thyme, ¼ tsp of the pepper and allspice; cover and refrigerate for 30 minutes or up to 1 hour. Meanwhile, in skillet, melt butter over medium heat; cook onion until softened, 6 minutes. Add liver, bay leaves, salt, nutmeg, and remaining thyme and pepper; cook for 5 minutes. Stir in wine; cook until no liquid remains, 2 minutes. Transfer to large bowl; let cool. Discard bay leaves. Cut pork belly and remaining duck breast into chunks; in food processor, purée until smooth. Stir into liver mixture along with eggs and cream.

On floured surface, roll out 1 pastry square to scant ¼-inch (5 mm) thickness; cut into 14- x 5-inch (35 x 12 cm) rectangle. Place on parchment paper–lined baking sheet. Leaving 1-inch (2.5 cm) border, spread with half of the pâté. Lay duck and pork slices lengthwise over top; spread with remaining pâté. Turn pastry up over sides. Whisk egg yolk with 2 tsp water; brush some over pastry. Roll out remaining pastry to 14- x 8-inch (35 x 20 cm) rectangle. Place over pâté, pressing to seal. Trim excess; cut decorations for top. Brush top with yolk mixture; press on decorations. Refrigerate for 1 hour. Cut 2 holes in top; insert rolled-up parchment paper into holes for steam vents. Brush with yolk mixture.

Bake in 400°F (200°C) oven for 20 minutes. Reduce heat to 350°F (180°C); bake, covering with foil if browning and spooning off any fat, until digital thermometer registers 170°F (77°C), 50 minutes. Transfer to clean parchment paper–lined baking sheet; let cool. *(Make-ahead: Cover and refrigerate for up to 3 days. Bring to room temperature to serve.)*

Makes 12 to 16 servings. PER EACH OF 16 SERVINGS: about 517 cal, 15 g pro, 43 g total fat (18 g sat. fat), 17 g carb, 1 g fibre, 182 mg chol, 237 mg sodium, 243 mg potassium. % RDI: 3% calcium, 30% iron, 77% vit A, 2% vit C, 40% folate.

French Puff pastry makes this classic tart easy to work with and gives it the richness and elegance that people love in appetizers. If anchovies are not a favourite, replace them with ⅓ cup sliced roasted red peppers.

Pissaladière

QUICK PUFF PASTRY: Set aside ¾ cup of the butter in refrigerator. In food processor, blend flour with salt. Sprinkle remaining butter over top; pulse until in fine crumbs, about 10 seconds. Sprinkle with reserved butter; pulse 4 or 5 times to cut into pea-size pieces. Drizzle cold water over mixture. Pulse 6 to 8 times until loose ragged dough forms (do not let ball form). Transfer to floured waxed paper; gather and press into rectangle. Dust with flour; top with waxed paper. Roll out into 15- x 12-inch (38 x 30 cm) rectangle.

Remove top paper. Starting at long edge and using bottom paper to lift pastry, fold over one-third; fold opposite long edge over top, bringing flush with edge of first fold to make 15- x 4-inch (38 x 10 cm) rectangle. Starting from 1 short end, roll up firmly; flatten into 5-inch (12 cm) square. Wrap and refrigerate until firm, about 1 hour. *(Make-ahead: Refrigerate for up to 2 days or freeze in airtight container for up to 2 weeks.)*

In large skillet, heat oil over medium-low heat; cook onions, garlic, thyme, bay leaf, pepper and sugar, stirring occasionally, until caramelized and reduced to about 1½ cups, 45 to 55 minutes. Stir in wine; set aside.

Meanwhile, divide puff pastry in half. On lightly floured surface, roll out each half into 9-inch (23 cm) square; place each on parchment paper–lined rimless baking sheet. Refrigerate until firm, about 30 minutes.

Drain and rinse anchovies; pat dry. Cut lengthwise in half. Divide onion mixture over puff pastry squares, spreading evenly; sprinkle with Gruyère cheese. Arrange anchovies over top. Place olive halves at 2-inch (5 cm) intervals over top to make 1 per serving when cut. Refrigerate for 15 minutes. *(Make-ahead: Refrigerate for up to 24 hours.)*

Bake in top and bottom thirds of 425°F (220°C) oven, switching and rotating pans halfway through, until golden and crusty, 20 to 25 minutes. Let cool for 5 minutes before cutting each into 16 squares.

Makes 32 pieces. PER PIECE: about 103 cal, 2 g pro, 8 g total fat (4 g sat. fat), 7 g carb, 1 g fibre, 16 mg chol, 110 mg sodium. % RDI: 4% calcium, 3% iron, 5% vit A, 7% folate.

¼ cup **extra-virgin olive oil**

3 **Spanish onions,** thinly sliced

3 cloves **garlic,** thinly sliced

2 tsp minced **fresh thyme**
   (or 1 tsp dried thyme)

1 **bay leaf**

¼ tsp **pepper**

¼ tsp **granulated sugar**

1 tbsp **white wine** or wine vinegar

1 can (50 g) **anchovy fillets**

1 cup shredded **Gruyère cheese**

16 **black olives,** pitted and halved

QUICK PUFF PASTRY:

1 cup cold **unsalted butter,** cut in
   ½-inch (1 cm) cubes

1⅔ cups **all-purpose flour**

¾ tsp **salt**

⅓ cup **cold water**

French This warm, rich and creamy fish dip never goes out of style. Serve it with a rustic flatbread, such as Lavash (page 101), or sliced baguette, such as our homemade Épi de Blé (page 94).

Brandade de Morue

Rinse fish well in cold water; place in large bowl. Pour in enough cold water to cover fish by 2 inches (5 cm); cover and refrigerate, changing water 3 times, for 24 hours. Drain.

In saucepan, cover fish with cold water and bring to boil over medium-high heat; reduce heat and simmer until fish flakes easily when tested, about 3 minutes. Drain; let cool. Remove skin and bones; flake with fork.

Peel potato; cut into chunks. In pot of boiling salted water, cover and cook potato until tender, about 20 minutes. Drain.

Meanwhile, in saucepan, bring cream, garlic, bay leaf, thyme and nutmeg to simmer over medium heat. Reduce heat to low; cover and simmer until garlic is tender, about 15 minutes. Discard bay leaf.

In food processor, purée together fish, potato, cream mixture, all but 1 tbsp of the oil, lemon juice and pepper just until smooth; scrape into 4-cup (1 L) ovenproof serving dish. *(Make-ahead: Let cool; cover and refrigerate for up to 3 days. Heat, covered, in 400°F/200°C oven, stirring once, until hot, about 20 minutes.)*

Drizzle with remaining oil. Broil about 8 inches (20 cm) from heat until golden, 3 to 5 minutes.

Makes 3 cups. PER 1 TBSP: about 40 cal, 5 g pro, 2 g total fat (trace sat. fat), 1 g carb, 0 g fibre, 13 mg chol, 412 mg sodium. % RDI: 2% calcium, 1% iron, 1% vit A, 2% vit C, 1% folate.

1 pkg (14 oz/400 g) **salt cod**

1 large **baking potato**

½ cup **10% cream**

2 cloves **garlic,** thinly sliced

1 **bay leaf**

1 tbsp chopped **fresh thyme** (or 1 tsp dried thyme)

Pinch **nutmeg**

¼ cup **extra-virgin olive oil**

2 tsp **lemon juice**

¼ tsp **pepper**

Baltic Sweet-sour pickled herring salad pairs beautifully with potato latkes. If it's not your thing, try any of the Assorted Latke Toppings (opposite).

Latkes With Herring Apple Salad

4 large **russet potatoes** (2½ lb/ 1.125 kg), peeled

1 large **onion,** quartered

1 **egg,** lightly beaten

¼ cup **all-purpose flour**

¾ tsp **salt**

½ tsp **baking powder**

¼ tsp **pepper**

Vegetable oil for frying

HERRING APPLE SALAD:

1 cup sliced **pickled herring**

Half **Granny Smith apple,** cored and cut in matchsticks

⅓ cup thinly sliced **red onion**

1 tsp **cider vinegar**

¼ tsp **granulated sugar**

¼ tsp each **salt** and **pepper**

HERRING APPLE SALAD: In bowl, gently toss together herring, apple and onion. Sprinkle with vinegar, sugar, salt and pepper; toss. *(Make-ahead: Cover and refrigerate for up to 24 hours.)*

Using coarse grater, alternately shred potatoes and onion quarters. Place in colander or sieve; with hands, squeeze out as much liquid as possible. In large bowl, stir together potato mixture, egg, flour, salt, baking powder and pepper.

In large skillet, pour in enough oil to come ½ inch (1 cm) up side; heat over medium-low heat. For each latke, spoon scant ¼ cup potato mixture into oil, pressing lightly with fork to flatten and leaving about 1 inch (2.5 cm) space between latkes.

Cook, turning once, until golden and crispy, 6 to 9 minutes. Drain on paper towel–lined baking sheet. Serve topped with herring apple salad.

Makes about 16 pieces. PER PIECE: about 202 cal, 5 g pro, 14 g total fat (1 g sat. fat), 16 g carb, 1 g fibre, 14 mg chol, 317 mg sodium, 278 mg potassium. % RDI: 3% calcium, 6% iron, 5% vit A, 15% vit C, 7% folate.

TIP | THESE CRISPY CAKES ARE BEST SERVED HOT, BUT YOU CAN MAKE THEM AHEAD AND SERVE THEM AT ROOM TEMPERATURE IF YOU PREFER.

ASSORTED LATKE TOPPINGS

DUCK CONFIT

• Heat in small pan in 400°F (200°C) oven, turning once, until hot, about 10 minutes. Remove skin; tear meat from bone into bite-size pieces. Top each latke with 1 tbsp Chunky Maple Pear Sauce (recipe, below), small piece of confit and fresh parsley leaf. Look for confit packages in fine food stores. Two legs (one 10-oz/280 g pkg) provide 6 oz (170 g) meat, enough for 36 latkes.

CHUNKY MAPLE PEAR SAUCE

• Peel, core and chop 3 pears into bite-size chunks. In saucepan, bring pears, 2 tbsp each lemon juice and water, and ¼ tsp nutmeg to boil. Cover and simmer, stirring, over medium-low heat until tender, about 20 minutes. Mash until chunky. Stir in 2 tbsp maple syrup. Let cool. *(Make-ahead: Refrigerate in airtight container for up to 3 days or freeze for up to 2 weeks.)* **Makes 2 cups.**

COLD SMOKED, HOT SMOKED OR CURED FISH

• Top each latke with 2 tsp crème fraîche or sour cream, small piece of smoked fish or gravlax and sprig of dill. Varieties to try include: cold smoked salmon or char; hot smoked salmon, trout or mackerel; and gravlax. You need about 8 oz (225 g) smoked fish or gravlax for 36 latkes.

CAVIAR

• Demand for this salted sturgeon roe has driven the species to the brink of extinction. Instead of beluga, osetra and sevruga caviar, try less-pricey, more eco-friendly farmed caviar from American sturgeon (black hackleback or pearly grey paddlefish). Or try salmon, whitefish or flying fish. Top each latke with crème fraîche or sour cream and about ¼ tsp caviar; sprinkle with finely chopped fresh chives. You need about 2 oz (55 g) caviar for 36 latkes.

GRILLED ARTICHOKES

• Drain oil-packed grilled artichoke hearts (available in jars in Italian grocery stores); cut into quarters. Top each latke with 2 tsp sour cream, crème fraîche or Roasted Red Pepper Relish (recipe, below), then artichoke quarter. You need 9 artichoke hearts for 36 latkes.

ROASTED RED PEPPER RELISH

• Drain 1 jar (500 mL) roasted red peppers and pat dry; finely chop. In bowl, combine red peppers; 1 green onion, sliced; 2 tbsp chopped fresh parsley; 1 small clove garlic, minced; 1 tbsp white balsamic or wine vinegar; 1 tbsp extra-virgin olive oil; ½ tsp granulated sugar; and pinch pepper. *(Make-ahead: Refrigerate in airtight container for up to 24 hours.)* **Makes 2 cups.**

Whisky Cheddar Spread (opposite)
with Oatcakes (page 90)

British A creamy, irresistible spread like this is an excellent make-in-advance dish to serve at a party. Stir up a classic manhattan to serve alongside for a very happy cocktail hour.

Whisky Cheddar Spread

On small rimmed baking sheet, toast hazelnuts in 350°F (180°C) oven until golden and fragrant, about 6 minutes. Let cool; coarsely chop.

In food processor, purée together Cheddar cheese, butter, whisky, mustard and pepper until smooth. Pulse in ¼ cup of the hazelnuts just until mixed. Scrape into bowl; sprinkle with remaining hazelnuts. *(Make-ahead: Cover and refrigerate for up to 3 days.)*

Makes 2 cups. PER 1 TBSP: about 57 cal, 3 g pro, 5 g total fat (3 g sat. fat), trace carb, trace fibre, 14 mg chol, 76 mg sodium. % RDI: 6% calcium, 1% iron, 4% vit A, 1% folate.

⅓ cup **hazelnuts**

2 cups diced **extra-old Cheddar cheese** (10 oz/280 g), at room temperature

¼ cup **butter,** softened

2 tbsp **Scotch whisky** or milk

1 tbsp **Dijon mustard**

½ tsp **pepper**

Baltic Tiny buckwheat pancakes are the ideal backdrop for a curl of tender, salty-sweet cured salmon. If you just can't wait five days, you can eat the gravlax as early as the third day of curing.

Gravlax Blini Bites

1 tbsp **black peppercorns**

⅓ cup **granulated sugar**

¼ cup **pickling salt** or kosher salt

2 lb (900 g) **skin-on centre-cut salmon fillet**

⅓ cup chopped **fresh dill**

2 tbsp **brandy** or aquavit

Small **fresh dill sprigs**

MUSTARD SAUCE:
3 tbsp **Dijon mustard**

2 tbsp **liquid honey**

1 tbsp chopped **fresh dill**

BUCKWHEAT BLINI:
1½ tsp **granulated sugar**

¼ cup **warm water**

1½ tsp **active dry yeast**

1 **egg**

1½ cups lukewarm **milk**

1 cup **all-purpose flour**

¾ cup **buckwheat flour**

½ tsp **salt**

¼ cup **butter**, melted

Five days before serving, coarsely crush peppercorns with bottom of heavy pan. Mix peppercorns, sugar and salt; spread over both sides of salmon. Spread one-third of the chopped dill down centre of large piece of plastic wrap; top with fish, skin side down.

Drizzle with brandy; **spread** remaining chopped dill over top. Wrap tightly in plastic wrap; place on small rimmed baking sheet. Place small cutting board on fish; weigh down with 2 full 28-oz (796 mL) cans. Refrigerate for 5 days, turning fish daily.

MUSTARD SAUCE: In small bowl, stir together mustard, honey and dill. *(Make-ahead: Cover and refrigerate for up to 3 days.)*

BUCKWHEAT BLINI: In liquid measure, dissolve ½ tsp of the sugar in warm water. Sprinkle in yeast; let stand until frothy, about 10 minutes. In bowl, beat together egg, milk and remaining sugar. Add all-purpose flour, buckwheat flour and salt; beat for 1 minute. Beat in yeast mixture and half of the butter. Cover and let rise in warm place until doubled in bulk, about 1 hour.

Heat nonstick skillet over medium heat; brush lightly with some of the remaining butter. Without stirring, spoon batter into pan by scant 2 tbsp to make 2¼-inch (5.5 cm) blini. Cook until bubbles form on top that do not fill in, about 1 minute. *Flip* and cook until bottom is golden, about 30 seconds.

Unwrap fish; using paper towel, brush off most of the dill. *(Make-ahead: Wrap in plastic wrap and refrigerate for up to 5 days.)* **Slice** thinly on 45-degree angle; cut each slice in half and place on blini. Drizzle with mustard sauce; garnish each with dill sprig.

Makes about 50 pieces. PER PIECE: about 71 cal, 5 g pro, 3 g total fat (1 g sat. fat), 6 g carb, trace fibre, 18 mg chol, 594 mg sodium. % RDI: 1% calcium, 2% iron, 2% vit A, 2% vit C, 5% folate.

~ spread ~   ~ flip ~   ~ slice ~

Danish This gorgeous spread also makes a nice sandwich filling, like those used to top Danish open-faced sandwiches called smørrebrød. A tasty partner is Lefse (page 99), a soft Norwegian potato-based flatbread.

Dilled Shrimp Spread

⅓ cup **light mayonnaise**

⅓ cup **light sour cream**

3 tbsp **chili sauce**

2 tbsp chopped **fresh dill**

½ tsp **celery seeds** (optional)

¼ tsp each **salt** and **pepper**

1 bag (1 lb/450 g) **frozen peeled deveined cooked shrimp,** thawed

1 rib **celery,** chopped

1 **green onion,** chopped

In food processor, purée together mayonnaise, sour cream, chili sauce, dill, celery seeds (if using), salt and pepper until smooth.

Add all but 3 of the shrimp, the celery and green onion; pulse until shrimp is roughly chopped.

Transfer to serving bowl; garnish with remaining shrimp. Cover and refrigerate for 1 hour. *(Make-ahead: Refrigerate for up to 24 hours.)*

Makes about 3 cups. PER 1 TBSP: about 18 cal, 2 g pro, 1 g total fat (trace sat. fat), 1 g carb, 0 g fibre, 19 mg chol, 61 mg sodium. % RDI: 1% calcium, 2% iron, 1% vit A, 2% vit C, 1% folate.

Guyanese Variations on these flavourful little fritters, called phulourie, are found all over the Caribbean. They are quick to whip up and best eaten hot and fresh. Serve with Mango Sauce (below).

Split Pea Fritters

In bowl, whisk together ground split peas, baking powder, cumin, salt and pepper. Whisk in ¾ cup water and hot pepper sauce; beat for 1 minute to make thick batter.

Into wok or Dutch oven, pour enough oil to come about 2 inches (5 cm) up side. Heat until deep-fry thermometer registers 375°F (190°C).

Drop batter, by heaping 1 tbsp, into hot oil; fry, turning once, until golden, 4 to 5 minutes. Drain on paper towel–lined tray.

Makes 8 servings. PER SERVING: about 129 cal, 5 g pro, 7 g total fat (1 g sat. fat), 13 g carb, 2 g fibre, 0 mg chol, 166 mg sodium. % RDI: 2% calcium, 6% iron, 18% folate.

1 cup **ground dried split peas**
½ tsp **baking powder**
½ tsp **ground cumin**
½ tsp **salt**
¼ tsp **pepper**
½ tsp **hot pepper sauce**
Vegetable oil for frying

TIP | GROUND DRIED SPLIT PEAS ARE AVAILABLE IN WEST INDIAN GROCERY STORES AND SOME SPECIALTY FOOD SHOPS. IF YOU CAN'T FIND THEM, FINELY GRIND SPLIT DRIED YELLOW PEAS IN A SPICE OR COFFEE GRINDER.

Mango Sauce

In saucepan, combine 1 mango, peeled, pitted and chopped; 1 small shallot, minced; ¼ cup cider vinegar; 2 tbsp packed brown sugar; 2 cloves garlic, minced; 1 tbsp minced fresh ginger; 2 whole cloves; 1 cinnamon stick; and ¼ tsp salt. Bring to boil. Reduce heat, cover and simmer until mango is tender, about 30 minutes. Discard cloves and cinnamon. In blender, purée mango mixture until smooth. *(Make-ahead: Refrigerate in airtight container for up to 2 days.)* **Makes about 1 cup.**

From left: Salt Fish Cakes with Tamarind Dip (opposite)
and Split Pea Fritters with Mango Sauce (page 41)

Caribbean Crispy and golden on the outside, soft and fluffy on the inside, these mild fish cakes come alive when served with Tamarind Dip (below). Sweet-and-sour tamarind is popular in many cuisines. Buy tamarind pulp in blocks in some grocery stores or specialty food shops.

Salt Fish Cakes

In bowl in refrigerator, soak cod in cold water for 12 hours, changing water twice. Taste cod; if still too salty, continue changing water and soaking for up to 4 hours. Drain and rinse; coarsely chop. Set aside.

In saucepan of boiling salted water, cover and cook potato until fork-tender, about 10 minutes. Drain and return to saucepan over medium heat; cook, stirring, for 1 minute. Transfer to bowl and mash.

Add fish, onion, garlic, 1 of the eggs, ¼ cup of the flour, thyme, salt and pepper; stir to combine. Form, by 2 tbsp, into 2-inch (5 cm) long logs.

In shallow dish, whisk remaining egg. Place remaining flour in separate shallow dish; place bread crumbs in another shallow dish. Coat fish cakes in flour, then egg, then bread crumbs, turning to coat all over. *(Make-ahead: Cover and refrigerate for up to 24 hours.)*

Into Dutch oven, pour enough oil to come 2 inches (5 cm) up side. Heat until deep-fry thermometer registers 375°F (190°C). Fry cakes, turning once, until golden, 4 to 5 minutes. Drain on paper towel–lined plate.

Makes 8 servings. PER SERVING: about 155 cal, 12 g pro, 6 g total fat (1 g sat. fat), 13 g carb, 1 g fibre, 68 mg chol, 812 mg sodium. % RDI: 4% calcium, 8% iron, 2% vit A, 3% vit C, 13% folate.

4 oz (115 g) **salt cod**

1 **Yukon Gold potato,** peeled and chopped

1 **small onion,** minced

2 cloves **garlic,** minced

2 **eggs**

½ cup **all-purpose flour**

1 tsp chopped **fresh thyme**

¼ tsp each **salt** and **pepper**

½ cup **dried bread crumbs**

Vegetable oil for frying

Tamarind Dip

Break up and soak ¼ cup tamarind pulp in 1 cup warm water for 5 minutes. Press through fine sieve; discard solids. In saucepan, toast 1 tsp cumin seeds over medium heat until popping, about 2 minutes; set aside. In same saucepan, heat 1 tbsp vegetable oil over medium heat. Fry 1 small onion, minced; 2 tsp minced fresh ginger; 1 clove garlic, minced; 1 tbsp granulated sugar; and ¼ tsp each salt and pepper, stirring occasionally, until softened and golden, about 7 minutes. Stir in tamarind mixture and cumin seeds; bring to boil. Boil for 2 minutes. *(Make-ahead: Refrigerate in airtight container for up to 2 days.)*
Makes about 1 cup.

Australian Enormous shrimp, grilled quickly and served with a piquant dipping sauce, is one of the hallmarks of Australian cuisine. Serve with a tall, cool glass of beer for the perfect summer starter.

Barbecued Jumbo Shrimp With Sweet Chili Dipping Sauce

2 lb (900 g) **raw jumbo shrimp** (size 8 to 12), peeled and deveined

1 tbsp **vegetable oil**

SWEET CHILI DIPPING SAUCE:

½ cup **unseasoned rice vinegar**

¼ cup packed **brown sugar**

1 tsp grated **lime zest**

4 tsp **lime juice**

2 tsp **Asian chili sauce** or hot pepper sauce

2 cloves **garlic,** minced

1 tsp **cornstarch**

1 tbsp chopped **fresh cilantro**

SWEET CHILI DIPPING SAUCE: In saucepan, bring vinegar, brown sugar, 2 tbsp water, lime zest, lime juice, chili sauce and garlic to boil over medium-high heat. Whisk cornstarch with 1 tbsp water; whisk into pan. Boil until thickened, about 1 minute. *(Make-ahead: Let cool. Refrigerate in airtight container for up to 2 days.)* Stir in cilantro.

Toss shrimp with oil and half of the dipping sauce; let stand for 10 minutes. Grill shrimp, covered, on greased grill over medium-high heat, turning once, until pink, about 6 minutes. Serve hot with remaining dipping sauce.

Makes about 18 pieces. PER PIECE: about 61 cal, 8 g pro, 1 g total fat (trace sat. fat), 4 g carb, 0 g fibre, 57 mg chol, 60 mg sodium. % RDI: 2% calcium, 7% iron, 2% vit A, 2% vit C, 1% folate.

Australian Dip crusty bread first in olive oil, then in this spread for an unusual and delicious appetizer. Dukka's place of origin is Egypt, but in Australia it is a popular ready-made companion to a glass of wine.

Dukka

½ cup **macadamia nuts** or Brazil nuts

¼ cup **hazelnuts**

¼ cup **sunflower seeds** or pumpkin seeds

¼ cup **unsweetened shredded coconut**

1 cup **sesame seeds**

½ cup **coriander seeds**

¼ cup **cumin seeds**

1 tsp **salt**

1 tsp **ground cumin**

½ tsp **pepper**

½ tsp **cinnamon**

¼ tsp **cayenne pepper**

On rimmed baking sheet, spread macadamia nuts, hazelnuts and sunflower seeds; toast in 350°F (180°C) oven for 9 minutes.

Sprinkle with coconut; toast, stirring occasionally, until nuts and coconut are fragrant and golden, about 3 minutes. Let cool.

Meanwhile, on separate rimmed baking sheet, toast sesame seeds, coriander seeds and cumin seeds, stirring occasionally, until sesame seeds are golden, about 8 minutes. Let cool.

In clean coffee grinder or mini food processor, chop nut mixture until fine with a few larger pieces; transfer to bowl.

Add seed mixture to grinder; pulse until finely chopped. Add to nut mixture along with salt, ground cumin, pepper, cinnamon and cayenne; stir to combine. *(Make-ahead: Refrigerate in airtight container for up to 1 week or freeze for up to 1 month.)*

Makes about 3 cups. PER 1 TBSP: about 45 cal, 1 g pro, 4 g total fat (1 g sat. fat), 2 g carb, 1 g fibre, 0 mg chol, 59 mg sodium. % RDI: 2% calcium, 6% iron, 2% folate.

Mexican This Mexican staple of cheese-stuffed fried peppers is worth the effort. Fresh poblano peppers are mildly hot and darker green than sweet green peppers, with more-tapered tips. If you can't find them or want a mild version, use small sweet red or yellow peppers.

Chiles Rellenos

ROAST TOMATO SAUCE: In roasting pan, toss together tomatoes, onion, garlic, oil, salt and pepper. Pour broth over top. Roast in 400°F (200°C) oven, stirring occasionally, until very tender, about 1 hour. Let cool slightly. In blender, purée tomato mixture until smooth. Keep warm. *(Make-ahead: Refrigerate in airtight container for up to 2 days.)*

On rimmed baking sheet, broil chilies, turning often, until charred and blistered all over, about 10 minutes. Transfer to bowl; cover and let stand until skins loosen, about 15 minutes. Peel off blackened skin. Cut lengthwise slit along 1 side of each chili; open and scrape out seeds.

In bowl, beat together Cheddar cheese, goat cheese and green onions. Divide into 8 portions; stuff inside chilies. Pinch slits to close. *(Make-ahead: Cover and refrigerate for up to 24 hours.)*

In large bowl, beat egg whites until stiff peaks form. Beat egg yolks with 1 tbsp of the flour; fold into whites.

Into heavy skillet, pour enough oil to come 1 inch (2.5 cm) up side. Heat until deep-fry thermometer registers 350°F (180°C). Roll chilies in remaining flour to coat, shaking off excess. In 2 batches and using metal tongs, dip each chili into egg batter to coat. Fry chilies, seam side down and turning once, until golden, 5 minutes. Drain on paper towel–lined plate.

Spoon roast tomato sauce onto platter; place chilies on top. Sprinkle with cilantro.

Makes 8 servings. PER SERVING: about 428 cal, 20 g pro, 33 g total fat (14 g sat. fat), 15 g carb, 3 g fibre, 124 mg chol, 554 mg sodium. % RDI: 34% calcium, 13% iron, 30% vit A, 115% vit C, 24% folate.

8 small **fresh poblano chilies**

3 cups shredded **Cheddar cheese** or Monterey Jack cheese

6 oz (170 g) **goat cheese,** softened

2 **green onions,** minced

3 **eggs,** separated

½ cup **all-purpose flour**

Vegetable oil for frying

2 tbsp chopped **fresh cilantro** or parsley

ROAST TOMATO SAUCE:

6 **plum tomatoes** (about 1½ lb/675 g), quartered

1 **onion,** coarsely chopped

3 cloves **garlic**

2 tbsp **extra-virgin olive oil**

¼ tsp each **salt** and **pepper**

1½ cups **sodium-reduced chicken broth**

Chilean Served all over Latin America, empanadas (filled pastries) have one thing in common: their aromatic street-food appeal. This version contains a typical Chilean beef and olive filling, but you can use chicken and chicken broth instead of beef and beef broth. Serve with Salsa (below).

Empanadas

3 cups **all-purpose flour**

¾ tsp **salt**

3 tbsp **lard** or shortening

2 **eggs**

¾ cup **milk**

FILLING:
2 lb (900 g) **boneless beef blade pot roast**

¾ tsp each **salt** and **pepper**

2 tbsp **vegetable oil**

2 **onions,** chopped

1 tbsp **sweet paprika**

1 tsp **ground cumin**

1 cup **beef broth**

2 tsp **wine vinegar**

2 **hard-cooked eggs,** chopped

1 cup halved **pimiento-stuffed green olives**

In bowl, whisk flour with salt. Using pastry blender or 2 knives, cut in lard until in very fine crumbs. Whisk 1 of the eggs with milk; pour over flour mixture and stir until mixture clumps together. Scrape onto floured surface; knead to form soft dough. Wrap and refrigerate for 30 minutes. *(Make-ahead: Refrigerate for up to 2 days.)*

FILLING: Trim beef. Cut into ½-inch (1 cm) chunks; sprinkle with salt and pepper. In Dutch oven, heat oil over medium-high heat; brown beef. Transfer to plate. Drain off fat; fry onions, paprika and cumin over medium heat until softened, about 3 minutes. Stir in broth, ½ cup water and vinegar, scraping up brown bits from bottom of pan.

Return beef and any accumulated juices to pan. Cover, reduce heat and simmer until tender, about 1 hour. Uncover and simmer until liquid is reduced by two-thirds, about 20 minutes; let cool slightly. Transfer to food processor; pulse until shredded. Transfer to bowl; refrigerate until cold. Stir in eggs and olives.

Divide dough into 12 rounds. On lightly floured surface, roll out each to 6-inch (15 cm) circle. Lightly beat remaining egg; lightly brush some over edge of each circle. Spoon rounded ⅓ cup filling onto half of each circle; mound slightly. Fold other half over; press seam to seal. At ½-inch (1 cm) intervals, fold seam over, pinching to seal. *(Make-ahead: Refrigerate for up to 4 hours, or freeze in airtight container for up to 1 month, then thaw.)*

Transfer to greased rimless baking sheet; brush lightly with remaining egg. Bake in 375°F (190°C) oven until golden and crisp, about 25 minutes.

Makes 12 pieces. PER PIECE: about 324 cal, 22 g pro, 14 g total fat (4 g sat. fat), 27 g carb, 1 g fibre, 106 mg chol, 737 mg sodium. % RDI: 5% calcium, 27% iron, 7% vit A, 2% vit C, 25% folate.

Salsa
Stir together 2 cups diced tomatoes, ⅓ cup finely chopped red onion, ¼ cup chopped fresh cilantro, 1 tbsp each minced jalapeño pepper and wine vinegar, and ¼ tsp salt. **Makes 2 cups.**

Indonesian This easy marinade also tastes great with beef, lamb and chicken. If you can't find sweet soy sauce, make your own (our recipe is below) and use the leftovers in stir-fries and fried rice.

Pork Satay

Slice pork lengthwise in half; cut diagonally into ½-inch (1 cm) thick slices. In large bowl, combine sweet soy sauce, garlic and 2 tsp each of the lime juice and oil; add pork, turning to coat. Cover and refrigerate for 1 hour. *(Make-ahead: Refrigerate for up to 3 hours.)*

Mix remaining oil with remaining lime juice. Thread 2 pieces of the pork onto each of 12 metal or soaked wooden skewers. Grill, covered, on greased grill over medium heat, turning and basting with oil mixture, until just a hint of pink remains inside, about 8 minutes. Serve sprinkled with peanuts and with lime wedges to squeeze over top.

Makes 12 skewers. PER SKEWER: about 81 cal, 9 g pro, 3 g total fat (1 g sat. fat), 4 g carb, trace fibre, 20 mg chol, 151 mg sodium. % RDI: 1% calcium, 4% iron, 3% vit C, 2% folate.

Sweet Soy Sauce

In saucepan, bring ⅓ cup granulated sugar, ¼ cup soy sauce and 2 tbsp fancy molasses to boil over medium-high heat, stirring, until sugar is dissolved. Let cool. **Makes ½ cup.**

1 **pork tenderloin** (1 lb/450 g)

3 tbsp **sweet soy sauce** (recipe, below left)

1 clove **garlic,** minced

4 tsp **lime juice**

4 tsp **peanut oil** or vegetable oil

1 tbsp chopped **peanuts**

Lime wedges

Vietnamese Cold rolls are totally refreshing on a hot summer day, and they're easier to make than they appear. Look for rice paper wrappers in the Asian section of your grocery store.

Fresh Rolls With Spicy Almond Dipping Sauce

SPICY ALMOND DIPPING SAUCE: Stir together almond butter, hoisin sauce, vinegar, soy sauce, sriracha sauce and 3 tbsp water. Set aside.

Break vermicelli into thirds; place in bowl. Pour boiling water over top; soak until tender, about 3 minutes. Drain; toss with sesame oil. Let cool.

Fill shallow bowl with warm water. Soak rice paper wrappers in water, 1 at a time, until softened and pliable, about 30 seconds. Spread wrappers on clean towel.

Along bottom third of wrapper, place 3 shrimp pieces. Top with scant ¼ cup noodles, ¼ cup lettuce and few pieces each of the red pepper, yellow pepper, cucumber and mango. Top with 2 or 3 pieces each of the mint and cilantro leaves.

From filled side, roll wrapper over filling. Fold sides in and tightly roll up. Place, seam side down, on tray; cover with damp towel. Repeat with remaining ingredients to make 12 rolls.

To serve, cut diagonally in half. Serve with dipping sauce.

Makes 24 pieces. PER PIECE: about 76 cal, 3 g pro, 2 g total fat (trace sat. fat), 11 g carb, 1 g fibre, 16 mg chol, 176 mg sodium, 93 mg potassium. % RDI: 2% calcium, 7% iron, 7% vit A, 20% vit C, 5% folate.

4 oz (115 g) **rice vermicelli noodles**

1 tsp **sesame oil**

12 large **rice paper wrappers**

36 cooked **large shrimp** (size 31 to 35)

3 cups thinly sliced **leaf lettuce**

Half each **sweet red pepper** and **sweet yellow pepper,** thinly sliced

1 piece (4 inches/10 cm) **English cucumber,** cut in thin strips

Half **mango,** peeled, pitted and thinly sliced

1 cup **fresh mint leaves**

1 cup **fresh cilantro leaves**

SPICY ALMOND DIPPING SAUCE:

¼ cup **crunchy natural almond butter**

¼ cup **hoisin sauce**

2 tbsp **seasoned rice vinegar**

2 tbsp **sodium-reduced soy sauce**

1 tbsp **sriracha sauce** or other hot pepper sauce

Thai Tender rounds of spiced shrimp garnished with a fruity topping make a tasty treat. Sambal oelek and sriracha sauce are Asian hot chili and garlic sauces, but you can use your favourite hot sauce. Play with the amount to suit your taste.

Shrimp Cakes With Pineapple Relish

2 tbsp **vegetable oil**

SHRIMP CAKES:

1 lb (450 g) **raw shrimp,** peeled and deveined

1 tbsp grated **fresh ginger**

1 **green onion,** chopped

2 tsp **fish sauce**

½ tsp **chili garlic sauce** (such as sambal oelek or sriracha sauce)

PINEAPPLE RELISH:

½ cup diced peeled cored **pineapple**

2 tbsp finely sliced **green onion**

2 tbsp minced **fresh cilantro**

2 tbsp diced **sweet red pepper**

2 tsp **unseasoned rice vinegar**

2 tsp **sesame oil**

SHRIMP CAKES: In food processor, coarsely chop together shrimp, ginger and green onion, pulsing 5 or 6 times; scrape into bowl. Stir in fish sauce and chili garlic sauce.

With wet hands, shape by heaping 1 tbsp into ½-inch (1 cm) thick patties. Place on plastic wrap–lined tray; cover and refrigerate for 30 minutes.

PINEAPPLE RELISH: In sieve, drain pineapple. In bowl, mix together onion, cilantro, red pepper, vinegar and sesame oil; set aside.

In large nonstick skillet, heat half of the oil over medium heat; fry half of the shrimp cakes, turning once, until pink throughout and firm to the touch, about 4 minutes. Drain on paper towel–lined tray. Wipe out pan. Repeat with remaining oil and shrimp cakes.

Arrange shrimp cakes on platter. Add pineapple to green onion mixture; spoon onto shrimp cakes.

Makes about 28 pieces. PER PIECE: about 27 cal, 3 g pro, 2 g total fat (trace sat. fat), 1 g carb, 0 g fibre, 18 mg chol, 54 mg sodium. % RDI: 1% calcium, 2% iron, 1% vit A, 3% vit C, 1% folate.

TIP | IT'S EASIER TO TURN PATTIES IN A SKILLET IF YOU USE TWO SPATULAS, OR A SPATULA AND A FORK. USE THE SECOND UTENSIL TO BRACE THE PATTY WHILE SLIPPING A SPATULA UNDERNEATH.

Vietnamese This is the perfect appetizer for a party because you can make it ahead, instead of at the last minute. The delicate lettuce cups are colourful and fun to eat.

Sautéed Pork in Lettuce Cups

FILLING: In skillet, heat oil over medium heat; fry pork, stirring occasionally, until no longer pink, about 5 minutes. Add onion, garlic, ginger, cinnamon, hot pepper flakes and cloves; fry until onion is softened, about 3 minutes.

Stir in fish sauce; cover and simmer over medium-low heat for 3 minutes. Stir together lime juice, soy sauce and cornstarch until smooth; stir into pork mixture and cook until slightly thickened, about 2 minutes. Let cool. *(Make-ahead: Refrigerate in airtight container for up to 2 days.)* Stir in cilantro.

Peel, pit and cut mango into ¼-inch (5 mm) thick slices; cut into ¼-inch (5 mm) thick sticks. Separate lettuce to make twenty-four 3-inch (8 cm) cups, trimming any large leaves if necessary. *(Make-ahead: Cover and refrigerate separately for up to 4 hours.)*

Mound 1 tbsp of the filling into each lettuce cup. Garnish with mango and red pepper.

Makes 24 pieces. PER PIECE: about 43 cal, 3 g pro, 3 g total fat (1 g sat. fat), 2 g carb, trace fibre, 8 mg chol, 94 mg sodium. % RDI: 1% calcium, 1% iron, 4% vit A, 13% vit C, 4% folate.

Half small **mango**

4 heads **Sweet Gem lettuce** or 1 head Bibb lettuce

½ cup finely diced **sweet red pepper**

FILLING:

1 tbsp **vegetable oil**

12 oz (340 g) **lean ground pork**

½ cup minced **red onion**

2 cloves **garlic,** minced

1 tbsp minced **fresh ginger**

½ tsp **cinnamon**

¼ tsp **hot pepper flakes**

Pinch **ground cloves**

1 tbsp **fish sauce**

1 tbsp **lime juice**

2 tsp **soy sauce**

1 tsp **cornstarch**

2 tbsp minced **fresh cilantro**

Japanese Sushi rolls, or maki-zushi, are a favourite treat across the globe. While they contain mostly typical Japanese ingredients, California rolls get their name and North American twist from the creamy avocado.

California Rolls

1½ cups **water**

1¼ cups **sushi rice**

3 tbsp **seasoned rice vinegar**

1 tbsp each **black sesame seeds** and **toasted sesame seeds**

1 tsp **salt**

3 sheets **nori**

Fish roe (optional)

FILLING:

1 tbsp **wasabi powder**

6 strips (7 x ⅜ inch/18 cm x 9 mm each) **cucumber**

6 **surimi crab legs,** halved lengthwise

1 small **avocado,** peeled, pitted and cut in strips

In saucepan, bring water and rice to boil; reduce heat to low. Cover and cook until tender, about 25 minutes. With rice paddle or fork, *toss* together rice, vinegar, sesame seeds and salt; let cool completely.

Meanwhile, using scissors, cut nori in half crosswise to make six 7- x 4-inch (18 x 10 cm) rectangles.

For each roll, place rolling mat on work surface with longest side closest. Cut plastic wrap same size as mat and place on mat; brush lightly with vegetable oil, if desired. With wet fingers, *press* rounded ½ cup rice onto wrap into same-size rectangle as nori, leaving 1-inch (2.5 cm) border at closest edge. Place nori sheet on rice.

FILLING: Stir wasabi powder with 2 tsp water; spread ¼ tsp into thin line about ½ inch (1 cm) from closest edge. Top with one-sixth of the cucumber, then crab; arrange one-sixth of the avocado in row beside. Holding filling in place with fingers and using mat and plastic wrap as support, bring mat up over filling.

Roll up tightly, lifting closest end of mat as you roll. Squeeze to compress. With wet sharp serrated knife, trim ends; cut roll into thirds. Cut each in half on diagonal. Place, flat side down, on serving plate. Top each with fish roe (if using).

Makes 36 pieces. PER PIECE: about 47 cal, 2 g pro, 1 g total fat (trace sat. fat), 7 g carb, trace fibre, 2 mg chol, 187 mg sodium. % RDI: 1% iron, 1% vit A, 2% vit C, 3% folate.

~ toss ~   ~ press ~   ~ roll ~

Spinach and Mushroom Dumplings (opposite) with Bok Choy, Mushroom and Tofu Soup (page 76)

Chinese Dumplings have always been a way to make a little meat – or a few humble ingredients – go a long way. Try this vegetarian recipe or our other filling options (page 58). For dumpling wrapping and cooking methods, turn to page 59.

Spinach and Mushroom Dumpling Filling

In heatproof bowl, cover bean threads with about 2 cups boiling water; soak for 10 minutes. Drain. With scissors, cut into 1-inch (2.5 cm) lengths; place in large bowl.

In pot of boiling water, blanch spinach for 1 minute. Drain; let cool enough to handle. Squeeze out excess moisture; chop finely. Add to bean threads.

Remove and discard mushroom stems; dice caps. In small skillet, heat peanut oil over medium-high heat; sauté mushrooms until lightly browned. Add soy sauce, rice wine and sugar; sauté until no liquid remains. Scrape into separate bowl; let cool.

Beat together eggs, sesame oil, ¼ tsp of the salt and pepper. Heat 8-inch (20 cm) nonstick or cast-iron skillet over medium heat; cook half of the egg mixture until set. Slide onto plate. Repeat with remaining egg mixture. Roll up egg sheets; cut into shreds and chop.

Add egg shreds, mushroom mixture, and remaining salt to spinach mixture; mix well.

Makes about 3 cups, or enough for about 60 dumplings. PER 2½ TSP: about 13 cal, 1 g pro, 1 g total fat (trace sat. fat), 1 g carb, trace fibre, 6 mg chol, 54 mg sodium. % RDI: 1% calcium, 4% iron, 12% vit A, 2% vit C, 8% folate.

1 pkg (50 g) **bean threads** (mung bean vermicelli)

2 bunches **fresh spinach** (about 12 oz/340 g each)

6 oz (170 g) **shiitake mushrooms**

1 tbsp **peanut oil** or vegetable oil

1 tbsp **soy sauce**

2 tsp **Chinese rice wine,** dry sherry or sake

½ tsp **granulated sugar**

2 **eggs**

1 tbsp **sesame oil**

¾ tsp **salt**

¼ tsp **white pepper**

Pork Dumpling Filling

If desired, soak 2 tbsp dried shrimp (optional) in cold water for 20 minutes; drain. In small skillet, toast shrimp over medium-low heat until fragrant and lightly toasted, 2 to 3 minutes; let cool. Mince and set aside.

Toss 3 cups finely chopped napa cabbage (8 oz/ 225 g) with 1 tsp salt; let stand for 20 minutes. Squeeze out moisture. Transfer to large bowl.

Add 1 lb (450 g) lean ground pork; 2 cups finely chopped Chinese or garlic chives (optional); ½ cup minced green onion; 1 egg, beaten; 1 tbsp soy sauce; 1 tsp grated fresh ginger; 1 tsp sesame oil; ¼ tsp white or black pepper; pinch cayenne pepper; and shrimp (if using). Mix well.

Makes about 3 cups, or enough for about 60 dumplings.
PER 2½ TSP: about 19 cal, 2 g pro, 1 g total fat (trace sat. fat), trace carb, 0 g fibre, 8 mg chol, 39 mg sodium. % RDI: 1% iron, 1% folate.

Shrimp and Leek Dumpling Filling

Toss 2 cups minced leeks (white and light green parts only) with 1 tsp salt; let stand for 30 minutes. Squeeze out moisture. Transfer to large bowl.

Peel and devein 1 lb (450 g) shrimp. On cutting board and using side of cleaver, pound 1 shrimp until pulpy; chop a few times and add to leeks. Repeat with remaining shrimp. Mix in 3 oz (85 g) ground pork; 1 egg yolk; ¼ cup finely chopped fresh cilantro; 2 tsp light or sodium-reduced soy sauce; 2 tsp Chinese rice wine, dry sherry or sake; 1 tsp grated fresh ginger; 1 tsp fish sauce or light soy sauce; 1 tsp sesame oil; and pinch white or black pepper.

Makes about 2½ cups, or enough for about 45 dumplings.
PER 2½ TSP: about 17 cal, 2 g pro, 1 g total fat (trace sat. fat), 1 g carb, 0 g fibre, 17 mg chol, 56 mg sodium. % RDI: 1% calcium, 2% iron, 1% vit A, 1% folate.

Beef and Dill Dumpling Filling

Toss 2 cups finely chopped napa cabbage (5 oz/ 140 g) with ½ tsp salt; let stand for 20 minutes. Squeeze out moisture. Transfer to large bowl.

Add 1 lb (450 g) medium or lean ground beef; 1½ cups finely chopped fresh dill; ⅔ cup minced green onion; 1 egg, beaten; 1 hot pepper, seeded and minced; 1 tbsp soy sauce; 2 tsp sesame oil; 1 tsp grated fresh ginger; and ¼ tsp each salt and pepper. Mix well.

Makes about 3 cups, or enough for about 60 dumplings.
PER 2½ TSP: about 21 cal, 2 g pro, 1 g total fat (trace sat. fat), trace carb, 0 g fibre, 8 mg chol, 36 mg sodium. % RDI: 1% iron, 1% vit A, 1% folate.

DUMPLINGS 101

Chinese dumpling (jiaozi) wrappers are available at Asian grocery stores and many supermarkets. They are white, round, and thicker and chewier than wonton wrappers.

WRAP DUMPLINGS

1 | With finger, wet edge of wrapper with water.
2 | Place about 2½ tsp filling in centre [A]; fold wrapper over and pinch edge together.
3 | Pleat edge, pinching to secure [B].
4 | Stand dumplings on cornstarch-dusted tray and cover with tea towel.

MAKE-AHEAD

• **To refrigerate:** Cover towel with plastic wrap; refrigerate for up to 8 hours.
• **To freeze:** Transfer dumplings to airtight container and freeze for up to 3 months. Cook from frozen.

COOK DUMPLINGS

• **Boiled:** Drop dumplings into pot of boiling water; return to boil. Add 1 Chinese rice bowl (about 1½ cups) of cold water. When water returns to boil, dumplings are cooked. Remove with Chinese wire strainer [C] or slotted spatula.
• **Boiled frozen:** Proceed as for boiled dumplings (above), but add second bowl of water after first bowl comes back to boil.
• **Fried:** Add 2 tbsp peanut oil or vegetable oil to cast-iron or nonstick skillet; add enough dumplings to fit snugly without touching. Heat over medium-high heat until oil sizzles; pour in ½ cup water. Cover; cook until water is evaporated and spattering stops. Uncover and cook, if necessary, until bottoms are golden .

REHEAT LEFTOVERS

Cooked dumplings can be reheated and crisped by cooking in a skillet with a little bit of oil.

A

B

C

Chinese It's best to use small pickling, Persian or immature English (baby seedless) cucumbers for this garlicky salad. Mature English cucumbers will work, but remove any seeds and the watery core.

Garlic Cucumber Strips

12 oz (340 g) **cucumbers**
½ tsp **salt** (approx)
1 tbsp **unseasoned rice vinegar**
1 tsp **granulated sugar**
3 or 4 cloves **garlic,** minced
½ tsp **sesame oil**

Cut cucumbers into 1½- x ⅓-inch (4 cm x 8 mm) sticks.

Mix cucumbers with salt; let stand for 30 minutes. Transfer to colander or sieve; press out as much liquid as possible.

In bowl, stir vinegar with sugar until sugar is dissolved; add cucumbers and toss to coat.

Place garlic on cutting board. Sprinkle with pinch more salt; finely mince. With side of knife, scrape garlic back and forth on board until paste; stir into cucumber mixture. Stir in oil. Let stand for 5 minutes. *(Make-ahead: Cover and refrigerate for up to 8 hours.)*

Makes 6 to 8 servings. PER EACH OF 8 SERVINGS: about 13 cal, trace pro, trace total fat (0 g sat. fat), 3 g carb, trace fibre, 0 mg chol, 72 mg sodium. % RDI: 1% calcium, 1% iron, 3% vit C, 1% folate.

*Clockwise from top right: Garlic Cucumber Strips
(opposite), Beijing-Style Boiled Peanuts (page 62) and
Kelp With Szechuan Peppercorns (page 63)*

Chinese Peanuts are called nuts, but they're really legumes. With a pleasant toothsome crunch, these spiced boiled peanuts look more like the beans they really are.

Beijing-Style Boiled Peanuts

8 oz (225 g) raw or blanched **skinned peanuts**

3 thin slices **fresh ginger**

2 whole **star anise**

½ cup finely diced **daikon radish**

½ cup finely diced **carrot**

⅓ cup finely chopped **Chinese celery** or regular celery

½ tsp **salt**

1¼ tsp **fish sauce**

In saucepan, bring peanuts, ginger, star anise and 2¾ cups water to boil; reduce heat to medium. Boil, adding water if necessary to just cover, until nuts are tender-crisp, about 30 minutes. If there is more water than to barely cover, boil over high heat until reduced. Transfer to bowl; let cool.

Meanwhile, combine radish, carrot, celery and salt; mix well. Let stand for 30 minutes.

Add vegetable mixture to peanuts; mix in fish sauce. Refrigerate for 2 hours. *(Make-ahead: Cover and refrigerate up to 3 days.)*

Makes 6 to 8 servings. PER EACH OF 8 SERVINGS: about 177 cal, 7 g pro, 12 g total fat (2 g sat. fat), 13 g carb, 3 g fibre, 0 mg chol, 232 mg sodium. % RDI: 3% calcium, 4% iron, 9% vit A, 3% vit C, 21% folate.

TIP | CHINESE CELERY HAS A SLIGHTLY MILDER FLAVOUR THAN REGULAR CELERY. LOOK FOR IT IN THE PRODUCE AISLE IN CHINESE GROCERY STORES.

Chinese Look for dried kelp, black rice vinegar and Szechuan peppercorns at Chinese or other Asian markets. The kelp has a lovely flavour reminiscent of the ocean, where it grows.

Kelp With Szechuan Peppercorns

Rinse kelp several times in cold water. Soak in 8 cups water until tender and not salty, 20 to 30 minutes. Drain well, squeezing out excess moisture. Place in heatproof bowl; mound garlic, hot pepper and sugar on top.

In small saucepan, heat oil with Szechuan peppercorns over medium heat until bubbling, fragrant and peppercorns darken, 4 to 5 minutes. Strain through heatproof sieve over garlic mixture, making garlic sizzle.

Return peppercorns to skillet. Add soy sauce and vinegar; boil until reduced by half, about 1 minute. Strain through sieve over kelp; discard peppercorns. Toss to mix well; let cool. Mix in green onion.

Makes 6 to 8 servings. PER EACH OF 8 SERVINGS: about 73 cal, 1 g pro, 7 g total fat (1 g sat. fat), 3 g carb, trace fibre, 0 mg chol, 291 mg sodium. % RDI: 3% calcium, 4% iron, 2% vit C, 1% folate.

1 oz (30 g) shredded **dried kelp**

2 cloves **garlic,** minced

1 **hot pepper,** thinly sliced

½ tsp **granulated sugar**

¼ cup **sesame oil**

4 tsp **Szechuan peppercorns**

2 tbsp **soy sauce**

1 tbsp **black rice vinegar** or balsamic vinegar

1 **green onion,** thinly sliced

Root Soup With Cashel
Blue Cheese (page 86) and
Brown Bread (page 87)

{soups & breads}

Italian Tuscany is renowned for its simple, earthy cuisine, and soups like this are one of its hallmarks. White beans, good olive oil and freshly picked vegetables are all Tuscan staples, and together they make a hearty bowl of soup.

Tuscan Bean Soup

1 tbsp **extra-virgin olive oil** (approx)

1 large **leek** (white and light green parts only), diced

1 **potato,** peeled and diced

2 cloves **garlic,** sliced

4 cups **vegetable broth**

3 cups shredded **savoy cabbage**

1 can (14 oz/398 mL) **white kidney beans** or mixed beans, drained

1 tbsp minced **fresh oregano** or parsley (approx)

¼ tsp each **salt** and **pepper**

Grated **Parmesan cheese**

GARLIC TOASTS:
Half **baguette**

2 tbsp **extra-virgin olive oil**

1 large clove **garlic,** halved

In Dutch oven, heat oil over medium-high heat; sauté leek, potato and garlic until softened, about 5 minutes.

Add broth and 2½ cups water; bring to boil. Reduce heat, cover and simmer for 10 minutes.

Stir in cabbage, beans, oregano, salt and pepper; cook for 10 minutes. Transfer 1 cup to blender and purée; return to pot and heat through. Serve sprinkled with more oil and oregano, and Parmesan cheese.

GARLIC TOASTS: Meanwhile, cut baguette into 12 slices; brush with oil. Broil until golden. Rub with cut sides of garlic.

Makes 4 to 6 servings. PER EACH OF 6 SERVINGS: about 221 cal, 7 g pro, 8 g total fat (1 g sat. fat), 32 g carb, 6 g fibre, 0 mg chol, 488 mg sodium, 348 mg potassium. % RDI: 6% calcium, 13% iron, 4% vit A, 18% vit C, 28% folate.

Eastern European Borscht is a Ukrainian staple that's popular all over eastern Europe, with variations from town to town and family to family. This one doesn't contain the traditional beets but gets its hit of red colour from tomatoes. Serve with Onion Bialys (page 88).

Beef and Cabbage Borscht

Cut ribs in half. In Dutch oven, cover beef ribs and soup bone with water; bring to boil. Reduce heat and simmer until meat is no longer pink, about 10 minutes. Drain and rinse ribs and bone; return to Dutch oven.

Add onions, tomatoes and 4 cups water; cover and simmer over medium-low heat for 1 hour.

Add cabbage, salt and pepper; simmer, covered, for 1 hour.

Remove ribs and bone. Remove meat from ribs; trim off fat and chop meat. Remove marrow from bone. Return meat and marrow to pot.

Stir in lemon juice, tomato paste and sugar; simmer for 20 minutes.

Makes 10 to 12 servings. PER EACH OF 12 SERVINGS: about 208 cal, 10 g pro, 14 g total fat (5 g sat. fat), 11 g carb, 2 g fibre, 26 mg chol, 355 mg sodium, 365 mg potassium. % RDI: 5% calcium, 11% iron, 2% vit A, 33% vit C, 9% folate.

2 lb (900 g) **beef simmering short ribs**

1 **beef marrow soup bone**

2 cups chopped **onions**

1 can (28 oz/796 mL) **stewed tomatoes**

8 cups shredded **cabbage**

1¼ tsp **salt**

¼ tsp **pepper**

¼ cup **lemon juice**

3 tbsp **tomato paste**

2 tbsp **granulated sugar**

Portuguese Seafood is usually prepared simply in Portugal, emphasizing its freshness and flavour – and this soup is a shining example. Make it with a dry white wine, preferably from the Douro Valley, or with a Vinho Verde, and serve the remainder with the finished soup.

Clam Soup

¼ cup **extra-virgin olive oil**

1 cup chopped **Spanish onion** or white onion

¼ tsp **salt**

¾ cup **dry white wine**

3 lb (1.35 kg) **Manila clams** or littleneck clams

2 cloves **garlic,** minced

⅓ cup chopped **fresh parsley**

⅓ cup chopped **fresh cilantro**

¼ tsp **pepper**

4 thick slices **day-old crusty bread**

In large saucepan, heat half of the oil over medium heat; cook onion and pinch of the salt, stirring often, until translucent and softened, about 5 minutes.

Add wine; bring to boil over high heat. Stir in 1 cup water; return to boil. Add clams, garlic, parsley, cilantro, pepper and remaining salt; bring to boil. Reduce heat, cover and simmer until clams open, 4 to 8 minutes. Uncover and simmer for 1 minute. Discard any clams that do not open.

Tear up bread and distribute among 4 soup bowls; ladle clam soup over top. Drizzle with remaining oil.

Makes 4 servings. PER SERVING: about 281 cal, 10 g pro, 15 g total fat (2 g sat. fat), 22 g carb, 2 g fibre, 17 mg chol, 356 mg sodium, 329 mg potassium. % RDI: 7% calcium, 62% iron, 9% vit A, 20% vit C, 35% folate.

Eastern European Beet soups are well-loved across eastern Europe. In this version, a potato added to the beets thickens the soup and gives it a smooth texture. After puréeing, add more stock or water to thin, if desired.

Beet and Caraway Soup

In large saucepan, heat oil over medium heat; cook onion, garlic, caraway seeds, salt and pepper, stirring, until onion is softened, about 5 minutes. Add broth, beets and potato; bring to boil. Reduce heat, cover and simmer until vegetables are tender, about 30 minutes.

In blender or food processor, purée soup, in batches, until smooth. *(Make-ahead: Let cool for 30 minutes. Refrigerate, uncovered, until cold. Cover and refrigerate for up to 3 days.)* Return to pan; reheat.

Meanwhile, in small bowl, stir sour cream with horseradish. Ladle soup into bowls; garnish each with dollop of sour cream mixture.

Makes 4 to 6 servings. PER EACH OF 6 SERVINGS: about 131 cal, 6 g pro, 4 g total fat (1 g sat. fat), 19 g carb, 3 g fibre, 1 mg chol, 628 mg sodium. % RDI: 5% calcium, 9% iron, 1% vit A, 12% vit C, 37% folate.

Variation
BEET AND CUMIN SOUP: Replace caraway seeds with 1 tsp ground cumin. Replace horseradish with 1 tbsp finely chopped fresh dill.

1 tbsp **vegetable oil**

1 small **red onion,** chopped

1 clove **garlic,** minced

¼ tsp **caraway seeds**

¼ tsp each **salt** and **pepper**

3½ cups **chicken broth** or vegetable broth

3 cups chopped peeled **beets** (about 5, or 1 lb/450 g)

1 large **potato,** peeled and chopped

¼ cup **light sour cream**

1 tbsp **horseradish**

Hungarian Served warm or cold, this thick, creamy soup makes taste buds sing with its vibrant accents of vinegar and sour cream. Sesame-topped egg bread is a delicious partner.

Creamy Potato Soup

8 **black peppercorns**

2 **bay leaves**

1 tbsp **vegetable oil**

2 ribs **celery,** diced

1 **onion,** diced

½ tsp **salt**

4 **russet potatoes** (1½ lb/675 g)

2 cups **sodium-reduced chicken broth**

3 tbsp **white vinegar**

⅓ cup **sour cream**

2 tbsp chopped **fresh parsley**

In cheesecloth square, tie peppercorns and bay leaves with string to make spice bag; set aside.

In large saucepan, heat oil over medium heat; cook celery, onion and salt, stirring occasionally, until tender but not browned, about 8 minutes.

Meanwhile, peel and cube potatoes. Add to pan; cook, stirring, for 2 minutes. Add 3 cups water, broth, vinegar and spice bag; bring to boil. Reduce heat, cover and simmer until potatoes are tender, about 45 minutes. Discard spice bag.

With immersion blender or food mill, purée soup until smooth. *(Make-ahead: Let cool for 30 minutes; refrigerate in airtight container for up to 2 days.)*

Whisk in sour cream and parsley. Heat through over medium heat, stirring occasionally.

Makes 4 servings. PER SERVING: about 201 cal, 5 g pro, 6 g total fat (2 g sat. fat), 33 g carb, 3 g fibre, 8 mg chol, 626 mg sodium. % RDI: 5% calcium, 5% iron, 5% vit A, 23% vit C, 11% folate.

TIP | AN IMMERSION BLENDER OR FOOD MILL WILL GIVE THIS SOUP THE PERFECT SILKY TEXTURE. IF YOU DON'T HAVE EITHER, PULSE SOUP (DO NOT PURÉE) IN BATCHES IN A REGULAR BLENDER.

Moroccan This soup is eaten to break the fast at sunset during Ramadan, the month of prayer and piety in the Islamic religious calendar. Fragrant with herbs and spices, harira is easy to prepare in large quantities and makes a substantial supper.

Harira

Chop ¼ cup each of the cilantro and parsley; set aside. Tie together remaining cilantro and parsley; place in large saucepan. Add broth; bring to boil. Reduce heat to low, cover and simmer for 15 minutes. Discard herb bundle. Add lentils; cover and simmer for 15 minutes.

Add tomatoes, chickpeas, onions, cinnamon, cumin, ginger, turmeric and pepper; cover and simmer for 30 minutes.

In food processor or blender, purée 3 cups of the soup. Return to pot and heat through. Stir in lemon juice, oil and reserved chopped herbs.

GARNISH: Ladle soup into bowls. Top with lemon slices and dates; sprinkle with cinnamon.

Makes 8 servings. PER SERVING: about 285 cal, 16 g pro, 6 g total fat (1 g sat. fat), 44 g carb, 7 g fibre, 0 mg chol, 1,031 mg sodium. % RDI: 8% calcium, 36% iron, 6% vit A, 27% vit C, 76% folate.

1 large bunch **fresh cilantro**

1 large bunch **fresh parsley**

8 cups **chicken broth** or vegetable broth

1 cup **dried green lentils** or dried brown lentils

2 cans (19 oz/540 mL each) **tomatoes,** drained and chopped

1 can (19 oz/540 mL) **chickpeas,** drained and rinsed

2 **onions,** chopped

2 tsp **cinnamon**

1 tsp **ground cumin**

1 tsp **ground ginger**

1 tsp **turmeric**

1 tsp **pepper**

¼ cup **lemon juice**

2 tbsp **extra-virgin olive oil**

GARNISH:
1 **lemon,** thinly sliced

12 **dates,** pitted and halved

1 tbsp **cinnamon**

Mexican This broth-based soup made with meat and hominy (a type of corn) traditionally takes many hours to prepare, but this quicker version still tastes wonderfully authentic. Pozole is served with a garnish tray so everyone can add his or her own personal touches.

Pozole

½ cup **pepitas** (hulled green pumpkin seeds)

1 jar (430 mL) **salsa verde** (see Tip, below right)

4 tsp **dried Mexican oregano** or regular oregano

1 **onion,** chopped

4 cloves **garlic,** sliced

1 **bay leaf**

3 lb (1.35 kg) **chicken thighs** or breasts

2 cups **sodium-reduced chicken broth**

2 cans (15 oz/425 g each) **white hominy,** drained and rinsed

4 tsp **chili powder**

¼ tsp each **salt** and **pepper**

TORTILLA STRIPS:
4 small **flour tortillas**

1 tbsp **vegetable oil**

GARNISHES:
Diced **avocado** tossed with **lime juice**

Shredded **iceberg lettuce**

Diced **radishes**

Thinly sliced **green onions**

Chopped **fresh cilantro**

Lime wedges

TORTILLA STRIPS: Brush tortillas all over with oil; stack and cut in half. Stack again and slice crosswise into thin strips. Separate strips and arrange on rimmed baking sheet. Bake in 350°F (180°C) oven until crisp and golden, about 10 minutes. Let cool. *(Make-ahead: Store in airtight container for up to 2 days.)*

In dry small skillet, toast pepitas over medium heat, stirring occasionally, until puffed and popping, about 6 minutes. Let cool. In blender, blend together pepitas, salsa verde and oregano until smooth. Set aside.

In Dutch oven, bring 8 cups water, onion, garlic and bay leaf to boil; reduce heat and simmer for 10 minutes. Add chicken; cover and simmer, skimming off any foam, until juices run clear when chicken is pierced, about 25 minutes. Reserving cooking liquid, transfer chicken to plate; let cool enough to handle. Shred chicken into bowl, discarding skin and bones. Cover and refrigerate.

Strain cooking liquid into clean Dutch oven. Add salsa mixture, broth, hominy, chili powder, salt and pepper; bring to boil. Reduce heat and simmer, uncovered and skimming off any fat or foam, for 30 minutes. Stir in chicken. *(Make-ahead: Let cool for 30 minutes; refrigerate in airtight container for up to 2 days. Reheat.)*

GARNISHES: Ladle soup into bowls. Top with tortilla strips; sprinkle with garnishes to taste.

Makes 8 to 10 servings. PER EACH OF 10 SERVINGS: about 316 cal, 29 g pro, 14 g total fat (3 g sat. fat), 19 g carb, 4 g fibre, 71 mg chol, 677 mg sodium. % RDI: 4% calcium, 31% iron, 6% vit A, 2% vit C, 53% folate.

TIP | SALSA VERDE IS MADE FROM TOMATILLOS. IT IS MILD, AND THINNER AND SMOOTHER THAN TOMATO-BASED SALSAS. PRESIDENT'S CHOICE AND HERDEZ BRANDS ARE WIDELY AVAILABLE. THOUGH THE JAR SIZES VARY, IT'S NOT ENOUGH TO MAKE A DIFFERENCE IN THE RECIPE.

Chinese This light-tasting soup, made with fresh, nutritious greens, is terrific with homemade dumplings (pages 57 and 58). If you make the Chinese Chicken Stock (below), you'll end up with more than you need, but leftovers freeze well.

Bok Choy, Mushroom and Tofu Soup

5 cups **Chinese Chicken Stock** (recipe, below right)

1 pkg (300 g) **medium tofu,** drained and cut in ¾-inch (2 cm) cubes

1 cup thinly sliced **mushrooms**

4 cups chopped **bok choy,** fresh spinach or napa cabbage (12 oz/340 g)

Salt (optional)

1 **green onion,** thinly sliced

½ tsp **sesame oil**

Pinch **white pepper**

Fresh cilantro leaves (optional)

In Dutch oven, bring stock to boil; add tofu and mushrooms. Reduce heat and simmer until mushrooms are tender, about 3 minutes.

Add bok choy; simmer until tender-crisp, about 3 minutes. Taste and add salt if desired. Ladle into bowls. Sprinkle with green onion, sesame oil and white pepper. Top with cilantro (if using).

Makes 6 to 8 servings. PER EACH OF 8 SERVINGS: about 59 cal, 6 g pro, 3 g total fat (trace sat. fat), 3 g carb, 1 g fibre, 1 mg chol, 325 mg sodium. % RDI: 8% calcium, 10% iron, 20% vit A, 22% vit C, 18% folate.

Chinese Chicken Stock

In Dutch oven, combine 10 cups water and 2 lb (900 g) chicken backs, legs or pieces. Bring to boil; reduce heat to simmer. Skim off scum. Add 3 slices fresh ginger, 2 green onions (white and light green parts only), 1 sprig fresh cilantro (root and stems only), 2 tbsp Chinese rice wine, 1 tsp black peppercorns and ½ tsp salt. Cook until flavourful, about 2 hours. Strain through fine sieve. Skim off any fat. *(Make-ahead: Let cool. Cover and refrigerate for up to 2 days.)*

Makes about 8 cups. PER 1 CUP: about 26 cal, 3 g pro, 1 g total fat (0 g sat. fat), 1 g carb, 0 g fibre, 1 mg chol, 163 mg sodium. % RDI: 1% iron, 1% folate.

TIP | THE STOCK FOR THIS SOUP IS LIGHT IN FLAVOUR. IF YOU WANT TO SUBSTITUTE STORE-BOUGHT BROTH, COMBINE 3 CUPS BROTH WITH 2 CUPS WATER TO GET THE PROPER BALANCE.

Malaysian Chinese and native Malay culinary traditions meet in this fabulously tasty meal in a bowl. Almost any kind of fish is suitable, but we recommend halibut or catfish. Look for blocks of tamarind pulp in Asian supermarkets.

Seafood Laksa

In small saucepan, bring 2 cups water and tamarind pulp to boil; reduce heat and simmer for 10 minutes. Strain through sieve into large saucepan, pressing to extract liquid; discard solids. Set aside.

In small skillet, toast coriander seeds, cumin seeds, fennel seeds and peppercorns over medium-low heat until fragrant, about 5 minutes. In clean coffee grinder, grind to fine powder; set aside. In same pan and using fork, mash shrimp paste; cook over medium heat, mashing, until crumbly, dry and very smelly. Transfer to food processor.

Add lemongrass to food processor. Break dried hot peppers in half; shake out and discard seeds. In clean coffee grinder, grind until coarse powder. Add to food processor along with chopped shallots, finger hot peppers, garlic, ginger and 1 cup water; purée until fairly smooth. Add to tamarind liquid in saucepan. Stir in 8 cups water, sugar, turmeric, salt and coriander seed mixture; bring to boil. Reduce heat to medium; simmer, stirring occasionally, for 20 minutes. Add fish; cook over medium-high heat for 3 minutes. Add shrimp; cook for 2 minutes. Add squid; cook for 1 minute.

Meanwhile, bring large pot of water to boil; add noodles. Remove from heat; cover and let stand for 15 minutes. (Or, if using rice stick noodles, cook according to package instructions.) Drain; divide among 6 warmed large soup bowls. Keep warm.

Ladle soup over noodles. Top with pineapple, cucumber, onion, pickled shallots, then mint. Serve with lime wedges to squeeze over top.

Makes 6 servings. PER SERVING: about 574 cal, 45 g pro, 4 g total fat (1 g sat. fat), 87 g carb, 5 g fibre, 251 mg chol, 1,053 mg sodium. % RDI: 16% calcium, 52% iron, 12% vit A, 37% vit C, 25% folate.

TIP | FOR A MILDER VERSION, CUT BACK TO FIVE DRIED HOT PEPPERS AND REPLACE FRESH HOT PEPPERS WITH A SWEET RED PEPPER.

¼ cup **tamarind pulp**

1 tbsp **coriander seeds**

1½ tsp each **cumin seeds** and **fennel seeds**

½ tsp **black peppercorns**

2 tbsp **shrimp paste**

4 stalks tender **lemongrass,** trimmed and sliced paper-thin

15 **dried red hot peppers**

8 **shallots** (or 2 onions), chopped

4 **red finger hot peppers** or 8 Thai bird's-eye peppers, chopped

1 clove **garlic,** chopped

2 tbsp minced **fresh ginger**

¼ cup packed **palm sugar** or light brown sugar

1 tbsp **turmeric**

2 tsp **salt**

1½ lb (675 g) **fish fillets,** cut in 2-inch (5 cm) chunks

1 lb (450 g) **raw large shrimp** (size 31 to 35), peeled and deveined

8 oz (225 g) cleaned **squid,** sliced

1 pkg (400 g) **laksa noodles** or rice stick noodles

1 cup chopped peeled **pineapple**

1 **English cucumber,** coarsely grated

Half **sweet onion,** thinly sliced

¼ cup sliced **pickled shallots** or pickled onions

½ cup loosely packed small **fresh mint leaves**

Lime wedges

Filipino This fish and vegetable soup, called diningding (pronounced with short i's, as in "thing"), is an Ilocano specialty from northern Philippines. In Canada, black cod (sablefish), salmon or halibut are especially good, but freshwater fish, such as pickerel or whitefish, are also tasty.

Grilled Fish and Vegetable Soup

Sprinkle fish with ¼ tsp of the pepper and salt. Grill or broil until fish flakes easily when tested, 8 to 10 minutes per 1 inch (2.5 cm) of thickness.

Meanwhile, bring 4 cups water, shallots, fish sauce, ginger and remaining pepper to boil. Add oyster and king mushrooms, squash, lima beans, okra and bamboo shoots; return to boil. Reduce heat and simmer until vegetables are tender, about 7 minutes.

Add spinach and enoki mushrooms; simmer until tender, 2 to 3 minutes. Ladle into bowls; top with fish. Serve with lime wedges.

Makes 4 to 6 servings. PER EACH OF 6 SERVINGS: about 228 cal, 15 g pro, 12 g total fat (3 g sat. fat), 16 g carb, 4 g fibre, 37 mg chol, 863 mg sodium, 848 mg potassium. % RDI: 7% calcium, 21% iron, 48% vit A, 17% vit C, 25% folate.

TIP | USE THIS RECIPE AS A GUIDELINE AND VARY THE VEGETABLES ACCORDING TO AVAILABILITY AND FRESHNESS. TRY SQUASH BLOSSOMS, ANY KIND OF CULTIVATED OR WILD MUSHROOMS, LONG BEANS, BITTER MELON AND/OR VEGETABLE MARROW.

4 **fish fillets** or steaks (about 1 lb/450 g)

¾ tsp **pepper**

¼ tsp **salt**

½ cup finely sliced **shallots**

3 tbsp **fish sauce** or Filipino anchovy sauce (bagoong na isda)

1 tbsp grated **fresh ginger**

3 oz (85 g) **oyster mushrooms,** torn in strips

1 cup sliced **king mushrooms** or shiitake mushroom caps

1 cup diced **orange-fleshed squash** or sweet potato

1 cup thawed **frozen lima beans** or fresh soybeans (edamame)

½ cup chopped **okra**

½ cup sliced **bamboo shoots**

2 cups lightly packed **fresh spinach**

2 oz (55 g) **enoki mushrooms**

Lime wedges

Filipino Bicol province in the Philippines is known for its spicy food, often made with coconut. Here, the coconut is in the accompanying buns, called Puto (page 113).

Bicol-Style Mussel Soup

2 lb (900 g) **mussels**

1 stalk **lemongrass** (optional)

2 tbsp **olive oil** or vegetable oil

½ cup thinly sliced **shallots**

3 cloves **garlic,** minced

6 **Thai bird's-eye peppers** (or 2 finger hot peppers), finely chopped

1 tbsp finely grated **fresh ginger**

¼ tsp **pepper**

3 **tomatoes,** peeled and chopped

3 cups **water**

1 tbsp **fish sauce**

2 cups lightly packed **fresh spinach**

2 tbsp **lime juice**

¼ tsp **salt**

Rinse mussels; pull off and discard any beards. Discard any mussels that do not close when tapped. Cut off dry tip of lemongrass (if using); peel off outer layer(s) if hard and dry. Cut into 2-inch (5 cm) long pieces; with side of chef's knife, hit pieces to bruise and split slightly. Set aside.

In heavy soup pot or large saucepan, heat oil over medium-high heat; sauté shallots until golden. Add garlic; sauté until light golden.

Stir in hot peppers, ginger, pepper and lemongrass; sauté until peppers are softened. Stir in tomatoes; sauté until softened, about 2 minutes.

Stir in water and fish sauce; bring to boil. Add mussels; cover and boil until mussels open. Discard any mussels that do not open. Stir in spinach. Remove from heat. Stir in lime juice and salt.

Makes 6 to 8 servings. PER EACH OF 8 SERVINGS: about 79 cal, 5 g pro, 4 g total fat (1 g sat. fat), 6 g carb, 1 g fibre, 10 mg chol, 319 mg sodium, 211 mg potassium. % RDI: 3% calcium, 12% iron, 14% vit A, 17% vit C, 14% folate.

Bicol-Style Mussel Soup (opposite)
with Puto (page 113)

Thai Perfect for entertaining, this lightly spiced soup can be prepared a few days in advance. Use the stems and the carefully cleaned roots of the cilantro for the fullest flavour.

Squash and Coconut Soup With Shrimp

In Dutch oven, bring half of the broth to boil; add half of the squash. Reduce heat to medium; cover and cook until squash is very tender, about 20 minutes.

Meanwhile, in large nonstick skillet, heat oil over medium-high heat; sauté sweet red pepper, onion, minced cilantro, chopped hot pepper, garlic and ginger until onion starts to brown, about 10 minutes.

Add fish sauce, brown sugar and pepper; cook for 30 seconds. Transfer to blender along with cooked squash and liquid; purée until very smooth. Pour into saucepan.

Add remaining broth and squash; cover and simmer over medium-low heat until squash is almost tender, about 6 minutes. *(Make-ahead: Let cool for 30 minutes. Refrigerate until cold. Transfer to airtight container and refrigerate for up to 3 days.)*

Add coconut milk; bring to boil. Add shrimp. Reduce heat; simmer until shrimp are pink and opaque, about 3 minutes. Remove from heat; stir in lime juice. Garnish each serving with cilantro sprigs, and sliced hot pepper (if using).

Makes 6 servings. PER SERVING: about 286 cal, 18 g pro, 18 g total fat (13 g sat. fat), 17 g carb, 2 g fibre, 86 mg chol, 926 mg sodium. % RDI: 7% calcium, 31% iron, 81% vit A, 70% vit C, 19% folate.

4 cups **chicken broth**

4 cups cubed **butternut squash**

1 tbsp **vegetable oil**

½ cup finely chopped **sweet red pepper**

¼ cup chopped **onion**

¼ cup minced **fresh cilantro**

1 tbsp chopped **red finger hot pepper**

1 clove **garlic,** minced

2 tsp chopped **fresh ginger**

4 tsp **fish sauce** (or 3 anchovies, chopped)

1 tsp packed **brown sugar**

½ tsp **pepper**

1 can (400 mL) **coconut milk**

1 lb (450 g) **raw medium shrimp** (size 41 to 50), peeled and deveined

1 tbsp **lime juice**

Fresh cilantro sprigs

Sliced **red finger hot pepper** (optional)

Spanish Gazpacho is a treat when you have ripe tomatoes. This version of the beloved cold soup tastes authentic but has about half the usual amount of oil. The secret is to use a tasty extra-virgin olive oil for maximum flavour.

Classic Gazpacho

1 cup cubed crustless **white bread**

1½ lb (675 g) very ripe **tomatoes,** chopped

¾ cup chopped **sweet onion**

½ cup chopped **sweet green pepper**

1 piece (4 inches/10 cm) **cucumber,** peeled and chopped

⅓ cup **extra-virgin olive oil**

2 tbsp **sherry vinegar**

1 tbsp **white wine vinegar** or 1½ tbsp lemon juice

2 small cloves **garlic,** smashed

1 tsp **salt**

¾ tsp **granulated sugar**

TOPPINGS:

¼ cup chopped **tomato**

¼ cup chopped **sweet green pepper**

¼ cup chopped peeled **cucumber**

Extra-virgin olive oil (optional)

Sprinkle bread with 3 tbsp water; gently squeeze out excess moisture.

In blender in batches, purée together bread, tomatoes, ¾ cup cold water, onion, green pepper, cucumber, oil, sherry vinegar, wine vinegar, garlic, salt and sugar until smooth. Strain through fine sieve into large bowl, pressing any solids to extract juice. Discard solids. Cover and refrigerate for 2 hours. *(Make-ahead: Refrigerate for up to 24 hours.)*

TOPPINGS: Ladle gazpacho into bowls; top with tomato, green pepper and cucumber. Drizzle with oil (if using).

Makes 6 servings. PER SERVING: about 157 cal, 2 g pro, 13 g total fat (2 g sat. fat), 10 g carb, 2 g fibre, 0 mg chol, 419 mg sodium, 386 mg potassium. % RDI: 3% calcium, 6% iron, 11% vit A, 53% vit C, 15% folate.

TIP | SHERRY VINEGAR IS A BIT PRICEY BUT IS ESSENTIAL IN THE SPANISH PANTRY. IT'S ALSO ONE OF THE BEST VINEGARS FOR DRESSING GREEN SALADS, SO IT'S WELL WORTH THE EXPENSE.

Scottish Leeks thrive in Scotland, so this soup has been around forever. Allspice is a later inclusion due to trade with the West Indies. Prunes are a more mysterious ingredient: No one seems to know where this addition came from. But who cares? They're a delicious, unexpected bonus.

Cock-a-Leekie Soup

Halve leeks lengthwise; wash well under cold water, separating layers to remove grit. Cut off dark green tops; slice white and light green parts. Set tops and sliced leeks aside separately.

In large pot, bring 14 cups water and 1 tsp of the salt to boil; add chicken. Return to boil; skim off any foam. Add onion, celery, garlic, thyme, bay leaf, peppercorns, allspice and reserved dark green tops of leeks. Bring to boil; reduce heat, cover and simmer gently until chicken is tender (drumstick will feel loose in joint), 1 to 1¼ hours.

Remove chicken; let cool enough to handle. Separate meat from bones and skin. Return bones and skin to pot; shred meat and set aside. Continue simmering soup, uncovered, for 45 minutes.

Skim 3 tbsp fat off soup. In separate large pot, heat fat over medium heat; fry sliced leeks, barley and remaining salt, stirring often, until leeks are soft, 10 to 15 minutes. Skim remaining fat from soup and discard.

Strain soup into leek mixture; add prunes. Bring to boil; reduce heat and simmer until barley is tender, 30 to 40 minutes. Add chicken meat to pot; heat through.

Makes 8 servings. PER SERVING: about 204 cal, 18 g pro, 6 g total fat (2 g sat. fat), 19 g carb, 3 g fibre, 63 mg chol, 512 mg sodium, 385 mg potassium. % RDI: 4% calcium, 13% iron, 5% vit A, 7% vit C, 9% folate.

3 **leeks**

1½ tsp **salt**

1 **whole chicken** (about 3 lb/1.35 kg)

1 **onion,** quartered

2 ribs **celery,** chopped

2 cloves **garlic,** halved

3 sprigs **fresh thyme** (or ½ tsp dried thyme)

1 **bay leaf**

½ tsp **black peppercorns**

8 **whole allspice**

⅓ cup **pot barley** or rice

12 **pitted prunes**

TIP | FOR A HEARTIER, THICKER SOUP, INCREASE BARLEY TO ½ CUP.

Irish Rich with vegetables, this puréed soup has highlights of Cashel Blue, one of Ireland's most well-known creamy blue-veined cheeses. For a vegetarian version, replace the chicken broth with vegetable broth.

Root Soup With Cashel Blue Cheese

3 tbsp **butter**

2 **leeks** (white and light green parts only), thinly sliced

1 **onion,** thinly sliced

4 cups diced peeled **rutabaga**

1 **carrot,** peeled and diced

1 **russet potato,** peeled and diced

¾ tsp **salt**

¼ tsp **pepper**

¼ tsp **nutmeg**

4 cups **sodium-reduced chicken broth**

2 cups **water**

1 cup **10% cream** or milk

1 tsp **cider vinegar** or white wine vinegar

⅓ cup crumbled **Cashel Blue cheese**

2 tbsp finely chopped **fresh chives** or parsley

In large pot or Dutch oven, melt butter over medium heat; fry leeks and onion, stirring often, until translucent, about 12 minutes. Add rutabaga, carrot, potato, salt, pepper and nutmeg; cook for 5 minutes.

Stir in broth and water; bring to boil. Reduce heat, cover and simmer until vegetables are tender, about 30 minutes.

In blender in batches, purée soup until smooth. *(Make-ahead: Refrigerate in airtight container for up to 3 days; thin with a little water, if desired.)*

Return to pot. Stir in cream and vinegar; bring just to boil over medium heat. Ladle into bowls. Garnish with cheese and chives.

Makes 8 servings. PER SERVING: about 164 cal, 5 g pro, 9 g total fat (6 g sat. fat), 16 g carb, 2 g fibre, 26 mg chol, 662 mg sodium. % RDI: 11% calcium, 6% iron, 27% vit A, 28% vit C, 12% folate.

TIP | IF YOU CAN'T GET YOUR HANDS ON ANY CASHEL BLUE CHEESE, GORGONZOLA OR CREAMY DANISH BLUE MAKE WORTHY SUBSTITUTES.

Irish This easy soda-leavened bread is dense and slightly crumbly, with a rich nutty flavour and just a hint of sweetness. It's divine with Root Soup With Cashel Blue Cheese (opposite) or with lashings of butter.

Brown Bread

In large bowl, whisk together all-purpose flour, whole wheat flour, oats, wheat germ, baking soda, caraway seeds and salt. With pastry blender or 2 knives, cut in butter until in fine crumbs. Whisk buttermilk with molasses; stir into flour mixture to make soft dough.

Turn out onto lightly floured surface; knead lightly about 10 times. Shape into 8-inch (20 cm) long oval; dust top with flour. With serrated knife, cut shallow slash lengthwise down centre; transfer to greased 9- x 5-inch (2 L) loaf pan.

Bake in 375°F (190°C) oven until loaf sounds hollow when tapped on bottom, about 45 minutes. Let cool in pan on rack for 5 minutes. Turn out onto rack; let cool completely before slicing. *(Make-ahead: Store in airtight container for up to 4 days or freeze for up to 2 weeks.)*

Makes 1 loaf, or 12 slices. PER SLICE: about 183 cal, 4 g pro, 9 g total fat (5 g sat. fat), 23 g carb, 2 g fibre, 21 mg chol, 332 mg sodium. % RDI: 4% calcium, 10% iron, 7% vit A, 14% folate.

1 cup **all-purpose flour** (approx)

1 cup **whole wheat flour**

½ cup **rolled oats** (not instant)

¼ cup **wheat germ**

1½ tsp **baking soda**

1½ tsp **caraway seeds**

½ tsp **salt**

½ cup cold **butter,** cubed

1 cup **buttermilk**

2 tbsp **cooking molasses** or fancy molasses

Polish Bialystok is the hometown of bialys, the onion and poppy seed buns made popular by the city's Jewish community. Served warm or at room temperature, they're a flavourful partner to Beef and Cabbage Borscht (page 67).

Onion Bialys

1½ tsp **granulated sugar**

1¼ cups **warm water**

2 tsp **active dry yeast**

⅓ cup **whole wheat flour**

1½ tsp **salt**

2⅔ cups **bread flour**

½ cup finely chopped **mild white onion**

1 tbsp **dry bread crumbs**

1 tbsp **poppy seeds**

1 tsp **vegetable oil**

In large bowl, dissolve sugar in warm water. Sprinkle in yeast; let stand until frothy, about 10 minutes. Stir in whole wheat flour and salt. Gradually add bread flour, mixing with wooden spoon to form shaggy dough. Turn out onto lightly floured surface; knead until smooth and elastic, about 15 minutes. Place in greased bowl, turning to grease all over. Cover with plastic wrap; let rise in warm draft-free place until doubled in bulk, about 2 hours.

Punch down dough; pull edges to centre and pinch to form ball. Turn dough and cover; let rise until doubled in bulk, about 1½ hours. (Or place in large bowl, cover and refrigerate overnight.)

Punch down dough; divide in half. Shape each into ball; cover and let rest for 15 minutes. Shape each into 10-inch (25 cm) long rope; cut each rope into 5 pieces. Shape each piece into ball, stretching and pinching dough underneath to smooth tops. Flatten to about 3 inches (8 cm) in diameter. Place on floured work surface; cover with damp cloth and let rise until doubled in bulk, about 45 minutes.

Mix together onion, bread crumbs, poppy seeds and oil. Make a well in centre of each bun. Stretch well to 2 inches (5 cm) in diameter with ¼-inch (5 mm) thick base, being careful not to deflate dough around well. Spoon heaping 1 tsp onion mixture into each well, pressing to adhere. Cover and let rise for 30 minutes.

Heat baking stone or baking sheet in 450°F (230°C) oven. With floured spatula, carefully slide half of the bialys, 1 at a time, onto stone. With spritzer bottle, spray cold water onto walls and floor of oven (avoiding lightbulb) until steam fills oven, about 10 seconds. Quickly close oven door to trap steam. Bake until golden, 13 to 15 minutes. Transfer to rack; let cool. Repeat with remaining bialys. *(Make-ahead: Let cool. Store in airtight container for up to 24 hours or freeze for up to 2 weeks.)*

Makes 10 buns. PER BUN: about 165 cal, 6 g pro, 2 g total fat (trace sat. fat), 32 g carb, 2 g fibre, 0 mg chol, 351 mg sodium, 88 mg potassium. % RDI: 2% calcium, 14% iron, 28% folate.

Onion Bialys (opposite)
with Beef and Cabbage
Borscht (page 67)

Scottish These crunchy home-baked crackers are the perfect base for rich, flavourful Whisky Cheddar Spread (page 37).

Oatcakes

2 cups **large-flake rolled oats**

½ cup **walnut pieces**

1 cup **all-purpose flour**

2 tbsp packed **brown sugar**

1 tsp **baking powder**

½ tsp **salt**

½ cup cold **butter**

¾ cup **buttermilk**

In food processor, pulse oats with walnuts until powdery with some small pieces remaining; transfer to bowl. Whisk in flour, brown sugar, baking powder and salt. Using pastry blender or 2 knives, cut in butter until crumbly; stir in buttermilk to form stiff smooth dough. Form into disc; wrap and refrigerate for 30 minutes. *(Make-ahead: Refrigerate for up to 24 hours.)*

On lightly floured surface, roll out dough to scant ¼-inch (5 mm) thickness. With 2-inch (5 cm) round cookie cutter, cut out rounds, rerolling scraps. Place, 1 inch (2.5 cm) apart, on parchment paper–lined or greased rimless baking sheets.

Bake in top and bottom thirds of 350°F (180°C) oven, switching and rotating pans halfway through, until edges are crisp and golden, about 28 minutes. Let cool on pans on racks for 5 minutes; transfer to racks and let cool completely. *(Make-ahead: Store in airtight container for up to 2 days or freeze for up to 1 month.)*

Makes about 40 pieces. PER PIECE: about 64 cal, 1 g pro, 4 g total fat (2 g sat. fat), 7 g carb, 1 g fibre, 7 mg chol, 64 mg sodium. % RDI: 1% calcium, 3% iron, 2% vit A, 3% folate.

Italian This dough makes a crisp, airy crust. It's a dream to work, especially after 24 hours, because the gluten is relaxed and easy to roll. Try it in our Calabrese Potato Provolone Pizza (page 153) or Alpine Cheese Pie (page 163).

Pizza Dough

In bowl, combine 2¾ cups of the flour, yeast and salt. With wooden spoon, gradually stir in water and oil until ragged dough forms, using hands if necessary.

Turn out onto lightly floured surface; knead, adding remaining flour 1 tbsp at a time as necessary, until smooth and elastic, about 8 minutes.

Place in greased bowl, turning to grease all over. Cover with plastic wrap; let rise in warm draft-free place until doubled in bulk, about 1 hour. *(Make-ahead: Refrigerate unrisen dough and let rise for 24 hours. Or freeze in plastic bag for up to 1 month, then thaw. Let rise in refrigerator overnight.)*

Makes about 1½ lb (675 g) dough, enough for one 14-inch (35 cm) pizza base.

Variations
BREAD MACHINE PIZZA DOUGH: Into pan of 2-lb (900 g) machine, place (in order) water, oil, salt, flour and yeast. (Do not let yeast touch liquid.) Choose dough setting.

SUN-DRIED TOMATO AND HERB FOCACCIA: Prepare Pizza Dough as directed. Pat 1 lb (450 g) of the dough evenly into greased 9-inch (2.5 L) square cake pan. Cover and let rise for 30 minutes. With fingertip, make 12 indentations in dough; brush with 2 tsp oil from oil-packed sun-dried tomatoes. Sprinkle with ¼ tsp coarse salt and ¼ tsp dried rosemary, thyme or oregano. Press ¼ cup chopped drained oil-packed sun-dried tomatoes into dough. Bake in 450°F (230°C) oven until golden, about 30 minutes. Remove from pan; let cool slightly on rack. *(Make-ahead: Let stand at room temperature for up to 8 hours; rewarm, if desired.)* Cut into 4 strips; cut each in half. **Makes 8 pieces.**

3 cups **all-purpose flour** (approx)
2 tsp **quick-rising (instant) dry yeast**
1 tsp **salt**
1¼ cups **hot water** (120°F/50°C)
1 tbsp **extra-virgin olive oil**

~ stir ~   ~ cross ~   ~ boil ~

German Oktoberfest is the perfect time to pair large pretzels with mustard, wurst and a stein of your favourite ale. Enjoy these pretzels warm out of the oven or later on the same day that they are baked.

Soft Pretzels

In large bowl, dissolve sugar in ¼ cup of the warm water. Sprinkle in yeast; let stand until frothy, about 10 minutes.

Stir in remaining warm water and oil. *Stir* in 3 cups of the flour and salt to make sticky dough.

Turn out onto lightly floured surface; knead, adding as much of the remaining flour as necessary to make firm dough, until smooth and elastic, about 10 minutes.

Place in greased bowl, turning to grease all over. Cover with plastic wrap; let rise in warm draft-free place until doubled in bulk, about 1 hour.

Punch down dough. Cut into 8 pieces. On lightly floured surface, roll each piece into 20-inch (50 cm) long rope. Form into circle, crossing left end over right end above circle 3 inches (8 cm) from ends. Pick up ends and *cross* left end over right end again. Bring ends over and down to bottom of circle, overlapping by ¼ inch (5 mm) to create pretzel shape; press to seal. Place on 2 parchment paper–lined baking sheets. Cover and let rise for 15 minutes.

Add baking soda to large wide saucepan of boiling water. *Boil* pretzels, 2 or 3 at a time, turning once with slotted spatula, until puffed and set, about 1 minute. Using spatula, transfer to rack; let cool.

TOPPING: Return 4 pretzels to each prepared pan. Brush with egg; sprinkle with salt. Bake in top and bottom thirds of 400°F (200°C) oven, switching and rotating pans halfway through, until golden and bottoms sound hollow when tapped, 25 to 30 minutes. Transfer to rack; let cool just until warm. *(Make-ahead: Let cool completely. Freeze in airtight container for up to 2 weeks.)*

Makes 8 large pretzels. PER PRETZEL: about 252 cal, 8 g pro, 2 g total fat (trace sat. fat), 49 g carb, 2 g fibre, 23 mg chol, 684 mg sodium. % RDI: 1% calcium, 22% iron, 1% vit A, 70% folate.

1 tsp **granulated sugar**

1½ cups **warm water**

1 pkg **active dry yeast** (2¼ tsp)

2 tsp **vegetable oil**

4 cups **all-purpose flour** (approx)

1 tsp **salt**

2 tbsp **baking soda**

TOPPING:
1 **egg,** beaten

2 tsp **coarse salt**

French This loaf, shaped like a wheat sheaf, is traditionally served during harvest time. The starter, fermented for 18 hours ahead of time, is the key to its classic baguette flavour.

Épi de Blé

½ cup **warm water**
½ tsp **active dry yeast**
2½ cups **all-purpose flour**
1½ tsp **sea salt**

STARTER:
¼ tsp **active dry yeast**
¾ cup **room-temperature water**
1 cup **all-purpose flour**

STARTER: In large bowl, sprinkle yeast over water; let stand for 1 minute. Stir in flour until smooth and slightly elastic, about 2 minutes. Scrape down side of bowl. Cover with plastic wrap; let stand at room temperature for 18 hours or up to 24 hours.

Mix water and yeast into starter until broken up and slightly foaming, 2 minutes. Stir in flour and salt to form soft ragged dough. Turn out onto well-floured surface; knead until smooth and elastic, about 6 minutes. Shape into ball. Place in greased bowl, turning to grease all over. Cover with plastic wrap; let **rise** in warm place until doubled in bulk and indentation remains after pressing finger into dough, about 1½ hours.

Punch down dough; divide in half. Knead into balls; cover and let rest for 15 minutes. Flatten balls; **roll** into 15-inch (38 cm) long logs. Place on lightly floured tea towel, pleating towel between loaves. Cover with greased plastic wrap; let rise until doubled in bulk, 45 to 60 minutes.

Place loaves, 3 inches (8 cm) apart, on large flour-dusted baking sheet. Starting 2 inches (5 cm) from end and using sharp scissors at 45-degree angle, make 1 **cut** three-quarters of the way through loaf. Turn cut section to right. Repeat 6 more times, cutting 2 inches (5 cm) apart and turning each piece to alternate side to resemble wheat sheaf.

Place in 450°F (230°C) oven. With spritzer bottle, spray cold water onto walls and floor of oven (avoiding lightbulb) until steam fills oven, about 10 seconds. Quickly close oven door to trap steam; wait for 3 minutes then repeat steaming. Bake until golden and loaves sound hollow when tapped on bottoms, about 20 minutes. Let cool on rack.

Makes 2 loaves, or 8 pieces each. PER PIECE: about 100 cal, 3 g pro, trace total fat (0 g sat. fat), 21 g carb, 1 g fibre, 0 mg chol, 146 mg sodium. % RDI: 9% iron, 27% folate.

Variation
CLASSIC BAGUETTE: Omit cutting with scissors. Score loaf 7 times diagonally, 2 inches (5 cm) apart, along top of loaf.

~ rise ~ *~ roll ~* *~ cut ~*

French Don't let the two-step process of this round loaf turn you off. The first step takes a mere 10 minutes and is key to developing the loaf's deep granary flavour. Spraying the oven during the initial baking produces a thick, chewy, deep golden crust.

Olive Boule

¾ cup **warm water**

2½ cups **all-purpose flour** (approx)

½ cup **whole wheat flour**

2 tsp **salt**

⅓ cup halved pitted **oil-cured black olives**

SPONGE:

1 cup **rye flour**

½ cup **all-purpose flour**

¾ cup **warm water**

½ tsp **active dry yeast** or quick-rising (instant) dry yeast

SPONGE: In bowl, stir together rye flour, all-purpose flour, warm water and yeast. With wooden spoon, beat until smooth and thick. Cover with plastic wrap; let rise at room temperature for 12 hours or up to 24 hours.

Stir warm water into sponge. Add 2 cups of the all-purpose flour, whole wheat flour and salt, stirring until shaggy dough forms.

Turn out onto lightly floured surface; knead, adding as much of the remaining all-purpose flour as necessary, until smooth and elastic, about 10 minutes.

Place in greased bowl, turning to grease all over. Cover and let rise in warm draft-free place until doubled in bulk, about 2 hours.

Punch down dough; gently knead in olives. Form into ball; place on greased rimless baking sheet. Cover with damp tea towel; let rise in warm draft-free place until nearly doubled in bulk, about 45 minutes.

With sharp knife, cut 3 shallow slits in top of loaf. Place in 400°F (200°C) oven. With spritzer bottle, spray cold water onto walls and floor of oven (avoiding lightbulb) until steam fills oven, about 10 seconds. Quickly close oven door to trap steam; wait for 5 minutes then repeat steaming. Bake until golden and loaf sounds hollow when tapped on bottom, 55 to 60 minutes. Transfer to rack; let cool.

Makes 1 loaf, or 16 slices. PER SLICE: about 134 cal, 4 g pro, 2 g total fat (trace sat. fat), 26 g carb, 2 g fibre, 0 mg chol, 380 mg sodium. % RDI: 1% calcium, 13% iron, 25% folate.

Scandinavian These deep yellow, rich, perfectly textured buns rise and bake together in the pans, so all that's left is to pull them apart at the table.

Saffron Butter Buns

Using mortar and pestle or in bowl with back of spoon, crush saffron with sugar; mix in warm water until sugar is dissolved. Sprinkle with yeast; let stand until foamy, 5 to 10 minutes.

In large bowl, whisk together buttermilk, honey, egg, egg yolks and salt; stir in yeast mixture. Stir in about one-third of the all-purpose flour; beat with wooden spoon until smooth and sticky. Beat in butter until smooth.

Stir in spelt flour and all but about ¼ cup of the remaining all-purpose flour to form soft dough. Turn out onto lightly floured surface; knead, adding remaining all-purpose flour as necessary, until moist but silky smooth, 5 to 10 minutes. Place in greased bowl, turning to grease all over; cover with plastic wrap and let rise in warm draft-free place until doubled in bulk, about 1½ hours.

Lightly punch down dough; knead lightly. Turn out onto lightly floured surface. Divide in half and form into 2 balls; cover and let rest for 15 minutes. Roll each ball into rope; cut into 10 equal pieces. Form each piece into ball, pinching bottom to make top smooth. Place, evenly spaced, in 2 greased 9-inch (2.5 L) round cake pans.

GLAZE: Brush tops with butter. Cover and let rise in warm draft-free place until doubled in bulk, 30 to 45 minutes.

Bake in 400°F (200°C) oven until golden (or instant-read thermometer inserted in centre registers 190° to 195°F/87° to 90°C), about 17 minutes. Serve warm.

Makes 20 buns. PER BUN: about 160 cal, 4 g pro, 5 g total fat (3 g sat. fat), 25 g carb, 1 g fibre, 39 mg chol, 271 mg sodium. % RDI: 2% calcium, 11% iron, 4% vit A, 30% folate.

Pinch **saffron threads**

1 tbsp **granulated sugar**

¼ cup **warm water**

2 tsp **active dry yeast**

1 cup **buttermilk**

3 tbsp **liquid honey**

1 **egg**

2 **egg yolks**

2 tsp **salt**

4 cups **all-purpose flour** (approx)

¼ cup **butter,** softened

½ cup **whole spelt flour** or whole wheat flour

GLAZE:
2 tbsp **butter,** melted

*Lefse (opposite) with Dilled
Shrimp Spread (page 40)*

Norwegian This soft flatbread made from potatoes is the usual accompaniment to lutefisk, a pungent preserved fish dish that's an acquired taste. Dilled Shrimp Spread (page 40) makes a less-challenging, delicious partner to this bread.

Lefse

In large bowl and using electric mixer, beat together potatoes, milk, butter, sugar and salt until smooth. Mix in flour, in 2 additions, until no longer sticky.

Turn out onto lightly floured surface; knead until soft and elastic, about 3 minutes. Form into log; cut into 24 pieces. Roll out each into 5-inch (12 cm) round.

Heat electric griddle to medium-low or heat skillet over medium heat; brush with just enough of the oil to coat. In batches and brushing pan lightly with remaining oil each time, cook rounds, turning once, until spots appear, about 4 minutes. Let cool on rack. *(Make-ahead: Refrigerate layered between waxed paper in airtight container for up to 1 week or freeze for up to 1 month.)*

Makes 24 pieces. PER PIECE: about 98 cal, 2 g pro, 3 g total fat (1 g sat. fat), 16 g carb, 1 g fibre, 6 mg chol, 118 mg sodium. % RDI: 1% calcium, 4% iron, 2% vit A, 5% vit C, 11% folate.

4 cups mashed cooked peeled **baking potatoes,** cooled (about 5 potatoes)

¼ cup **milk**

¼ cup **butter,** melted

1 tbsp **granulated sugar**

1 tsp **salt**

2 cups **all-purpose flour**

2 tbsp **vegetable oil**

Scandinavian Finland, Denmark and Sweden all enjoy this type of dense cracker-like bread as a base for spreads and open-faced sandwiches. Dilled Shrimp Spread (page 40) is particularly nice on top.

Rye Crispbread

1 tbsp **caraway seeds**

¼ tsp **granulated sugar**

1¼ cups **warm water**

1 tsp **active dry yeast**

1¼ cups **rye flour**

1⅓ cups **all-purpose flour**

1 tsp **salt**

1 tbsp **vegetable oil**

In small skillet, toast caraway seeds over medium heat, shaking pan occasionally, until fragrant, 3 to 5 minutes. Using spice grinder or in mortar with pestle, grind caraway seeds to fine powder. Set aside.

In large bowl, dissolve sugar in warm water. Sprinkle in yeast; let stand until frothy, about 10 minutes. With wooden spoon, stir in rye flour, 1 cup of the all-purpose flour, caraway seeds and salt to form shaggy dough. Turn out onto floured surface; knead, adding as much of the remaining all-purpose flour as necessary, until smooth and elastic, 5 minutes. Form into ball.

Place in large greased bowl, turning to grease all over. Cover with plastic wrap; let rise in warm, draft-free place until almost doubled in bulk, about 1½ hours.

Punch down dough; turn out onto floured surface. Divide into 12 pieces. Dusting with all-purpose flour as necessary, roll out each piece as thinly as possible into long rectangle with rounded edges. Transfer to greased rimless baking sheets; prick all over with fork. Let stand for 15 minutes.

Bake in top and bottom thirds of 400°F (200°C) oven, switching and rotating pans halfway through, until crisp, 10 to 12 minutes. Transfer to racks; brush with oil. Let cool. *(Make-ahead: Store in airtight container for up to 1 week or freeze for up to 1 month.)* Break each into 4 pieces.

Makes about 48 pieces. PER PIECE: about 27 cal, 1 g pro, trace total fat (0 g sat. fat), 5 g carb, 1 g fibre, 0 mg chol, 48 mg sodium. % RDI: 3% iron, 5% folate.

Armenian This cracker bread is popular in countries from the Middle East through the southern part of the Caucasus Mountains. You'll achieve super-crisp lavash by rolling the dough out paper-thin. Break it into shards and serve with dips, spreads or your favourite cheeses.

Lavash

In bowl, whisk together flour, salt and yeast; stir in oil and honey. Stir in warm water to form stiff dough.

Turn out onto lightly floured surface; knead until smooth, about 5 minutes. Place in greased bowl, turning to grease all over; cover with tea towel or plastic wrap and let rise in warm draft-free place until doubled in bulk, about 1½ hours.

Turn out onto lightly floured surface; roll out into 17- x 12-inch (42 x 30 cm) paper-thin rectangle. Transfer to large greased or parchment paper–lined rimless baking sheet; gently stretch edges to hang ½ inch (1 cm) over edge of pan. Let rest for 5 minutes; release edges, letting overhang shrink back.

Lightly brush top with water; sprinkle with caraway seeds, poppy seeds and kosher salt. Bake in 375°F (190°C) oven until golden and crisp, 16 to 20 minutes. Let cool on pan on rack. *(Make-ahead: Store in airtight container for up to 1 week.)*

Makes 1 sheet, or 16 pieces. PER PIECE: about 66 cal, 2 g pro, 2 g total fat (trace sat. fat), 10 g carb, trace fibre, 0 mg chol, 121 mg sodium. % RDI: 1% calcium, 4% iron, 8% folate.

1½ cups **bread flour**

½ tsp **salt**

½ tsp **quick-rising (instant) dry yeast**

2 tbsp **vegetable oil**

2 tsp **liquid honey**

½ cup **warm water**

1 tsp **caraway seeds**

1 tsp **poppy seeds**

½ tsp **kosher salt** or coarse salt

Afghan This soft, chewy naan bread, shaped like a snowshoe, is a staple in Afghanistan but is also common in Turkey and Iran. Our recipe has a deep sesame flavour because of the tahini, a paste made of ground sesame seeds.

Snowshoe Flatbread

1¼ cups **warm water**

½ tsp **active dry yeast**

¼ tsp **granulated sugar**

¾ cup **whole wheat flour**

2 cups **all-purpose flour** (approx)

¼ cup **tahini**

3 tbsp **sesame seeds**

1½ tsp **salt**

1 tbsp **vegetable oil**

1½ tsp **kosher salt** or coarse salt

In large bowl, stir together warm water, yeast and sugar until sugar is dissolved. Stir in whole wheat flour and ½ cup of the all-purpose flour for 1 minute. Cover and let stand for 30 minutes.

Stir in tahini, 2 tbsp of the sesame seeds and salt until combined; stir in remaining all-purpose flour.

Turn dough out onto floured surface; knead, dusting with more flour as necessary, until smooth and elastic, about 5 minutes. Place in greased bowl, turning to grease all over. Cover with tea towel or plastic wrap; let rise in warm draft-free place until doubled in bulk, about 2 hours.

Punch down dough. On lightly floured surface, divide into 8 pieces. Shape each into 5- x 2½-inch (12 x 6 cm) oval; cover and let rise for 15 minutes.

Meanwhile, heat baking stone in 475°F (240°C) oven for 10 minutes, or heat heavy baking sheet for 5 minutes.

Using fingertips, press through dough to make 12 holes in each piece. Gently stretch dough lengthwise until about 8 inches (20 cm) long. Brush all over with oil; sprinkle top with remaining sesame seeds and kosher salt.

Bake, 4 pieces at a time, on hot baking stone or baking sheet for 5 minutes. Turn over; bake until golden, about 3 minutes. Brush any loose sesame seeds off baking stone or sheet before baking remaining bread.

Wrap in tea towel to keep warm and soft; serve warm or at room temperature. *(Make-ahead: Store in airtight container for up to 24 hours. Wrap in foil; reheat in 400°F/200°C oven until hot, about 8 minutes.)*

Makes 8 pieces, or 16 servings. PER SERVING: about 129 cal, 3 g pro, 4 g total fat (1 g sat. fat), 20 g carb, 2 g fibre, 0 mg chol, 366 mg sodium. % RDI: 2% calcium, 10% iron, 19% folate.

Mediterranean Sephardic Jews – especially those from the Mediterranean – often add aniseed and/or sesame seeds to challah for flavour and to represent fruitfulness. The spiral loaf is a must at Rosh Hashanah so that holiday prayers will ascend to heaven.

Swirled Challah With Aniseed

In small bowl, dissolve sugar in warm water. Sprinkle yeast over top; let stand until frothy, about 10 minutes.

In large bowl, whisk together 3 cups of the flour, aniseed and salt. Add yeast mixture, oil, honey, eggs and egg yolks; using wooden spoon, stir to form soft, sticky dough.

Turn out onto lightly floured surface; knead, dusting with enough of the remaining flour to prevent dough from sticking, until smooth and elastic, about 10 minutes.

Place in large greased bowl, turning to grease all over. Cover with plastic wrap; let rise in warm draft-free place until doubled in bulk and indentation remains when dough is poked with 2 fingers, about 1¼ hours. (Or let rise in refrigerator for up to 12 hours; bring to room temperature for 45 to 60 minutes before proceeding.)

Punch down dough; with lightly floured hands, squeeze and roll dough out into 36-inch (90 cm) long rope. Using fingertips, press to flatten into 4-inch (10 cm) wide strip. Press raisins evenly along strip; fold long edges together over raisins and pinch to enclose. Gently roll to make smooth, seamless log.

Fold 2 inches (5 cm) of 1 end over and flatten; bend upward slightly. Wind remaining rope around flattened end to form fairly tight spiral, keeping centre slightly higher. Transfer to greased rimless baking sheet. Cover loosely with plastic wrap; let rise in warm draft-free place until doubled in bulk, about 1 hour.

GLAZE: Lightly beat egg with 1 tbsp water; brush over loaf. Bake in 350°F (180°C) oven until golden and loaf sounds hollow when tapped on bottom, 35 to 45 minutes. Let cool on rack.

Makes 1 loaf, or 10 slices. PER SLICE: about 311 cal, 8 g pro, 9 g total fat (1 g sat. fat), 51 g carb, 2 g fibre, 96 mg chol, 367 mg sodium. % RDI: 3% calcium, 19% iron, 4% vit A, 36% folate.

1 tbsp **granulated sugar**

½ cup **warm water**

1 pkg **active dry yeast** (2¼ tsp)

3½ cups **all-purpose flour** (approx)

2 tsp **aniseed,** crushed

1½ tsp **salt**

¼ cup **vegetable oil**

¼ cup **liquid honey**

2 **eggs**

2 **egg yolks**

¾ cup **golden raisins**

GLAZE:
1 **egg**

French This pretty little loaf is a holiday tradition in the French province of Alsace, along the German border. Its sweet, spicy flavours complement rich cheeses.

Alsatian-Style Fruit and Nut Bread

¾ cup chopped **dried pears**

¾ cup chopped **dried apples**

¾ cup **boiling water**

¾ cup chopped **dried figs**

½ cup **sultana raisins**

¼ cup **candied mixed peel**

¼ cup **kirsch**

½ cup chopped toasted **hazelnuts**

½ cup chopped toasted **almonds**

1½ tsp **cinnamon**

½ tsp **ground star anise**

¼ tsp **ground cloves**

Pinch each **grated nutmeg** and **pepper**

¼ cup **granulated sugar**

½ tsp **salt**

1 pkg **active dry yeast** (2¼ tsp)

2 cups **rye flour**

2¼ cups **all-purpose flour** (approx)

SUGAR SYRUP:

⅓ cup **granulated sugar**

⅓ cup **water**

1 tbsp **kirsch**

In heatproof bowl, combine pears, apples and boiling water; cover and let stand until at room temperature, about 1 hour. Reserving liquid, drain, pressing fruit to extract liquid. Add figs, raisins, mixed peel and kirsch; toss to combine. Cover and let stand for 2 hours. Add hazelnuts, almonds, cinnamon, star anise, cloves, nutmeg and pepper; toss to combine.

Add enough water to reserved soaking liquid to make 1¼ cups. In saucepan, heat soaking liquid, sugar and salt over medium heat until sugar is dissolved; let cool to lukewarm. Pour sugar mixture into large bowl; sprinkle yeast over top. Let stand until frothy, about 10 minutes. Stir in rye flour and 1 cup of the all-purpose flour to make sticky dough.

Turn out onto floured surface; knead, adding up to 1 cup of the remaining flour as necessary to prevent sticking, until smooth and elastic, about 6 minutes. Place in greased bowl, turning to grease all over. Cover and let rise until doubled in bulk, about 2 hours.

Toss fruit with ¼ cup of the remaining all-purpose flour. Punch down dough. On lightly floured surface, knead in fruit mixture. Transfer to large greased bowl; cover and let stand for 20 minutes. Divide dough in half. On lightly floured surface, pat each into 11- x 8-inch (28 x 20 cm) rectangle. Starting at narrow end, roll up each into cylinder; pinch edge and ends to seal. Fit, seam side down, into 2 greased 8- x 4-inch (1.5 L) loaf pans. Cover and let rise until doubled in bulk, 1½ to 2 hours.

Using razor or sharp serrated knife, cut ¼-inch (5 mm) deep slit along top of each loaf. Bake in 400°F (200°C) oven for 20 minutes. Reduce heat to 350°F (180°C); bake until tops are dark golden and bottoms sound hollow when tapped, about 30 minutes.

SUGAR SYRUP: In saucepan, boil sugar with water until reduced to ¼ cup, 3 to 5 minutes. Stir in kirsch; brush over warm loaves. Remove from pans; let cool on racks.

Makes 2 loaves, or 10 to 12 slices each. PER EACH OF 24 SLICES: about 190 cal, 4 g pro, 3 g total fat (trace sat. fat), 39 g carb, 5 g fibre, 0 mg chol, 55 mg sodium, 246 mg potassium. % RDI: 3% calcium, 14% iron, 2% vit C, 18% folate.

Portuguese This large round sweet loaf is just as tasty plain as it is topped with your favourite jam or spread. For a decadent treat, use it as a rich base for French toast.

Massa Sovada

¾ cup **granulated sugar**

¼ cup **warm water**

1 tbsp **active dry yeast**

1 cup **homogenized milk**

½ cup **unsalted butter**

1 tsp **salt**

4 **eggs**

1 tsp grated **lemon zest**

6 cups **all-purpose flour** (approx)

GLAZE:

1 **egg**

In large bowl, dissolve 1 tsp of the sugar in warm water. Sprinkle yeast over top; let stand until foamy, about 10 minutes.

Meanwhile, in saucepan, heat milk, remaining sugar, butter and salt over medium heat until butter is melted and sugar is dissolved, about 3 minutes. Let cool to lukewarm; whisk into yeast mixture along with eggs and lemon zest.

Stir 5 cups of the flour into yeast mixture to make soft dough. Transfer to well-floured surface; knead, adding as much of the remaining flour as necessary to prevent sticking, until smooth and elastic, 8 to 10 minutes.

Place in large greased bowl, turning to grease all over. Cover and let rise in warm draft-free place until doubled in bulk, about 2 hours.

Punch down dough and divide in half; form each into ball. Grease two 8-inch (1.2 L) round cake pans with 2-inch (5 cm) high sides. Place 1 ball in each. Cover and let rise until dough rises over tops of pans, about 2 hours.

GLAZE: Whisk egg with 2 tsp water; brush over loaves. Bake in 350°F (180°C) oven until golden and bottoms sound hollow when tapped, 35 to 40 minutes. Remove from pans; let cool on racks.

Makes 2 loaves, or 8 slices each. PER SLICE: about 292 cal, 8 g pro, 8 g total fat (5 g sat. fat), 46 g carb, 2 g fibre, 75 mg chol, 172 mg sodium, 110 mg potassium. % RDI: 3% calcium, 18% iron, 8% vit A, 55% folate.

Italian This tall Christmas loaf from Milan is made with egg yolks, which lend it a golden hue. A batterlike yeast mixture called a sponge gives it a light texture and tangy flavour. Cut panettone into wedges for a scrumptious breakfast or dessert.

Panettone

SPONGE: In large bowl, sprinkle yeast over milk; cover and let stand until yeast starts to rise to surface, about 10 minutes. Stir in flour to make sticky dough. Cover with greased plastic wrap; let rise in warm draft-free place until bubbly and doubled in bulk, about 1½ hours.

In glass measure, microwave brandy on high until hot, about 20 seconds. Add raisins; cover and let stand until plump, 1 hour. Reserving liquid, drain, pressing raisins to extract liquid. Set aside separately.

In large bowl with electric mixer, beat yolks, eggs, sugar, orange zest, lemon zest, vanilla, salt and soaking liquid until light and thickened. Beat in butter, 1 tbsp at a time, to form curdled-looking mixture. Add sponge and 3 cups of the flour; mix by hand until sticky dough forms. Transfer to well-floured surface; knead, adding remaining flour as necessary, until smooth and rather buttery, about 8 minutes. Let rest for 5 minutes.

Press down dough. Knead in raisins and mixed peel. Place in greased bowl; cover with greased plastic wrap. Let rise in warm draft-free place until doubled in bulk, 2 hours. Punch down dough. Turn out onto floured surface; form into ball, pinching bottom to make top smooth.

Grease panettone mould or 2-lb (900 g) coffee can. Line bottom and side with parchment paper, extending 1 inch (2.5 cm) above rim. Place dough, seam side down, in mould. Cover and let rise in warm draft-free place until doubled in bulk, about 2 hours. (Or let rise in refrigerator for up to 12 hours; remove from refrigerator 1 hour before baking.)

TOPPING: Cut ¼-inch (5 mm) deep X shape in top; brush with butter. Bake in bottom third of 350°F (180°C) oven until tester inserted in centre comes out clean, 1½ to 1¾ hours, covering with foil after 40 minutes if darker than milk chocolate. Let cool on rack for 1 hour. Pull paper to remove from can. *(Make-ahead: Wrap and store for up to 1 day or overwrap with heavy-duty foil and freeze for up to 2 weeks.)*

Makes 1 loaf, or 12 slices. PER SLICE: about 426 cal, 8 g pro, 16 g total fat (9 g sat. fat), 63 g carb, 2 g fibre, 132 mg chol, 402 mg sodium. % RDI: 4% calcium, 21% iron, 15% vit A, 2% vit C, 62% folate.

¼ cup **brandy** or rum

½ cup **golden raisins**

4 **egg yolks**

2 **eggs**

⅔ cup **granulated sugar**

1 tbsp grated **orange zest**

1 tbsp grated **lemon zest**

1 tbsp **vanilla**

1½ tsp **salt**

¾ cup **butter**, softened

4 cups **all-purpose flour** (approx)

½ cup chopped **candied mixed peel**

SPONGE:
1 pkg **active dry yeast** (2¼ tsp)

⅔ cup warm **milk**

1 cup **all-purpose flour**

TOPPING:
2 tsp **butter**, melted

~ mix ~   ~ roll ~   ~ cover ~

Croatian Easter calls for special treats. In Croatia, this traditional sweet bread, called makovnjaca, is the star on holiday tables. Serve it for brunch or enjoy a slice with an afternoon cup of tea.

Poppy Seed Roll

In small microwaveable bowl or saucepan, warm milk. In separate bowl, dissolve 1 tsp of the sugar in 2 tbsp of the warm milk. Sprinkle in yeast; let stand until frothy, about 20 minutes. Meanwhile, stir butter and remaining sugar into remaining milk; heat until butter is melted. Let cool to lukewarm.

In large bowl, whisk 2½ cups of the flour, lemon zest and salt. Make well in centre; add eggs, butter mixture and yeast mixture. With wooden spoon, *mix* to form soft, slightly sticky dough that comes away from side of bowl. Turn out onto floured surface; knead, adding as much of the remaining flour as necessary, until smooth, about 2 minutes. Place in greased bowl, turning to grease all over. Cover and let rise in warm draft-free place until doubled in bulk, about 1 hour.

POPPY SEED FILLING: Meanwhile, in clean coffee grinder, grind poppy seeds. In saucepan, bring milk, sugar and honey to boil. Stir in poppy seeds, currants, butter, lemon zest and cinnamon; return to boil. Reduce heat to medium; cook, stirring often, until fairly dry and stiff, about 8 minutes. Stir in rum; let cool for 10 minutes.

Punch down dough; turn out onto floured surface. Roll out into 14- x 12-inch (35 x 30 cm) rectangle. Leaving ½-inch (1 cm) border, spread with filling. Starting at long side, *roll* up; pinch seam to seal. Using metal spatulas, place roll diagonally, seam side down, on greased baking sheet. Cover loosely with greased plastic wrap; let rise in warm draft-free place for 1 hour.

TOPPING: Brush egg over dough. Bake in 350°F (180°C) oven until golden and loaf sounds hollow when tapped on bottom, 30 minutes. Transfer pan to rack; *cover* loaf with tea towel (for softer crust) and let cool for 20 minutes. Transfer loaf to rack; let cool completely.

Makes 1 roll, or 18 slices. PER SLICE: about 209 cal, 5 g pro, 9 g total fat (3 g sat. fat), 28 g carb, 2 g fibre, 43 mg chol, 80 mg sodium. % RDI: 13% calcium, 14% iron, 5% vit A, 2% vit C, 29% folate.

¾ cup **milk**

¼ cup **granulated sugar**

1 tbsp **active dry yeast**

¼ cup **butter**

2¾ cups **all-purpose flour** (approx)

2 tsp grated **lemon zest**

¼ tsp **salt**

2 **eggs,** beaten

POPPY SEED FILLING:

1 cup **poppy seeds**

¾ cup **milk**

⅓ cup **granulated sugar**

3 tbsp **liquid honey**

2 tbsp **dried currants** or chopped raisins

2 tbsp **butter**

1 tsp grated **lemon zest**

¼ tsp **cinnamon**

1 tbsp **amber rum** or water

TOPPING:

1 **egg,** lightly beaten

Eastern European Made in Czechoslovakia, Poland and Hungary, these bundles of sweet dough are stuffed with a variety of fillings. This cottage cheese and cream cheese filling is laced with refreshing lemon zest to balance the sweetness.

Double Cheese Kolaches

⅔ cup **milk**

¼ cup **unsalted butter**

3 tbsp **granulated sugar**

¾ tsp **salt**

¼ cup **warm water**

1½ tsp **active dry yeast**

2 **egg yolks**

2½ cups **all-purpose flour**

FILLING:
¼ cup **4% cottage cheese**

½ cup **cream cheese,** softened

2 tbsp **granulated sugar**

1 **egg yolk**

½ tsp grated **lemon zest**

TOPPING:
2 tbsp **all-purpose flour**

1½ tbsp **granulated sugar**

1 tbsp **butter,** softened

In small saucepan, heat milk, 3 tbsp of the butter, all but 2 tsp of the sugar and salt until butter is melted and sugar is dissolved. Let cool to lukewarm.

In large bowl, dissolve remaining sugar in warm water. Sprinkle in yeast; let stand until frothy, about 10 minutes. Whisk in milk mixture and egg yolks. Stir in 2 cups of the flour to form shaggy dough.

Turn out onto floured surface; knead, adding as much of the remaining flour as necessary, until smooth and elastic, about 10 minutes. Place in large greased bowl, turning to grease all over. Cover with plastic wrap; let rise in warm draft-free place until doubled in bulk, about 1½ hours.

Divide dough into 12 pieces. Shape each into ball, stretching and pinching dough underneath to smooth tops. Place, 1 inch (2.5 cm) apart, in parchment paper–lined 13- x 9-inch (3.5 L) cake pan, pressing to flatten slightly. Melt remaining butter; brush over tops. Cover with plastic wrap and let rise in warm draft-free place until doubled in bulk, about 1 hour.

TOPPING: In small bowl, whisk flour with sugar. Using fingertips, work in butter until crumbly. Set aside.

FILLING: In small strainer, press cottage cheese to drain off moisture. In bowl, beat together cottage cheese, cream cheese, sugar, egg yolk and lemon zest until smooth.

Using fingers, make indentation in each ball. Spoon about 1 tbsp filling into each; sprinkle with topping. Bake in 350°F (180°C) oven until golden, about 35 minutes. Let cool in pan on rack.

Makes 12 buns. PER BUN: about 231 cal, 6 g pro, 10 g total fat (6 g sat. fat), 29 g carb, 1 g fibre, 76 mg chol, 208 mg sodium, 81 mg potassium. % RDI: 4% calcium, 11% iron, 11% vit A, 35% folate.

Hungarian With dark trails of poppy seeds swirled inside sweet dough, this traditional wreath makes a dramatic centrepiece. Cooking the seeds makes them tender; grinding them ensures that none stick between your teeth.

Hungarian Christmas Bread

¼ cup packed **brown sugar**

⅓ cup **warm water**

1 pkg **active dry yeast** (2¼ tsp)

⅔ cup **milk**

¼ cup **butter,** melted

2 **eggs**

1 tbsp grated **lemon zest**

1½ tsp **salt**

4½ cups **all-purpose flour** (approx)

⅔ cup **golden raisins**

2 tbsp **lemon juice**

FILLING:

½ cup **poppy seeds**

1 cup **milk**

¼ cup **granulated sugar**

2 tbsp **cornstarch**

1 tsp **almond extract**

TOPPING:

1 **egg,** lightly beaten

In large bowl, dissolve 1 tsp of the brown sugar in warm water. Sprinkle in yeast; let stand until frothy, about 10 minutes.

Whisk in remaining sugar, milk, butter, eggs, lemon zest and salt. Whisk in 2 cups of the flour. With wooden spoon, stir in enough of the remaining flour, ½ cup at a time, to make soft slightly sticky dough. Turn out onto lightly floured surface; knead, adding remaining flour as necessary, until smooth and elastic, 8 minutes. Place in greased bowl, turning to grease all over. Cover and let rise in warm place until doubled in bulk, 1 hour.

FILLING: Meanwhile, in blender, chop poppy seeds finely. In saucepan, bring poppy seeds, ¾ cup of the milk and sugar to boil. Reduce heat to medium-low; simmer, stirring, until liquid is almost evaporated, 3 minutes. Combine remaining milk, cornstarch and almond extract. Whisk into poppy seed mixture; cook over medium heat, stirring, until thickened and clumped, 10 to 15 minutes. Refrigerate until room temperature.

In small saucepan, bring raisins and lemon juice to boil. Reduce heat to medium-low; cover and cook for 3 minutes. Set aside.

Punch down dough. Turn out onto floured surface; roll out into 17- x 14-inch (42 x 35 cm) rectangle. Leaving 1-inch (2.5 cm) border, spread with filling; sprinkle with raisin mixture, pressing lightly. Starting at long edge, tightly roll up; pinch seam to seal. Place, seam side down, on greased rimless baking sheet; shape into ring, pinching ends together. With serrated knife, make 17 slits, 1 inch (2.5 cm) apart, two-thirds of the way into centre of ring. Turn each section out, alternating sides. Cover and let rise in warm draft-free place until doubled in bulk, 40 minutes.

TOPPING: Brush egg over dough. Bake in 375°F (190°C) oven until golden and loaf sounds hollow when tapped on bottom, 20 to 30 minutes. Transfer to rack; let cool completely. *(Make-ahead: Wrap in plastic wrap and store at room temperature for up to 24 hours.)*

Makes 1 loaf, or 17 slices. PER SLICE: about 240 cal, 6 g pro, 6 g total fat (3 g sat. fat), 40 g carb, 2 g fibre, 47 mg chol, 257 mg sodium. % RDI: 10% calcium, 15% iron, 5% vit A, 2% vit C, 25% folate.

Filipino These small, sweet steamed buns are popular throughout the Philippines and are excellent at soaking up delicious sauces and broths. Try them with a steaming bowl of Bicol-Style Mussel Soup (page 80).

Puto

In small bowl, dissolve 2 tsp of the sugar in warm water. Sprinkle in yeast; let stand until frothy, about 10 minutes.

In separate bowl, whisk together rice flour, bread flour, remaining sugar and salt.

In stand mixer with paddle attachment or large bowl with wooden spoon, beat egg. Beat in coconut milk, ½ cup water and yeast mixture. Add flour mixture; beat until smooth and thick, about 5 minutes. Cover and let rise in warm draft-free place until bubbly and increased about 1½ times in bulk, 1½ to 2 hours.

Beat batter down lightly. Spoon into greased mini muffin cups, filling to just below top. Place on rack over wok of boiling water, or in bamboo steamer. Cover and steam until buns rise and tester inserted In centre comes out dry, 6 to 8 minutes. Let cool in pan on rack for 3 minutes. *(Make-ahead: Let cool. Freeze in airtight container for up to 1 week; heat in microwave for 20 seconds.)* Serve warm.

Makes 36 buns. PER BUN: about 56 cal, 1 g pro, 2 g total fat (1 g sat. fat), 9 g carb, trace fibre, 5 mg chol, 35 mg sodium, 26 mg potassium. % RDI: 3% iron, 4% folate.

3 tbsp **granulated sugar**

¼ cup **warm water**

¾ tsp **active dry yeast**

1½ cups **rice flour**

1 cup **bread flour** or all-purpose flour

½ tsp **salt**

1 **egg**

1 cup **coconut milk**

TIP | BE SURE TO BUY FULL-FAT COCONUT MILK. BEFORE OPENING IT, SOAK THE CAN IN HOT WATER FOR FIVE MINUTES TO MELT THE SOLIDS THAT CONGEAL ON TOP. SHAKE BEFORE OPENING.

Israeli Latkes may be the most popular Hanukkah treat in Canada, but these jam-filled doughnuts (singular: sufganiyah in Hebrew) can't be far behind.

Sufganiyot

In large bowl, dissolve 1 tbsp of the sugar in warm water. Sprinkle in yeast; let stand until frothy, about 10 minutes. Beat in egg yolks, butter, vanilla and remaining sugar. With wooden spoon, beat in flour and salt, adding more flour if necessary to make soft sticky dough.

Transfer to lightly floured surface; knead until smooth and elastic, 5 to 8 minutes. Place in greased bowl, turning to grease all over. Cover with plastic wrap; let rise in warm draft-free place until doubled in bulk, about 1½ hours.

Punch down dough. On lightly floured surface, roll out to ½-inch (1 cm) thickness. Using 2-inch (5 cm) round cookie cutter, cut out circles, gently pressing scraps together and rerolling. Transfer to lightly floured baking sheet. Cover loosely and let rise in warm draft-free place until doubled in bulk and rounded, about 1 hour.

In deep fryer, wok or deep saucepan, heat about 2 inches (5 cm) oil until deep-fry thermometer registers 350°F (180°C). Deep-fry doughnuts, 3 at a time and turning once, until golden, 3 to 4 minutes. With slotted spoon, transfer to paper towel–lined plate to drain.

Spoon jam into pastry bag fitted with small plain tip. Cut small slit in side of each doughnut. Insert pastry tip into slit; inject 1 tsp jam into centre of each.

TOPPING: Place sugar on plate; roll warm doughnuts in sugar to coat completely. *(Make-ahead: Store in airtight container for up to 1 day.)*

Makes about 24 doughnuts. PER DOUGHNUT: about 149 cal, 2 g pro, 7 g total fat (1 g sat. fat), 21 g carb, 1 g fibre, 21 mg chol, 36 mg sodium. % RDI: 1% calcium, 5% iron, 2% vit A, 12% folate.

¼ cup **granulated sugar**

⅔ cup **warm water**

1 pkg **active dry yeast** (2¼ tsp)

2 **egg yolks**

2 tbsp **butter** or hard pareve margarine, softened

1 tsp **vanilla**

2½ cups **all-purpose flour** (approx)

¼ tsp **salt**

Vegetable oil for frying

½ cup **raspberry jam**

TOPPING:
½ cup **granulated sugar** or icing sugar

Danish Red Cabbage (page 130)

{salads & sides}

Greek This salad has all the flavours of a traditional Greek village salad in a pretty presentation. Greece has won the right to call its tangy white goat cheese "feta." Other countries that produce similar cheese must add the country of origin, such as Danish feta, to distinguish it from the real thing.

Tomato and Feta Salad

8 small **tomatoes**

12 **sun-dried black olives**

12 oz (340 g) **feta cheese**

Quarter **English cucumber,** thinly sliced

¼ cup **extra-virgin olive oil**

1 tbsp chopped **fresh parsley**

Core tomatoes. Cut each into 8 wedges from stem end almost to base, leaving base intact so wedges form flower shape. Arrange on serving platter.

Place olive in centre of each tomato; surround with remaining olives. Slice feta thickly; add to platter along with cucumber. Drizzle with oil; sprinkle with parsley.

Makes 8 servings. PER SERVING: about 194 cal, 7 g pro, 17 g total fat (8 g sat. fat), 5 g carb, 1 g fibre, 39 mg chol, 553 mg sodium. % RDI: 21% calcium, 6% iron, 9% vit A, 17% vit C, 10% folate.

French Toasted goat cheese croûtes enhance this simply dressed bistro-style salad. Choose the inner lighter green leaves of curly endive, or use frisée or spinach.

Curly Endive With Goat Cheese Croûtes

Arrange baguette slices on baking sheet. Broil 1 side until golden and crisp, about 30 seconds; let cool.

Rub toasted side of each slice with cut side of garlic. Spread untoasted side of each slice with goat cheese. *(Make-ahead: Cover with plastic wrap and refrigerate for up to 2 hours.)* Broil until cheese is just starting to brown, about 2 minutes.

DRESSING: In large bowl, whisk together oil, vinegar, mustard, garlic, salt and pepper.

Add endive to dressing; toss to coat. Divide salad among plates; top each with 2 croûtes.

Makes 4 servings. PER SERVING: about 291 cal, 9 g pro, 21 g total fat (7 g sat. fat), 17 g carb, 2 g fibre, 14 mg chol, 455 mg sodium. % RDI: 9% calcium, 14% iron, 19% vit A, 7% vit C, 44% folate.

8 thin slices **baguette**

Half large clove **garlic**

½ cup **soft goat cheese**

4 cups torn **light green curly endive**

DRESSING:
¼ cup **extra-virgin olive oil**

1 tbsp **wine vinegar**

1 tsp **Dijon mustard**

1 clove **garlic,** minced

¼ tsp each **salt** and **pepper**

Middle Eastern This aromatic salad – traditionally a mixture of crumbled toasted pitas, purslane greens and ground sumac – is popular throughout the Middle East. Sumac is a dried red berry with a lemony taste.

Fattoush

1 cup thinly sliced **red onion**

2 **green onions,** thinly sliced

1 **English cucumber** (about 12 inches/30 cm long), seeded and diced

1 **sweet green pepper,** diced

6 **radishes,** sliced

¼ cup shredded **fresh mint**

⅓ cup **extra-virgin olive oil**

¼ cup **lemon juice**

2 cloves **garlic,** minced

1 tbsp **balsamic vinegar**

1½ tsp **ground sumac** or grated lemon zest

1 tsp **salt**

3 **pitas**

4 cups torn **romaine lettuce**

2 **tomatoes,** diced

In large bowl, combine red onion, green onions, cucumber, pepper, radishes and mint. Whisk together oil, lemon juice, garlic, vinegar, sumac and salt; pour over vegetables and toss to coat. *(Make-ahead: Cover and refrigerate for up to 3 hours.)*

Toast pitas in 375°F (190°C) oven or toaster oven until crisp, about 7 minutes. Let cool. Break into bite-size chunks.

Add pita bread chunks, lettuce and tomatoes to bowl; toss to coat. Let stand for 10 minutes before serving.

Makes 8 servings. PER SERVING: about 175 cal, 4 g pro, 10 g total fat (1 g sat. fat), 20 g carb, 2 g fibre, 0 mg chol, 418 mg sodium. % RDI: 5% calcium, 10% iron, 12% vit A, 57% vit C, 37% folate.

Australian The large tropical papaya, or *Carica papaya* fruit, is called "pawpaw" in Australia. Its vibrant burnt-orange, tender-firm flesh is refreshing in a salad.

Pawpaw and Avocado Salad

Half small **red onion,** thinly sliced
  into rings

2 **avocados,** pitted, peeled
  and cubed

2 cups cubed seeded peeled
  papaya

2 tbsp torn **fresh mint**

DRESSING:
3 tbsp **white wine vinegar**

1 tbsp **sodium-reduced soy sauce**

½ tsp cracked **black peppercorns**

Pinch **granulated sugar**

DRESSING: In small bowl, whisk together vinegar, soy sauce, cracked peppercorns and sugar.

Place onion, avocados and papaya in separate bowls. Divide dressing among bowls; toss gently to coat.

Arrange onion on serving platter; top with papaya and avocados. Sprinkle with mint.

Makes 6 servings. PER SERVING: about 134 cal, 2 g pro, 10 g total fat (2 g sat. fat), 11 g carb, 4 g fibre, 0 mg chol, 109 mg sodium. % RDI: 2% calcium, 7% iron, 14% vit A, 58% vit C, 21% folate.

Thai Your first whiff of fish sauce may be a bit overwhelming, but its salty, umami-rich flavour is vital to a delicious green mango salad – and many other Thai dishes. Choose unripe, firm, green-skinned mangoes for the best flavour and texture.

Green Mango Salad

In dry skillet over medium heat, toast cashews until fragrant and golden, about 8 minutes. Set aside.

Cut pointy ends off mangoes. Set each mango on cut end; cut off skin. Cut flesh on either side of flat pit into thin slices; stack and cut into thin strips.

In bowl, whisk together cilantro, mint, lime juice, sugar, fish sauce, oil and chili sauce. Add mangoes, red pepper and onion; toss to coat. *(Make-ahead: Cover and refrigerate for up to 2 days.)*

Sprinkle with cashews just before serving.

Makes 6 servings. PER SERVING: about 189 cal, 3 g pro, 6 g total fat (1 g sat. fat), 35 g carb, 4 g fibre, 0 mg chol, 318 mg sodium. % RDI: 3% calcium, 8% iron, 71% vit A, 137% vit C, 18% folate.

⅓ cup chopped **raw cashews** or peanuts

2 **unripe mangoes** (2 lb/ 900 g total)

⅓ cup chopped **fresh cilantro**

⅓ cup chopped **fresh mint**

2 tbsp **lime juice**

4 tsp **granulated sugar**

4 tsp **fish sauce**

1 tbsp **vegetable oil**

¼ tsp **Asian chili sauce** or hot pepper sauce

1 **sweet red pepper,** thinly sliced

1 cup thinly sliced **red onion**

Korean A refreshing dish on a hot summer day, this salad has a fabulous mix of textures and flavours. To make kimchi juice, gently squeeze kimchi or pour out the excess from the jar. You'll need to seek out the kimchi and gochujang at an Asian market, but their authentic flavours are worth the effort.

Cold Somen Noodle Salad

PICKLED DAIKON: Combine daikon, vinegar and sugar; refrigerate for 15 minutes.

Meanwhile, in large pot of boiling water, cook noodles according to package instructions, about 2 minutes. Drain and rinse under cold running water until no longer starchy. Drain well; shake. Set aside to air-dry for 10 minutes.

SAUCE: Meanwhile, stir together gochujang, vinegar, sesame seeds, sesame oil, sugar and soy sauce.

In bowl, combine noodles, cucumber, ham (if using), pear, kimchi, green onion and kimchi juice; add half of the sauce and toss to coat.

Add endive and nori, tossing gently. Divide among bowls; top with pickled daikon. Add remaining sauce to taste at the table.

Makes 4 to 6 servings. PER EACH OF 6 SERVINGS: about 257 cal, 6 g pro, 7 g total fat (1 g sat. fat), 43 g carb, 6 g fibre, 0 mg chol, 908 mg sodium, 269 mg potassium. % RDI: 4% calcium, 12% iron, 22% vit A, 23% vit C, 30% folate.

9 oz (255 g) **somen noodles**

Half **cucumber,** cored and julienned

4 oz (115 g) **deli ham,** julienned (optional)

1½ cups sliced cored **Asian pear**

1 cup **kimchi,** chopped

½ cup finely chopped **green onion**

¼ cup **kimchi juice**

4 cups shredded **curly endive** or red leaf lettuce

1 sheet **nori,** cut in strips

SAUCE:

3 tbsp **gochujang** (Korean hot pepper paste)

3 tbsp **unseasoned rice vinegar**

2 tbsp toasted **sesame seeds**

2 tbsp **sesame oil**

4 tsp **granulated sugar**

1 tbsp **sodium-reduced soy sauce**

PICKLED DAIKON:

½ cup thinly sliced peeled **daikon radish**

1 tbsp **unseasoned rice vinegar**

½ tsp **granulated sugar**

Cuban Yuca, also known as cassava, is starchy and sticky when cooked but has a sweetness that has made it a favourite the world over. Serve with Pork Roast With Mojo Criollo (page 226) and Tostones (opposite) for an authentic Cuban menu.

Yuca With Red Onion

2 lb (900 g) **fresh yuca** or potatoes, peeled and cut in 1-inch (2.5 cm) cubes

¾ tsp **salt**

¼ cup **extra-virgin olive oil**

1 small **red onion,** thinly sliced

4 cloves **garlic,** minced

2 tbsp **lime juice**

In saucepan, cover yuca with cold water; add ½ tsp of the salt. Cover and bring to boil over medium-high heat; reduce heat and boil until tender but not mushy, about 20 minutes.

Drain yuca and peel away any remaining pink fibrous layers. Arrange in serving dish.

Meanwhile, in small skillet, heat oil over medium heat; fry onion for 3 minutes. Remove from heat. Stir in garlic and lime juice; pour over yuca. Sprinkle with remaining salt; toss to coat.

Makes 8 servings. PER SERVING: about 170 cal, 3 g pro, 7 g total fat (1 g sat. fat), 25 g carb, trace fibre, 0 mg chol, 223 mg sodium. % RDI: 8% calcium, 3% iron, 50% vit C, 7% folate.

TIP | WHEN SHOPPING FOR YUCA, LOOK FOR HEAVY TUBERS THAT ARE COMPLETELY COVERED WITH BARK. SCRUB WELL. BECAUSE YUCA IS HARD, CUT CROSSWISE INTO 3-INCH (8 CM) ROUNDS. THEN SET CUT SIDE DOWN AND SLICE DOWNWARD WITH A CHEF'S KNIFE TO CUT OFF THE BARK, TURNING THE ROUND AFTER EACH CUT.

Cuban Like french fries, these crisp fried plantains are irresistible. Tostones are traditionally made with green plantains (cooking bananas); the name changes to maduros when they're made with sweeter ripe brown plantains. We've used both here for a taste sensation.

Tostones

Peel green and ripe plantains; cut into 1-inch (2.5 cm) slices. Set plantains aside separately.

Pour about 1 inch (2.5 cm) oil into large deep skillet or wide saucepan. Heat over medium-high heat until deep-fry thermometer registers 375°F (190°C). In batches, fry green plantains, turning often, until softened, 8 to 10 minutes. Transfer to paper towel–lined baking sheet; cover with paper towel. With hands or bottom of glass, flatten fried plantains to half of the slice's thickness. Repeat with ripe plantains, frying for 2 to 3 minutes.

In batches, return all slices to same hot oil; fry, turning once, for 1 minute. Drain on paper towel–lined baking sheet. Sprinkle with salt. Serve warm.

Makes 8 servings. PER SERVING: about 229 cal, 1 g pro, 14 g total fat (1 g sat. fat), 30 g carb, 2 g fibre, 0 mg chol, 76 mg sodium. % RDI: 4% iron, 9% vit A, 17% vit C, 11% folate.

2 large **green plantains**
2 large **ripe plantains**
Vegetable oil for frying
¼ tsp **salt**

Italian Cipollini are small, sweet Italian pearl onions that are disc-shaped. They make an excellent side dish with grilled meats, especially poultry.

Orange Balsamic Cipollini Onions

3 pkg (10 oz/284 g each) **cipollini onions** (about 48 onions)

2 tbsp **butter** or vegetable oil

¼ cup **orange juice**

¼ cup **white balsamic vinegar**

½ tsp each **salt** and **pepper**

In large saucepan of boiling water, blanch onions for 1 minute; drain and chill in ice water. Peel onions, trimming root end if necessary.

In large skillet, melt butter over medium-high heat; sauté onions until golden, shaking pan often, about 10 minutes.

Add orange juice, vinegar, salt and pepper; bring to boil. Cover and simmer over medium-low heat for 5 minutes. Uncover and simmer until onions are glazed and just tender, 5 to 7 minutes. *(Make-ahead: Let cool. Cover and refrigerate for up to 24 hours. Reheat in covered casserole dish in 400°F/200°C oven for 20 minutes, or in microwave on high for 5 minutes.)*

Makes 12 servings. PER SERVING: about 70 cal, 2 g pro, 2 g total fat (1 g sat. fat), 12 g carb, 1 g fibre, 6 mg chol, 123 mg sodium. % RDI: 2% calcium, 6% iron, 9% vit A, 3% vit C, 8% folate.

TIP | IF YOU CAN'T FIND CIPOLLINI ONIONS, SUBSTITUTE TWICE AS MANY PEARL ONIONS, OR QUARTER AND PEEL SIX COOKING ONIONS, LEAVING ROOT ENDS INTACT.

Danish In Denmark, braised red cabbage is a must with Christmas roast goose. It's also often served alongside roast pork with cracklings, a favourite throughout the country.

Danish Red Cabbage

2 tbsp **butter,** goose or duck fat, or lard

½ cup finely chopped **onion**

1 **red cabbage** (about 3 lb/1.35 kg), shredded

⅓ cup **red wine vinegar**

⅓ cup **dry red wine**

1 tbsp **granulated sugar**

½ tsp **salt**

Pinch **cinnamon**

⅓ cup **red currant jelly**

In Dutch oven, melt butter over medium heat; fry onion until softened, about 5 minutes. Stir in cabbage, 1⅔ cups water, vinegar, wine, sugar, salt and cinnamon. Cover and cook, stirring occasionally, until cabbage is wilted, about 15 minutes.

Reduce heat to medium-low; braise, stirring occasionally and adding up to 2 tbsp more water if mixture starts to stick, until cabbage is soft, about 1½ hours.

Stir in jelly; cook, stirring, for 2 minutes.

Makes 8 servings. PER SERVING: about 105 cal, 2 g pro, 4 g total fat (2 g sat. fat), 18 g carb, 2 g fibre, 8 mg chol, 181 mg sodium, 164 mg potassium. % RDI: 4% calcium, 3% iron, 4% vit A, 45% vit C, 13% folate.

Irish This hearty side dish always pairs potatoes with cabbage or kale, and often adds other tasty ingredients. You'll find similar dishes throughout the British Isles, peppered with parsnips, turnips, leeks or carrots – or even bacon or ham.

Colcannon

In saucepan of boiling salted water, cook potatoes, parsnips and onion over medium heat until tender, about 20 minutes. Drain; return to pan. Reduce heat and dry over medium-low heat, about 1 minute. Add milk; mash well.

Meanwhile, in separate saucepan, melt butter over medium-high heat; add cabbage, salt and pepper. Pour in ½ cup water; bring to boil. Cover and steam until no liquid remains, 8 to 10 minutes.

Uncover; reduce heat to medium and cook, stirring and reducing heat if cabbage is browning, until cabbage is tender and sweet, 5 to 10 minutes. Stir into mashed potato mixture.

Makes 6 to 8 servings. PER EACH OF 8 SERVINGS: about 173 cal, 3 g pro, 5 g total fat (3 g sat. fat), 31 g carb, 4 g fibre, 12 mg chol, 572 mg sodium, 553 mg potassium. % RDI: 6% calcium, 5% iron, 5% vit A, 43% vit C, 22% folate.

TIP | SHAPE ANY LEFTOVERS INTO PATTIES, COAT THEM WITH BREAD CRUMBS OR FLOUR AND PAN-FRY THEM IN BACON FAT, BUTTER OR OIL.

2 lb (900 g) **potatoes,** peeled and halved

2 **parsnips** or white turnips, peeled and cut in large chunks

1 **white onion,** coarsely chopped

⅓ cup hot **milk**

3 tbsp **butter**

6 cups chopped **cabbage**

½ tsp **salt**

Pinch **pepper**

Swiss Forcing the batter for these Swiss or southern German dumplings, also called knöpfli, through a large-holed colander is easier than the traditional method of cutting the batter into strips. Beating the batter very well brings out the gluten in the flour and gives spaetzli their characteristic texture.

Spaetzli

2 cups **all-purpose flour**

¼ cup **whole spelt flour** or whole wheat flour

½ tsp **salt**

Pinch **nutmeg**

3 **eggs**

2 tbsp **butter,** melted

In stand mixer with paddle attachment or in bowl with wooden spoon, stir together all-purpose flour, spelt flour, salt and nutmeg.

Make well in centre; beat in eggs at low speed until incorporated. Gradually beat in 1 cup water to make thick smooth batter (mixture should be thicker than pancake batter), adding up to 3 tbsp more water if too thick. Beat at medium speed until bubbles appear on surface, about 2 minutes (or beat vigorously with wooden spoon in bowl for about 5 minutes). Cover and let stand at room temperature for 30 minutes or up to 2 hours.

Place batter in large-holed colander over large pot of boiling salted water. With spatula, push batter through holes into water. Boil until spaetzli float to surface, 2 to 3 minutes. Drain. Mix gently with butter until coated. *(Make-ahead: Do not mix with butter. Chill drained spaetzli in ice water; drain well. Refrigerate in airtight container for up to 1 day. In nonstick skillet, melt butter over medium heat; cook spaetzli until heated through but not browned.)*

Makes 6 servings. PER SERVING: about 246 cal, 9 g pro, 7 g total fat (3 g sat. fat), 37 g carb, 2 g fibre, 103 mg chol, 426 mg sodium, 105 mg potassium. % RDI: 2% calcium, 18% iron, 7% vit A, 44% folate.

TIP | THE WHOLE SPELT OR WHOLE WHEAT FLOUR GIVES THE SPAETZLI A FULLER, MORE RUSTIC FLAVOUR, BUT YOU CAN MAKE THEM FROM ALL WHITE FLOUR IF YOU PREFER.

Indian This attractive combo, called aloo hari matar foogath, is typical of the many Indian vegetarian dishes that combine starch and protein-filled vegetables and legumes. They ensure nutritional balance and have nice contrasting textures.

Potatoes and Peas

Cut slit down centre of hot pepper. In large heavy saucepan, heat ghee over medium heat; stir-fry hot pepper, ginger, garlic, mustard seeds and cumin seeds until mustard seeds begin to pop, about 2 minutes.

Add tomatoes, turmeric and cayenne pepper; cook, stirring, for 4 minutes. Add potatoes and 1¼ cups water; bring to boil. Reduce heat to medium; cover and simmer for 20 minutes.

Stir in ¼ cup of the cilantro; cook, uncovered, until potatoes are tender, about 12 minutes. Add peas and salt; cook for 2 minutes. Garnish with remaining cilantro.

Makes 6 servings. PER SERVING: about 177 cal, 4 g pro, 9 g total fat (5 g sat. fat), 21 g carb, 3 g fibre, 22 mg chol, 393 mg sodium. % RDI: 3% calcium, 13% iron, 15% vit A, 33% vit C, 15% folate.

TIP | WHEN FRESH PEAS ARE AVAILABLE, USE THEM INSTEAD OF THE FROZEN ONES AND ADD TO PAN ALONG WITH THE CILANTRO.

1 **green finger hot pepper**
¼ cup **ghee** (recipe, page 134) or vegetable oil
1 tbsp minced **fresh ginger**
1 clove **garlic,** minced
1 tsp **black mustard seeds**
½ tsp **cumin seeds**
1 cup chopped drained **canned tomatoes**
½ tsp **turmeric**
¼ tsp **cayenne pepper**
2 **red potatoes** (1 lb/450 g), cut in 1½-inch (4 cm) cubes
⅓ cup chopped **fresh cilantro**
2 cups **frozen peas**
¾ tsp **salt**

THE INDIAN PANTRY

Indian cuisine opens home cooks up to a world of exotic spices and flavours. Here are the ones you need to make the recipes in this book.

DRIED SPICES

- Allspice (whole and ground)
- Aniseed
- Black mustard seeds* (yellow can be substituted)
- Black peppercorns
- Caraway seeds
- Cardamom pods* (choose green pods over white pods)
- Cayenne pepper
- Cinnamon (sticks and ground)
- Cloves (whole)
- Coriander seeds
- Cumin seeds
- Dried whole hot peppers
- Fennel seeds
- Fenugreek seeds*
- Garam masala (for recipe, see page 19)
- Ground ginger
- Mace (whole and ground)
- Nutmeg (whole stays fresh longer than ground)
- Saffron
- Sesame seeds
- Sweet paprika
- Turmeric

PANTRY STAPLES

- Chutneys
- Coconut milk
- Palm sugar or jaggery* (raw cane sugar)
- Pappadams
- Rice (long-grain basmati and shorter-grain Patna)
- Tamarind* (blocks, with or without seeds, and concentrate)

FRESH STAPLES

- Curry leaves* (dried leaves add little taste; omit from recipe if fresh are unavailable)
- Dates*
- Fresh cilantro
- Fresh ginger
- Hot peppers (red and green finger hot peppers)

Might be easier to find at Indian grocery stores than at supermarkets

GHEE

The preferred cooking oil in many Indian dishes, ghee is a rich, nutty-flavoured fat made by removing the milk solids from unsalted butter. It doesn't burn at high temperatures like some oils and can last for up to six months in the refrigerator.

To make your own: In heavy-bottomed pot, melt 1 lb (450 g) unsalted butter over medium heat. Increase heat and bring to boil; immediately reduce heat to low. Simmer gently until all solids sink to bottom and turn golden. Carefully ladle out oil, leaving milky liquid behind; strain oil through fine sieve or cheesecloth. Discard milky liquid. As it cools, ghee turns yellow and hard.

Indian This sautéed spinach dish, known as saag bhaji, must be cooked just before serving, but it's a snap if you prep ahead. Garam masala formulas vary by region – even household – but generally include most or all of the spices in our version.

Spinach With Ginger and Hot Pepper

In large shallow Dutch oven, heat oil over medium heat; cook ginger and hot pepper for 2 minutes.

Add spinach; cook until spinach is just beginning to wilt, about 5 minutes. Add salt and garam masala; stir to combine.

Makes 6 servings. PER SERVING: about 43 cal, 3 g pro, 3 g total fat (trace sat. fat), 4 g carb, 2 g fibre, 0 mg chol, 250 mg sodium. % RDI: 11% calcium, 22% iron, 70% vit A, 20% vit C, 55% folate.

TIP | GARAM MASALA IS AVAILABLE COMMERCIALLY, BUT IT LOSES ITS FLAVOUR QUICKLY. IT'S BETTER TO MAKE SMALL BATCHES AT HOME WHEN YOU NEED IT.

1 tbsp **vegetable oil**

2 tbsp minced **fresh ginger**

1 tbsp finely chopped seeded **green finger hot pepper**

2 bags (10 oz/284 g each) **fresh spinach,** trimmed

½ tsp **salt**

½ tsp **garam masala** (recipe, page 19)

Afghan Rice is the centrepiece of any Afghan menu. This dish, called kabli, is traditionally made with lamb, but this vegetarian version is an extremely tasty, beautiful side dish.

Basmati Rice With Carrots, Raisins and Spices

2 cups **basmati rice**

1 tbsp **salt**

¼ cup **vegetable oil**

1 tbsp **granulated sugar**

¼ tsp **ground cardamom**

¼ tsp **cinnamon**

¼ tsp **ground cumin**

¼ tsp **pepper**

4 **carrots** (12 oz/340 g total)

1 cup **golden raisins**

Rinse rice under running water until water is clear. In large bowl, cover rice with water; soak for 1 hour. Drain.

Add salt to large pot of boiling water; add rice. Cover and simmer until tender, 6 to 8 minutes. Drain, reserving 1 cup of the cooking liquid; set cooking liquid aside. Pour rice into large Dutch oven.

In skillet, heat 1 tbsp of the oil over medium-high heat. Add sugar; stir until dissolved. Add reserved cooking liquid; bring to boil. Slowly pour over rice, stirring to coat. Stir in cardamom, cinnamon, cumin and pepper.

Bake in 450°F (230°C) oven until no liquid remains, about 10 minutes. Reduce heat to 200°F (100°C); bake, covered, for 1 hour. Scrape into serving dish, mounding attractively.

Meanwhile, peel carrots and cut into thin strips or grate coarsely. In skillet, heat remaining oil over medium-high heat; sauté carrots and raisins until tender, about 2 minutes. Spoon over rice.

Makes 8 servings. PER SERVING: about 310 cal, 5 g pro, 7 g total fat (1 g sat. fat), 57 g carb, 3 g fibre, 0 mg chol, 251 mg sodium. % RDI: 3% calcium, 6% iron, 91% vit A, 2% vit C, 4% folate.

Italian The delicate licorice flavour of fennel sings when paired with Parmesan. Real Parmigiano-Reggiano, though pricey, adds the richest flavour to this simple baked side dish. You can replace it with less-expensive grana Padano or even Romano cheese, if desired.

Baked Fennel Parmesan

Remove fennel stalks; chop fronds and set aside for garnish. Cut fennel in half lengthwise and core. Cut lengthwise into generous ¼-inch (5 mm) thick slices.

In large saucepan of boiling salted water, cook fennel, covered, until tender, about 8 minutes. Drain; chill under cold water. Drain on towels.

Place fennel in 13- x 9-inch (3 L) baking dish or casserole dish. Add oil, salt and pepper; toss gently to coat. *(Make-ahead: Cover and refrigerate for up to 5 hours.)* Sprinkle with Parmesan cheese.

Bake in 400°F (200°C) oven until hot, about 15 minutes. Broil until cheese is crisp, about 2 minutes. Garnish with reserved fennel fronds.

Makes 8 to 10 servings. PER EACH OF 10 SERVINGS: about 75 cal, 3 g pro, 4 g total fat (1 g sat. fat), 9 g carb, 4 g fibre, 2 mg chol, 227 mg sodium. % RDI: 9% calcium, 7% iron, 2% vit A, 22% vit C, 11% folate.

2 **fennel bulbs** (3 lb/1.35 kg total)
2 tbsp **extra-virgin olive oil**
½ tsp each **salt** and **pepper**
¼ cup grated **Parmesan cheese**

Swiss A traditional Swiss rösti is prepared with the previous day's boiled potatoes; it's best to use slightly undercooked ones. If you boil potatoes the same day, refrigerate them until they're cool for easy grating.

Rösti With Gruyère Cheese

1 lb (450 g) **potatoes** (unpeeled), scrubbed

Half **onion,** finely chopped

½ tsp **salt**

¼ tsp **pepper**

2 tbsp **butter**

1 cup shredded **Gruyère cheese** (about 4 oz/115 g)

In saucepan of boiling salted water, cook potatoes, covered, until tender but still a little firm. Drain and let cool. Refrigerate, uncovered, for 12 hours. *(Make-ahead: Refrigerate for up to 24 hours.)*

Peel potatoes; coarsely grate into bowl. Mix in onion, salt and pepper. In cast-iron or nonstick skillet, melt two-thirds of the butter over medium heat; press potato mixture into pan to cover bottom. Cook until bottom is well browned, 10 to 12 minutes. Invert plate over rösti; carefully flip rösti onto plate.

Add remaining butter to skillet. Slip rösti back into skillet, uncooked side down; cook until bottom is light golden, about 6 minutes. Slide onto plate; cut into halves or quarters. Top with Gruyère cheese.

Makes 2 to 4 servings. PER EACH OF 4 SERVINGS: about 243 cal, 10 g pro, 15 g total fat (9 g sat. fat), 19 g carb, 2 g fibre, 45 mg chol, 624 mg sodium, 371 mg potassium. % RDI: 26% calcium, 3% iron, 13% vit A, 20% vit C, 6% folate.

Guyanese All over the Caribbean, there are rice-and-pea dishes. This version from Guyana gets its richness and flavour from a mixture of coconut and salt pork.

Cookup Rice

¼ cup **dried pigeon peas**

4 oz (115 g) cubed **salt pork**

3 **green onions,** chopped (white and green parts separated)

1 **onion,** finely chopped

2 cloves **garlic,** minced

1 **carrot,** diced

1 **hot red pepper,** halved and seeded

2 sprigs **fresh thyme**

1 **cinnamon stick**

¼ tsp each **salt** and **pepper**

2 cups **long-grain rice**

1 can (400 mL) **coconut milk**

Soak peas overnight in 2 cups cold water. (Or for quick-soak method, bring to boil and boil gently for 2 minutes. Remove from heat, cover and let stand for 1 hour.) Drain.

In saucepan, cover peas again with 3 times their new volume in water; bring to boil. Reduce heat, cover and simmer until tender, about 40 minutes. Drain, reserving cooking liquid.

In Dutch oven, fry salt pork over medium heat, stirring, until golden, about 5 minutes. Transfer to paper towel–lined plate; set aside.

Drain all but 1 tbsp fat from pan; fry white parts of green onions, onion, garlic, carrot, hot pepper, thyme, cinnamon stick, salt and pepper until onion is softened and golden, about 5 minutes. Return pork to pan. Stir in rice; cook, stirring, for 1 minute.

In large glass measure, whisk together coconut milk and enough of the reserved cooking liquid (and water if needed) to make 4 cups; stir into rice mixture.

Add peas; bring to boil. Reduce heat, cover and simmer until rice is tender and no liquid remains, 15 to 18 minutes. Remove from heat; let stand, covered, for 5 minutes. Discard hot pepper, thyme and cinnamon stick; stir in green parts of onions.

Makes 8 servings. PER SERVING: about 380 cal, 7 g pro, 20 g total fat (13 g sat. fat), 44 g carb, 3 g fibre, 10 mg chol, 285 mg sodium. % RDI: 4% calcium, 16% iron, 16% vit A, 3% vit C, 15% folate.

Mexican The red, green and white of this dish represent the bars of the Mexican flag. The best part: You don't have to cook this tasty rice in three separate pots. Serve with Mole Turkey Wings (page 224) for a perfect backyard fiesta.

Tricolour Rice

In large saucepan, bring 3½ cups water, rice and salt to boil; reduce heat to low. Cover and cook until no liquid remains, about 25 minutes. Fluff with fork.

RED SAUCE: Meanwhile, in small saucepan or skillet, heat oil over medium heat; fry onion, garlic, chili powder, chipotle chili powder, cumin and salt, stirring often, until onion is softened, 3 to 4 minutes. Stir in paprika; fry for 20 seconds. Stir in tomatoes, 2 tbsp water, sugar and vinegar. Cover and simmer over medium-low heat for 10 minutes. Scrape into bowl; keep warm.

GREEN SAUCE: Meanwhile, in small saucepan or skillet, heat oil over medium heat; fry green onions, garlic, jalapeño pepper and salt, stirring, for 3 minutes. Stir in cilantro; cook for 1 minute. Stir in spinach and 3 tbsp water; cook, stirring occasionally, for 2 minutes. Scrape into bowl; keep warm.

Mix one-third of the rice with Red Sauce. Mix another third with Green Sauce. Mix remaining rice with oil.

In warmed 13- x 9-inch (3 L) baking dish, arrange rice colours like bars on Mexican flag: green on left, white in centre and red on right. Place cilantro sprigs in circle in centre of white rice to represent coat of arms.

Makes 6 to 8 servings. PER EACH OF 8 SERVINGS: about 290 cal, 5 g pro, 7 g total fat (1 g sat. fat), 50 g carb, 2 g fibre, 0 mg chol, 439 mg sodium, 192 mg potassium. % RDI: 5% calcium, 13% iron, 23% vit A, 7% vit C, 17% folate.

2½ cups **long-grain rice**

¾ tsp **salt**

1 tbsp **olive oil**

Fresh cilantro sprigs

RED SAUCE:
1 tbsp **olive oil**

1 small **onion,** minced

1 clove **garlic,** minced

½ tsp **chili powder**

¼ tsp **chipotle chili powder** (or half canned chipotle pepper, minced)

¼ tsp **ground cumin**

¼ tsp **salt**

½ tsp **sweet paprika**

1 cup **canned crushed tomatoes** or bottled strained tomatoes (passata)

¼ tsp **granulated sugar**

¼ tsp **vinegar**

GREEN SAUCE:
2 tbsp **olive oil**

2 **green onions,** minced

1 clove **garlic,** minced

1 **jalapeño pepper,** seeded and minced

¼ tsp **salt**

½ cup minced **fresh cilantro**

1 cup chopped blanched **fresh spinach** (or frozen chopped spinach, thawed)

Chinese Usually included on Chinese New Year menus, this dish is made with a combination of long-grain and glutinous rice for an overall less-sticky texture. If you can get fresh water chestnuts, use ¾ cup, diced.

Sticky Rice

1 oz (30 g) **dried shiitake mushrooms**

3 pieces **Chinese sweet sausage** (5 oz/140 g total)

8 oz (225 g) **lean pork loin**

2 cups **glutinous rice**

½ cup **long-grain rice**

¼ cup **soy sauce**

3 tbsp **oyster sauce**

1 tbsp **Chinese rice wine** or sherry

2 tsp **sesame oil**

1 tsp **vegetable oil**

1 can (10 oz/284 mL) **water chestnuts,** drained, rinsed and finely diced

6 **green onions** (white parts only), finely diced

1 clove **garlic,** minced

Place mushrooms in small bowl; cover with 2 cups warm water. Soak until plump, about 30 minutes. Squeeze out water, reserving for another use. Cut mushrooms into ⅛-inch (3 mm) cubes. Place in bowl; set aside.

In saucepan, bring 1 cup water to boil; add sausage. Reduce heat and simmer until plump, about 8 minutes. Transfer to cutting board; let cool. Cut into ⅛-inch (3 mm) cubes. Add to mushrooms.

Cut pork crosswise into ¼-inch (5 mm) thick slices; cut into ¼-inch (5 mm) cubes. Add to mushroom mixture.

In large saucepan, bring 3½ cups cold water to boil. Stir in glutinous rice and long-grain rice. Cover and reduce heat to low; simmer until tender and no liquid remains, about 20 minutes. Remove from heat; fluff with fork.

Meanwhile, stir together soy sauce, oyster sauce, wine and sesame oil. In large nonstick skillet, heat vegetable oil over medium heat; cook pork mixture, water chestnuts, green onions, garlic and soy sauce mixture, stirring often, until pork is no longer pink inside, about 5 minutes. Add to rice; stir well. *(Make-ahead: Transfer to microwaveable casserole dish; let cool for 30 minutes. Refrigerate until cold; cover and refrigerate for up to 24 hours. Reheat in microwave on high, stirring once, until hot, about 5 minutes.)*

Makes 10 servings. PER SERVING: about 302 cal, 13 g pro, 7 g total fat (2 g sat. fat), 45 g carb, 2 g fibre, 25 mg chol, 833 mg sodium. % RDI: 2% calcium, 9% iron, 3% vit C, 6% folate.

THE CHINESE PANTRY

China is a vast country, and every region has its own specialties and special ingredients. These are just a few of the most common ingredients you'll need for the recipes this book.

SPICES AND SEASONING PASTES

- Black bean and garlic sauce*
- Chili broad bean paste*
- Chili garlic sauce*
- Cinnamon
- Fermented black beans*
- Five-spice powder (for homemade, see page 19)
- Hoisin sauce
- Oyster sauce
- Star anise
- Szechuan pepper*
- White pepper

PANTRY STAPLES

- Canned water chestnuts (or fresh*)
- Chicken broth
- Chili oil*
- Chinese rice wine* or dry sherry
- Cornstarch
- Dark sesame oil
- Dried shiitake mushrooms
- Long-grain rice
- Peanut oil or vegetable oil
- Rice vinegar (clear and red* are generally mild; aged black* is stronger)
- Soy sauce (we prefer light-coloured soy sauce over the dark, syrupy kind)
- Sweet or sticky rice
- Wide rice noodles

FRESH STAPLES

- Dumpling and spring roll wrappers
- Fresh cilantro
- Fresh ginger
- Garlic
- Green onions

Might be easier to find at Chinese grocery stores than at supermarkets

{salads & sides}

Bulgogi (page 178)

{everyday mains}

Italian Pancetta is cured, rather than smoked, bacon. It's a frequently used flavour accent in Italian dishes. Look for it in the deli section of your supermarket, or use thick-cut bacon instead.

Radicchio and Pancetta Risotto

4½ cups **water** or sodium-reduced chicken broth

1 tbsp **extra-virgin olive oil**

2 oz (55 g) **pancetta** or bacon, diced

½ cup finely chopped **onion**

3 cups shredded **radicchio**

1⅓ cups **short-grain rice** (such as arborio, carnaroli or Vialone Nano)

¼ cup **red wine** (optional)

½ cup grated **Parmesan cheese**

1 tbsp **butter**

1 tbsp **balsamic vinegar**

1 tsp **salt**

¼ tsp **pepper**

In saucepan, bring water to boil; reduce heat to low and keep warm.

In large deep skillet, heat oil over medium-high heat; fry pancetta until starting to crisp. Add onion; sauté until softened and translucent, about 2 minutes. Add radicchio and rice; sauté until radicchio is wilted and rice is coated, about 2 minutes. Stir in wine (if using) until absorbed.

Add water, ½ cup at a time, stirring after each addition and waiting until most of the liquid is absorbed before adding more, for about 20 minutes total. Taste before adding last ½ cup; rice should be loose and creamy but not mushy, and still slightly firm in centre.

Remove from heat. Stir in Parmesan cheese, butter, vinegar, salt and pepper.

Makes 4 to 6 servings. PER EACH OF 6 SERVINGS: about 287 cal, 8 g pro, 11 g total fat (6 g sat. fat), 38 g carb, 1 g fibre, 19 mg chol, 591 mg sodium, 142 mg potassium. % RDI: 10% calcium, 4% iron, 3% vit A, 2% vit C, 6% folate.

TIP | DIFFERENT SHORT-GRAIN RICES CREATE DIFFERENT TEXTURES, DEPENDING ON THEIR STARCHINESS. ARBORIO YIELDS A VERY CREAMY, SLIGHTLY STICKY RISOTTO. CARNAROLI BREAKS DOWN LESS THAN ARBORIO, MAKING A FLUFFIER RISOTTO. VIALONE NANO RETAINS ITS HARD INTERIOR WHEN COOKED, CREATING THE VERY LOOSE VENETIAN-STYLE ALL'ONDA (WAVY), RISOTTO.

Italian This dish of rice and peas is a classic from northern Italy. The rice should be creamy — much like a soupy risotto. Serve it as a light main course and pass Parmesan cheese to sprinkle on top, or divide it into six servings for an appetizer.

Risi e Bisi

In saucepan, melt half of the butter over medium heat; cook pancetta and onion, stirring often, until onion is softened, about 7 minutes.

Add broth, rice, pepper and salt; bring to boil. Reduce heat and simmer, uncovered and stirring occasionally, for 18 minutes.

Stir in peas and parsley; cook until peas and rice are tender, about 4 minutes. Stir in Parmesan cheese and remaining butter; cover and let stand for 2 minutes. Serve in shallow soup bowls.

Makes 4 servings. PER SERVING: about 543 cal, 20 g pro, 20 g total fat (12 g sat. fat), 72 g carb, 5 g fibre, 44 mg chol, 1,234 mg sodium, 320 mg potassium. % RDI: 18% calcium, 14% iron, 20% vit A, 27% vit C, 24% folate.

TIP | IF AVAILABLE, USE HOMEMADE BROTH, OR BUY THE BEST-QUALITY BROTH YOU CAN FIND. MAKE AN EVEN MORE FLAVOURFUL STOCK BY SIMMERING THE EMPTY PEA PODS WITH THE BROTH IN A COVERED SAUCEPAN FOR 20 MINUTES. STRAIN, PRESSING THE PODS.

3 tbsp **butter**

2 oz (55 g) **pancetta,** diced

1 **onion,** diced

6 cups **sodium-reduced chicken broth** or vegetable broth

1½ cups **short-grain rice** (such as arborio or carnaroli)

¼ tsp **pepper**

Pinch **salt**

1½ cups **fresh peas** (about 1½ lb/ 675 g in pods)

½ cup chopped **fresh parsley**

½ cup grated **Parmesan cheese**

Italian The trinity of creamy Gorgonzola cheese, bitter-edged rapini and earthy walnuts give this pasta rich, rustic appeal. Bucatini has a nice, chewy texture, but spaghetti or linguine are good alternatives.

Pasta With Rapini, Gorgonzola and Walnuts

¼ cup **extra-virgin olive oil**

1 **red onion,** thinly sliced

½ tsp each **salt** and **pepper**

2 cloves **garlic,** minced

2 tsp **red wine vinegar**

1 bunch **rapini** (12 oz/340 g)

12 oz (340 g) **bucatini** or other long pasta

3 oz (85 g) **Gorgonzola cheese,** crumbled

1 cup toasted **walnut pieces**

In skillet, heat half of the oil over medium-low heat; cook onion and half each of the salt and pepper, stirring occasionally, until lightly caramelized, about 15 minutes. Stir in garlic; cook for 5 minutes. Stir in wine vinegar.

Meanwhile, trim ½ inch (1 cm) off rapini stems; cut rapini in half. In large pot of boiling salted water, cook rapini until tender, about 2 minutes; drain and stir into onion mixture.

Meanwhile, in separate saucepan of boiling salted water, cook pasta until al dente, about 8 minutes. Drain, reserving ⅓ cup of the cooking liquid. Return pasta to pot.

Stir in onion mixture, Gorgonzola cheese and remaining oil, salt and pepper. Add reserved cooking liquid if necessary to moisten. Sprinkle with walnuts.

Makes 4 servings. PER SERVING: about 760 cal, 23 g pro, 42 g total fat (8 g sat. fat), 78 g carb, 9 g fibre, 21 mg chol, 1,075 mg sodium, 480 mg potassium. % RDI: 25% calcium, 43% iron, 24% vit A, 20% vit C, 122% folate.

Italian A crunchy bread crumb topping adds texture and flavour to this simple seafood pasta. Most of the ingredients are pantry staples, so this can be a last-minute weeknight dinner, but it will taste like you cooked all day.

Spaghettini With Clams and Bread Crumbs

2 tbsp **butter**

1 cup **fresh bread crumbs**

2 cloves **garlic,** minced

¼ cup chopped **fresh parsley**

¼ cup **extra-virgin olive oil**

1 **onion,** chopped

4 **anchovy fillets,** minced

1 tbsp drained **capers,** chopped

1 can (28 oz/796 mL) **plum tomatoes,** drained

⅓ cup **dry white wine**

1 can (5 oz/142 g) **whole baby clams**

Pinch each **salt** and **pepper**

12 oz (340 g) **spaghettini**

In skillet, melt butter over medium heat; cook bread crumbs and half of the garlic, stirring often, until golden, about 5 minutes. Stir in half of the parsley; cook for 1 minute. Transfer to bowl.

In saucepan, heat half of the oil over medium heat; cook onion until softened, about 5 minutes.

Stir in anchovies, capers and remaining garlic; cook, stirring, until fragrant, about 2 minutes.

Add tomatoes, wine, clams, salt and pepper, breaking up tomatoes with spoon. Bring to boil; reduce heat and simmer for 25 minutes.

Meanwhile, cook pasta until al dente, about 8 minutes; drain and toss with sauce and remaining oil and parsley. Sprinkle with toasted bread crumb mixture.

Makes 4 to 6 servings. PER EACH OF 6 SERVINGS: about 391 cal, 12 g pro, 15 g total fat (4 g sat. fat), 52 g carb, 4 g fibre, 19 mg chol, 487 mg sodium, 357 mg potassium. % RDI: 7% calcium, 44% iron, 8% vit A, 30% vit C, 62% folate.

Italian Here's a pizza to please the meat-and-potato lovers. Calabrese sausage is an Italian salami with a bit of heat, but any sliced salami will do.

Calabrese Potato Provolone Pizza

Peel potato. Using mandoline, slice into paper-thin rounds. *(Make-ahead: Place in airtight container and cover with water; refrigerate for up to 24 hours. Drain and pat dry before using.)*

On lightly floured surface, roll out dough into 14-inch (35 cm) circle; centre on greased pizza pan. Spread with tomato sauce. Layer potato, sausage and sage on top; sprinkle with provolone cheese.

Bake in bottom third of 425°F (220°C) oven until cheese is bubbly and crust is golden and slightly puffed, about 20 minutes.

Makes 8 slices. PER SLICE: about 325 cal, 13 g pro, 11 g total fat (5 g sat. fat), 42 g carb, 2 g fibre, 22 mg chol, 652 mg sodium. % RDI: 17% calcium, 24% iron, 6% vit A, 15% vit C, 57% folate.

Tomato Pizza Sauce

Reserving juice, drain, seed and chop 1 can (28 oz/796 mL) plum tomatoes. In saucepan, heat 2 tbsp extra-virgin olive oil over medium heat. Fry 1 small onion, minced; 2 cloves garlic, minced; and ¼ tsp dried oregano, stirring, until onion is translucent, about 5 minutes. Add tomatoes and reserved juice, ½ tsp wine vinegar, and pinch each salt, pepper and granulated sugar. Simmer until thickened, about 20 minutes. Let cool for 5 minutes. In food processor, blend sauce until smooth. *(Make-ahead: Refrigerate in airtight container for up to 1 week or freeze for up to 1 month.)* **Makes about 2 cups.**

1 small **Yukon Gold potato** (about 5 oz/140 g)

Pizza Dough (recipe, page 91) or 1½ lb (675 g) prepared pizza dough

1 cup **Tomato Pizza Sauce** (recipe, below left)

3 oz (85 g) **Calabrese sausage** or other salami, thinly sliced

7 **fresh sage leaves,** chopped

1½ cups shredded **provolone cheese**

Spanish In Spain, sauces are often thickened with ground almonds. In this gourmet – but easy – dinner for two, saffron lends a subtle, earthy taste to the briny mussels. Serve with crusty bread to soak up the savoury broth.

Mussels Steamed in Tomato Saffron Broth

½ cup **dry white wine**

Pinch **saffron threads,** crumbled

2 lb (900 g) **mussels**

1 can (28 oz/796 mL) **plum tomatoes**

¼ cup **extra-virgin olive oil**

Half **Spanish onion,** chopped

1 clove **garlic,** minced

3 tbsp **ground almonds**

1 **roasted red pepper,** chopped

¼ cup chopped **fresh flat-leaf parsley**

Pinch **salt**

Stir wine with saffron; let stand for 10 minutes or up to 20 minutes.

Scrub mussels, removing any beards; discard any that do not close when tapped. Reserving ½ cup juice, drain tomatoes; seed and coarsely chop. Set aside separately.

In large saucepan, heat oil over medium heat; fry onion and garlic, stirring occasionally, until onion is translucent, about 6 minutes.

Add almonds; fry for 1 minute. Add red pepper, tomatoes, reserved tomato juice, saffron mixture, half of the parsley and the salt; bring to boil. Reduce heat to low; simmer until slightly thickened, about 10 minutes.

Add mussels; cover and simmer, stirring once, until mussels open, about 7 minutes. Discard any mussels that do not open. Sprinkle with remaining parsley.

Makes 2 servings. PER SERVING: about 520 cal, 22 g pro, 36 g total fat (4 g sat. fat), 30 g carb, 6 g fibre, 38 mg chol, 590 mg sodium. % RDI: 14% calcium, 62% iron, 28% vit A, 200% vit C, 44% folate.

Portuguese The piri-piri pepper grown in Africa made its way to Portugal via colonial trade routes. It's the basis of this typical spicy chicken dish, but hot pepper flakes are an easy-to-find substitute in North America.

Piri-Piri Chicken Legs

In glass bowl, combine lemon zest, lemon juice, garlic, oil, hot pepper flakes and salt. Add chicken, turning to coat and pushing some of the mixture under skin. Cover and refrigerate for 8 hours. *(Make-ahead: Refrigerate for up to 24 hours.)*

Arrange chicken, skin side up, on foil-lined baking sheet. Roast in 425°F (220°C) oven, brushing once with pan drippings, until juices run clear when chicken is pierced, about 35 minutes.

Makes 6 servings. PER SERVING: about 374 cal, 28 g pro, 27 g total fat (7 g sat. fat), 4 g carb, 1 g fibre, 120 mg chol, 499 mg sodium. % RDI: 3% calcium, 10% iron, 11% vit A, 17% vit C, 5% folate.

3 tbsp grated **lemon zest**

¼ cup **lemon juice**

1 head **garlic,** minced

2 tbsp **olive oil**

1 tbsp **hot pepper flakes**

1 tsp **salt**

3½ lb (1.5 kg) **bone-in skin-on chicken legs**

Hungarian Inspired by the traditional long-simmering stew, this creamy goulash (which is at its finest when made with real Hungarian paprika) is quick, easy and full of robust flavour. Serve it over egg noodles or Spaetzli (page 132).

20-Minute Chicken Goulash

½ tsp **caraway seeds**

1 lb (450 g) **boneless skinless chicken breasts**

2 tbsp **vegetable oil**

3 cups sliced **mushrooms** (8 oz/225 g)

1 **onion,** chopped

1 **sweet green pepper,** chopped

4 cloves **garlic,** minced

1 tbsp **sweet paprika**

½ tsp each **salt** and **pepper**

½ tsp **dried thyme**

3 tbsp **all-purpose flour**

1⅓ cups **chicken broth**

¼ cup **tomato paste**

¼ cup chopped **fresh parsley**

¼ cup **light sour cream**

Using mortar and pestle or side of chef's knife, crush caraway seeds.

Cut chicken into ¾-inch (2 cm) chunks. In Dutch oven, heat half of the oil over medium-high heat; fry chicken, in batches, until browned on outside and no longer pink inside, about 4 minutes. Transfer to bowl.

Add remaining oil to pan; cook mushrooms, onion, green pepper, garlic, paprika, salt, pepper, thyme and caraway seeds over medium heat, stirring occasionally, until onion is softened, about 5 minutes.

Add flour; cook, stirring, for 1 minute. Stir in broth and tomato paste; cook, stirring often, until thickened enough to coat back of spoon, about 5 minutes.

Return chicken and any accumulated juices to pan. Add parsley and sour cream; stir until heated through.

Makes 4 servings. PER SERVING: about 293 cal, 32 g pro, 11 g total fat (2 g sat. fat), 18 g carb, 3 g fibre, 68 mg chol, 637 mg sodium. % RDI: 7% calcium, 22% iron, 19% vit A, 60% vit C, 15% folate.

French Old-fashioned bouillabaisse takes hours of chopping and simmering, but this simplified version has all the flavour without a serious time commitment.

Easy Bouillabaisse

Scrub mussels, removing any beards; discard any that do not close when tapped. Set aside.

In large saucepan, heat oil with butter over medium heat; cook shallots and bay leaf, stirring often, until shallots are softened, about 3 minutes.

Stir in tomatoes, garlic and salt; cook, stirring, for 1 minute. Stir in clam juice, 1 cup water and wine; bring to boil. Reduce heat, cover and simmer for 10 minutes.

Add mussels and fish; cover and cook until mussels open and fish flakes easily when tested, about 6 minutes. Discard bay leaf and any mussels that do not open. Stir in parsley.

Makes 4 servings. PER SERVING: about 178 cal, 17 g pro, 8 g total fat (3 g sat. fat), 6 g carb, 1 g fibre, 37 mg chol, 395 mg sodium, 563 mg potassium. % RDI: 5% calcium, 17% iron, 13% vit A, 15% vit C, 14% folate.

1 lb (450 g) **mussels**

1 tbsp **olive oil**

1 tbsp **butter**

½ cup finely chopped **shallots** or onion

1 **bay leaf**

2 **plum tomatoes,** seeded and chopped

1 clove **garlic,** minced

¼ tsp **salt**

1 bottle (240 mL) **clam juice**

½ cup **white wine** or water

8 oz (225 g) **halibut fillets** or cod fillets, cubed

2 tbsp chopped **fresh parsley**

Greek Cafés across the globe serve up these juicy grilled skewers. Though this version is served sandwich-style in a fluffy Greek pita, you can make the souvlaki and tzatziki to serve with rice and Tomato and Feta Salad (page 118).

Pork Souvlaki

1½ lb (675 g) **pork tenderloins**

2 tbsp **lemon juice**

1 tbsp **extra-virgin olive oil**

1 large clove **garlic,** minced

½ tsp **dried oregano**

½ tsp **salt**

¼ tsp **pepper**

2 **plum tomatoes,** sliced

Half **red onion,** sliced

1 cup shredded **romaine lettuce**

4 **Greek-style pocketless pitas**

TZATZIKI:

1 cup shredded **cucumber**

½ tsp **salt**

¾ cup **Balkan-style plain yogurt**

2 cloves **garlic,** minced

2 tbsp chopped **fresh dill** (optional)

1 tbsp **lemon juice**

TZATZIKI: Mix cucumber with salt; let stand for 10 minutes. Squeeze out moisture. In small bowl, stir together cucumber, yogurt, garlic, dill (if using) and lemon juice.

Meanwhile, trim pork and cut into 1-inch (2.5 cm) cubes. In large bowl, whisk together lemon juice, oil, garlic, oregano, salt and pepper; add pork and stir to coat. Marinate for 10 minutes. *(Make-ahead: Cover and refrigerate for up to 6 hours.)*

Thread pork onto metal or soaked wooden skewers; brush with any remaining marinade. Grill, covered, on greased grill over medium-high heat, turning halfway through, until juices run clear when pork is pierced and just a hint of pink remains inside, about 12 minutes. Remove from skewers. Serve with tomatoes, onion, lettuce and tzatziki on pitas.

Makes 4 servings. PER SERVING: about 463 cal, 46 g pro, 10 g total fat (4 g sat. fat), 44 g carb, 3 g fibre, 100 mg chol, 863 mg sodium, 910 mg potassium. % RDI: 14% calcium, 28% iron, 12% vit A, 22% vit C, 49% folate.

Greek Fresh-from-the-sea fish is essential when dining in Greece. Here, where that's not always possible, pickerel is a delicious, convenient option. Any fish is tasty prepared this way, so choose whatever's freshest.

Grilled Fish With Olive Oil

Set aside half of the oil. Brush remaining oil over both sides of fillets. Season tops with oregano, salt and pepper.

Grill fish, covered and skin side down, on greased grill over medium heat, without turning, until fish is opaque and flakes easily when tested, about 10 minutes.

Transfer to warmed platter. Drizzle with reserved oil; sprinkle with capers. Surround with lemon and watercress.

Makes 8 servings. PER SERVING: about 223 cal, 29 g pro, 11 g total fat (2 g sat. fat), 1 g carb, trace fibre, 129 mg chol, 340 mg sodium. % RDI: 17% calcium, 16% iron, 9% vit A, 13% vit C, 10% folate.

⅓ cup **extra-virgin olive oil**

3 lb (1.35 kg) **skin-on pickerel fillets**

1 tbsp minced **fresh oregano**

1 tsp each **sea salt** and **pepper**

2 tbsp **capers,** drained

1 **lemon,** cut in wedges

1 bunch **watercress** or purslane

Ethiopian Beef, lamb, goat, chicken, pulses or vegetables stewed in a hot, spicy sauce are known in Ethiopia as wot. Most Ethiopian food is served with a sourdough pancake made from teff, an indigenous grain, but easier-to-find naan, tortillas or Italian-style bread are tasty substitutes.

Spicy Beef Wot

2 lb (900 g) **beef blade stewing steak** or other stewing steak

2 tbsp **lemon juice**

1 tsp **salt**

2 **red onions,** coarsely chopped

3 cloves **garlic,** smashed

2 tsp finely chopped **fresh ginger**

¼ cup **butter**

¼ tsp **turmeric**

5 tsp **sweet paprika**

4 tsp **ground dried red hot peppers** or regular chili powder

½ tsp **ground coriander**

¼ tsp **ground cardamom** or 3 cardamom pods, crushed

¼ tsp **ground fenugreek** or fenugreek seeds (optional)

Pinch **nutmeg**

Pinch **ground allspice**

Pinch **ground cloves**

⅔ cup **bottled strained tomatoes** (passata)

⅓ cup **dry red wine** or water

1 to 3 **red hot peppers** or green hot peppers, halved lengthwise and seeded

Cut beef into ½-inch (1 cm) cubes. Toss with lemon juice and half of the salt; set aside. In food processor, purée together onions, garlic and ginger, adding a little water if necessary, to make smooth paste.

In wok or heavy Dutch oven, melt butter over medium-low heat; cook turmeric for 3 minutes. Increase heat to medium-high; fry onion mixture, stirring constantly, until dry and just starting to colour, 8 to 10 minutes.

Reduce heat to medium; fry mixture, stirring occasionally, until golden, 12 to 15 minutes. Stir in paprika, ground hot peppers, coriander, cardamom, fenugreek (if using), nutmeg, allspice and cloves; fry, stirring, until fragrant, about 1 minute. Stir in ¼ cup water; continue frying, stirring and scraping up brown bits from bottom of pan, until very fragrant, 3 to 4 minutes. Stir in tomatoes and wine; cook, stirring, for 3 minutes.

Drain off any juices from beef. Stir beef into sauce; cook, stirring, until meat is browned, 3 to 4 minutes. Stir in 1 cup water and remaining salt. Simmer, covered, over medium-low heat for 45 minutes. Cut hot peppers diagonally into strips; stir into stew. Cook until beef is tender, 10 to 15 minutes.

Makes 4 to 6 servings. PER EACH OF 6 SERVINGS: about 362 cal, 33 g pro, 19 g total fat (9 g sat. fat), 15 g carb, 3 g fibre, 107 mg chol, 605 mg sodium, 785 mg potassium. % RDI: 5% calcium, 32% iron, 21% vit A, 23% vit C, 13% folate.

Variation
SPICY LAMB OR GOAT WOT: Substitute an equal amount of lamb or goat for the beef.

Swiss Cheese pies are baked throughout Switzerland, some with buttery short pastry or puff pastry crusts, others with yeast doughs. Here, we use simple homemade pizza dough. A combination of strong and mild cheeses, such as tangy Appenzeller with mild Emmenthal, makes a nice filling.

Alpine Cheese Pie

In skillet, melt butter over medium heat; fry onions until softened but not browned, about 8 minutes. Let cool.

In bowl, beat flour with milk; beat in cream, eggs, coriander, nutmeg, salt and white pepper.

On greased 16- x 12-inch (40 x 30 cm) rimmed baking sheet, stretch pizza dough, pressing with fingertips and gently pulling edges, to fit pan. Roll in edges and pinch to form ½-inch (1 cm) high lip; prick bottom all over with fork. Sprinkle with onion mixture, then cheese; pour cream mixture evenly over top.

Bake in bottom third of 425°F (220°C) oven until bottom and top are golden, about 25 minutes. Let cool for 10 minutes before cutting into 16 squares. Serve warm or at room temperature.

Makes 16 pieces. PER PIECE: about 154 cal, 4 g pro, 6 g total fat (3 g sat. fat), 21 g carb, 1 g fibre, 37 mg chol, 167 mg sodium, 79 mg potassium. % RDI: 2% calcium, 10% iron, 5% vit A, 2% vit C, 31% folate.

TIP | FOR A MORE RUSTIC CRUST, YOU CAN SUBSTITUTE WHOLE WHEAT FLOUR FOR ONE-QUARTER OF THE ALL-PURPOSE FLOUR IN THE PIZZA DOUGH.

2 tbsp **butter**

2 **onions,** finely chopped

3 tbsp **all-purpose flour**

⅓ cup **milk**

½ cup **whipping cream**

2 **eggs**

¾ tsp **ground coriander**

Pinch **nutmeg**

Pinch each **salt** and **white pepper**

Pizza Dough (recipe, page 91) or 1½ lb (675 g) prepared pizza dough, at room temperature

2½ cups shredded **Swiss cheese,** such as Appenzeller, Gruyère, Fribourgeois, Diabolo, Raclette or Emmenthal (about 6 oz/170 g)

Swiss Pounding the chicken until it's thin makes it cook quickly and evenly. Anchovy paste adds a depth of flavour to the sauce, so try not to leave it out; no one will know what is providing such deliciousness.

Chicken Schnitzel

4 **boneless skinless chicken breasts** (about 1½ lb/675 g)

⅓ cup **all-purpose flour**

¼ tsp each **salt** and **pepper**

¼ tsp **dried thyme**

1 **egg**

⅔ cup **dried bread crumbs**

¼ cup finely chopped **fresh parsley**

3 tbsp **vegetable oil**

2 cloves **garlic,** minced

1 tsp **anchovy paste** (optional)

½ cup **chicken broth**

1 tbsp **lemon juice**

1 tsp **cornstarch**

Between sheets of waxed paper and using mallet, pound chicken to ¼-inch (5 mm) thickness.

In shallow dish, whisk together flour, salt, pepper and thyme. In separate shallow dish, whisk egg with 2 tbsp water. In third shallow dish, combine bread crumbs with half of the parsley.

Dip chicken into flour mixture to coat both sides. Dip into egg mixture, letting excess drip off. Dip into bread crumb mixture, patting to coat evenly. *(Make-ahead: Place on waxed paper–lined baking sheet; cover with plastic wrap and refrigerate for up to 4 hours.)*

In large nonstick skillet, heat 1 tbsp of the oil over medium heat; fry chicken, in batches and using remaining oil as necessary, until no longer pink inside, about 4 minutes. Transfer to platter; keep warm.

Add garlic, and anchovy paste (if using) to pan; cook over medium heat just until garlic is golden, about 20 seconds. Add broth and lemon juice; bring to boil, scraping up brown bits from bottom of pan.

Stir cornstarch with 2 tsp cold water; stir into sauce and cook until thickened, 1 minute. Pour over chicken; sprinkle with remaining parsley.

Makes 4 servings. PER SERVING: about 419 cal, 44 g pro, 15 g total fat (2 g sat. fat), 23 g carb, 1 g fibre, 145 mg chol, 508 mg sodium. % RDI: 6% calcium, 20% iron, 5% vit A, 8% vit C, 15% folate.

Guyanese Exotic spices and pawpaw (papaya) hot sauce are tasty Caribbean accents for this juicy grilled chicken. Serve with Split Pea Fritters (page 41), Salt Fish Cakes (page 43) and Cookup Rice (page 142) for an island-themed party menu.

Island Grilled Chicken

¼ cup **vegetable oil**

1 **onion,** chopped

2 cloves **garlic,** chopped

1 piece (2 inches/5 cm) **fresh ginger,** chopped

2 tsp chopped **fresh thyme**

1 tsp **ground coriander**

1 tsp **hot pepper sauce**

½ tsp **ground cloves**

½ tsp **ground allspice**

2 **whole chickens** (about 3½ lb/1.5 kg each), cut in 10 pieces each

¾ tsp **salt**

½ tsp **pepper**

In food processor, pulse together oil, onion, garlic and ginger until chunky paste forms. Transfer to large shallow baking dish; stir in thyme, coriander, hot pepper sauce, cloves and allspice. Add chicken; rub all over with paste. Cover and refrigerate for 4 hours. *(Make-ahead: Refrigerate for up to 24 hours.)*

Sprinkle chicken with salt and pepper. Grill, covered, on greased grill over medium-high heat, turning once, until no longer pink inside for breasts, about 20 minutes, and until juices run clear when thighs and legs are pierced, about 40 minutes.

Makes 8 servings. PER SERVING: about 428 cal, 38 g pro, 29 g total fat (7 g sat. fat), 2 g carb, 1 g fibre, 139 mg chol, 339 mg sodium. % RDI: 2% calcium, 10% iron, 7% vit A, 2% vit C, 5% folate.

Pawpaw Hot Sauce

In food processor, pulse 2 carrots, peeled and chopped, with half English cucumber, peeled and seeded. Add 4 Scotch bonnet peppers, halved and seeded, and 2 cups chopped peeled seeded papaya. Finely chop. Scrape into saucepan; stir in ½ cup vinegar, ¼ cup water, 2 tsp packed brown sugar and ½ tsp salt. Bring to boil. Reduce heat and simmer for 30 minutes. *(Make-ahead: Refrigerate in airtight container for up to 3 weeks.)*

TIP | DECREASE THE PEPPERS TO TWO FOR A MILD HOT SAUCE; INCREASE TO SIX IF YOU LIKE IT HOT, HOT, HOT! BE WARNED THOUGH: THE HEAT INTENSIFIES WITH AGE.

Argentinian The grasslands of Argentina have sustained generations of happy steak eaters. This recipe, served with the quintessential Argentinian chimichurri sauce, is so simple and delicious you'll always want to serve it to guests.

Grilled Marinated Flank Steak

In glass bowl, combine lime juice, oil, garlic, cumin and pepper; add steak, turning to coat. Cover and refrigerate for 4 hours.

Sprinkle steak with salt to taste. Grill, covered, on greased grill over medium-high heat, turning once, until medium-rare, 8 to 10 minutes.

Transfer to cutting board and tent with foil; let stand for 10 minutes before thinly slicing across the grain. Serve with chimichurri sauces(s).

Makes 4 to 6 servings. PER EACH OF 6 SERVINGS: about 312 cal, 24 g pro, 22 g total fat (5 g sat. fat), 3 g carb, 1 g fibre, 48 mg chol, 146 mg sodium, 307 mg potassium. % RDI: 3% calcium, 22% iron. 9% vit A, 25% vit C, 10% folate.

Chimichurri Verde

In food processor, finely chop together 1 cup packed fresh parsley leaves; 2 tbsp packed fresh oregano leaves; 2 cloves garlic; half jalapeño pepper, seeded; and ¼ tsp each salt and pepper. Add ¼ cup extra-virgin olive oil, 2 tbsp water and 1 tbsp red wine vinegar. Pulse until combined. **Makes about ½ cup.**

3 tbsp **lime juice**

3 tbsp **extra-virgin olive oil**

3 cloves **garlic,** minced

¼ tsp **ground cumin**

¼ tsp **pepper**

1½ lb (675 g) **beef flank marinating steak**

Sea salt or salt

Chimichurri Verde (recipe, below left) and/or **Chimichurri Rojo** (recipe, page 228)

Japanese A salty, slightly sweet marinade based on miso paste gives excellent flavour to fish and makes for a lovely glazed exterior. It works best on thick, firm-fleshed fish fillets or steaks, such as halibut, salmon (especially wild) or swordfish.

Miso-Marinated Broiled Fish

⅔ cup **white miso paste** or red miso paste

¼ cup **sake,** dry sherry or Chinese rice wine

2 small inner ribs **celery with leaves,** finely chopped

1 tsp grated **fresh ginger**

4 **green onions**

4 **fish fillets** or steaks (1½ lb/ 675 g total)

Lemon wedges

In blender, purée together miso, sake, celery, ginger and 1 tbsp water, adding up to 1 tbsp more water if necessary.

Place onions in baking dish. Spread miso mixture evenly over fish; place on onions. Cover and refrigerate for 6 hours. *(Make-ahead: Refrigerate for up to 12 hours.)*

Scrape marinade off fish and discard. Place fish on greased rack on broiler pan; broil until top is golden, 6 to 7 minutes. Turn fish and add onions to rack; broil, turning onions once, until golden and fish flakes easily when tested, 6 to 7 minutes. Serve with lemon wedges.

Makes 4 servings. PER SERVING: about 198 cal, 36 g pro, 4 g total fat (1 g sat. fat), 2 g carb, 0 g fibre, 54 mg chol, 260 mg sodium. % RDI: 8% calcium, 11% iron, 7% vit A, 5% vit C, 10% folate.

Japanese Similar to schnitzel, this easy-to-prepare breaded chicken is tasty served hot with steamed rice and a salad, or cold in a sandwich. The key to the crunchy exterior is the layer of coarse Japanese bread crumbs called panko.

Chicken Katsu

KATSU SAUCE: In small saucepan, bring ketchup, Worcestershire sauce, sugar, soy sauce, mirin, garlic, ginger and mustard to boil. Reduce heat and simmer until reduced to ¾ cup, about 10 minutes. Let cool. *(Make-ahead: Refrigerate in airtight container for up to 1 week.)*

Meanwhile, between plastic wrap and using mallet, pound chicken to ¼-inch (5 mm) thickness. In bowl, combine soy sauce, garlic and half each of the salt and pepper; add chicken and toss to coat.

In shallow dish, whisk together flour and remaining salt and pepper. In separate shallow dish, whisk eggs with 2 tbsp water. Pour panko into third shallow dish. Dip chicken into flour mixture to coat both sides, shaking off excess. Dip into egg mixture, letting excess drip off. Dip into panko, patting to coat evenly.

In deep skillet or shallow Dutch oven, heat 1 inch (2.5 cm) oil over medium-high heat; cook chicken, in batches, until no longer pink inside, about 6 minutes. Cut chicken crosswise into ¾-inch (2 cm) wide strips. Place on platter; drizzle with katsu sauce. Serve with lemon slices.

Makes 4 servings. PER SERVING: about 634 cal, 43 g pro, 21 g total fat (3 g sat. fat), 67 g carb, 3 g fibre, 170 mg chol, 1,587 mg sodium, 802 mg potassium. % RDI: 12% calcium, 36% iron, 7% vit A, 23% vit C, 48% folate.

TIP | IF YOU CAN'T FIND MIRIN (JAPANESE SWEET RICE WINE), YOU CAN SUBSTITUTE 1 TBSP EACH BOILING WATER AND GRANULATED SUGAR.

4 **boneless skinless chicken breasts**

2 tsp **sodium-reduced soy sauce**

1 clove **garlic,** minced

½ tsp **salt**

¼ tsp **pepper**

½ cup **all-purpose flour**

2 **eggs**

1¾ cups **panko**

Vegetable oil for frying

Lemon slices

KATSU SAUCE:

½ cup **ketchup**

3 tbsp **Worcestershire sauce**

2 tbsp **granulated sugar**

2 tbsp **sodium-reduced soy sauce**

2 tbsp **mirin**

2 tsp minced **garlic**

2 tsp minced **fresh ginger**

¼ tsp **dry mustard**

Japanese Cold buckwheat noodle dishes like this are a summertime treat in Japan. The creamy texture of soft tofu is critical to this dish, so avoid the firmer varieties.

Soba Noodles With Spinach and Tofu

SOBA SAUCE: In saucepan, soak kelp in 2 cups water for 15 minutes. Bring just to boil over medium heat; remove kelp and discard. Stir bonito flakes into water in pan; simmer for 6 minutes. Add mirin, soy sauce, sugar and sake; return to boil. Strain through cheesecloth-lined sieve into heatproof measuring cup; let cool completely.

Meanwhile, in saucepan of boiling water, cook noodles according to package instructions, about 5 minutes. Drain and rinse under cold running water. Drain well; shake. Set aside to air-dry for 10 minutes.

Meanwhile, in covered skillet, steam spinach with ¼ cup water, stirring occasionally, just until wilted. Drain in colander; press out water.

Toss together noodles, spinach and about 1 cup of the soba sauce; divide among 4 bowls. Top with tofu; sprinkle with green onions, nori (if using), and sesame seeds. Serve with remaining soba sauce, adding as desired and tossing to coat.

Makes 4 servings. PER SERVING: about 369 cal, 20 g pro, 4 g total fat (1 g sat. fat), 64 g carb, 6 g fibre, 0 mg chol, 918 mg sodium, 725 mg potassium. % RDI: 22% calcium, 44% iron, 106% vit A, 18% vit C, 92% folate.

TIP | THE NOODLES, TOFU, DRIED KELP, BONITO FLAKES AND NORI ARE EASY TO FIND AT JAPANESE MARKETS. MANY OTHER ASIAN MARKETS AND SOME SUPERMARKETS CARRY THEM TOO.

1 pkg (250 g) **Japanese buckwheat (soba) noodles**

1 lb (450 g) **fresh spinach,** trimmed

1 pkg (10 oz/300 g) **soft tofu,** drained and cubed

2 **green onions,** thinly sliced diagonally

2 tbsp thin strips **nori** (optional)

1 tbsp toasted **sesame seeds**

SOBA SAUCE:
1 piece (about 4 inches/10 cm) **dried kelp** (konbu)

1 cup **bonito flakes**

½ cup **mirin**

⅓ cup **sodium-reduced soy sauce**

2 tbsp **granulated sugar**

1 tbsp **sake**

Vietnamese This popular salad (pronounced boon) of grilled meat, herbs and rice vermicelli is found on virtually every Vietnamese restaurant menu. Set out a platter of extra bean sprouts and sprigs of basil and mint so people can customize their salads.

Bun

8 **boneless skinless chicken thighs**

1 **green onion,** minced

2 cloves **garlic,** minced

2 tbsp **peanut oil** or vegetable oil

4 tsp **fish sauce**

1 tbsp **granulated sugar**

2 tsp minced **fresh lemongrass,** lemongrass paste or grated lime zest

¼ tsp **pepper**

⅓ cup chopped **roasted peanuts**

VERMICELLI SALAD:

8 oz (225 g) **rice vermicelli**

1 piece (5 inches/12 cm) **English cucumber**

¼ cup each chopped **fresh basil** and **mint**

2 cups shredded **romaine lettuce**

2 cups **bean sprouts**

1 **carrot,** julienned

SAUCE:

3 tbsp each **lime juice, fish sauce** and **unseasoned rice vinegar**

1 clove **garlic,** minced

4 tsp **granulated sugar**

½ tsp **Asian chili garlic sauce**

Between plastic wrap and using mallet, pound chicken to scant ¼-inch (5 mm) thickness. Cut each piece in half crosswise; place in bowl. Add green onion, garlic, oil, fish sauce, sugar, lemongrass and pepper; toss to coat. Cover and refrigerate for 1 hour.

SAUCE: Whisk together lime juice, fish sauce, rice vinegar, garlic, sugar, chili garlic sauce and ⅓ cup water. *(Make-ahead: Cover and refrigerate for up to 24 hours.)*

VERMICELLI SALAD: Meanwhile, in large bowl, cover vermicelli with boiling water; soak until tender, about 5 minutes. Drain and rinse in cold water, separating noodles. Drain and pat dry with towel. Divide among 4 large soup or pasta bowls. Cut cucumber in half crosswise. Cut each half lengthwise into ¼-inch (5 mm) thick slice. Cut slices lengthwise into ⅛-inch (3 mm) wide strips. Sprinkle vermicelli with half each of the basil and mint. In rows, neatly arrange lettuce, cucumber, bean sprouts and carrot on top.

Thread chicken onto metal or soaked wooden skewers (see photo, below). Grill, covered, on greased grill over medium-high heat, turning once, until well marked and juices run clear when chicken is pierced, about 8 minutes. (Or omit skewers and grill in grill pan.)

Pull chicken off skewers if desired; place on vermicelli salad. Sprinkle with peanuts and remaining basil and mint. While eating, pour sauce, a little at a time, over salad; toss to combine.

Makes 4 servings. PER SERVING: about 587 cal, 34 g pro, 20 g total fat (4 g sat. fat), 68 g carb, 6 g fibre, 95 mg chol, 1,714 mg sodium. % RDI: 8% calcium, 27% iron, 45% vit A, 30% vit C, 55% folate.

Thai This recipe can be gluten-free. Just check labels, including ketchup (Heinz is gluten-free), sriracha sauce, peanuts and fish sauce, and use homemade broth. Toast peanuts in a dry skillet over medium heat, shaking, until golden, about four minutes.

Pad Thai

In large bowl, soak noodles in warm water for 15 minutes; drain and set aside.

Meanwhile, in small bowl, whisk together ketchup, broth, fish sauce, lime juice, sugar and sriracha sauce; set aside.

In wok or large skillet, heat 1 tbsp of the oil over medium-high heat; cook eggs, stirring occasionally, until scrambled and set, about 30 seconds. Transfer to separate bowl.

Wipe out wok. Add 1 tbsp of the remaining oil and heat over high heat; stir-fry shrimp until pink, about 1 minute. Transfer to plate.

Heat 1 tbsp of the remaining oil in wok over high heat; stir-fry chicken until browned and no longer pink inside, about 1 minute. Add to shrimp.

Heat remaining oil in wok over high heat; cook shallots, garlic, red pepper and ginger until softened, about 2 minutes. Stir in ketchup mixture and noodles. Return shrimp mixture to pan; cook, stirring to coat, until noodles are tender, about 3 minutes.

Return scrambled eggs to pan along with tofu, bean sprouts and green onions; heat through just until sprouts begin to wilt, about 1 minute. Serve garnished with cilantro and peanuts, and with lime wedges to squeeze over top.

Makes 6 to 8 servings. PER EACH OF 8 SERVINGS: about 340 cal, 21 g pro, 13 g total fat (2 g sat. fat), 35 g carb, 2 g fibre, 100 mg chol, 931 mg sodium, 416 mg potassium. % RDI: 8% calcium, 15% iron, 12% vit A, 55% vit C, 23% folate.

Half pkg (454 g pkg) **wide rice stick noodles**

⅓ cup **ketchup**

⅓ cup **sodium-reduced chicken broth**

¼ cup **fish sauce**

3 tbsp **lime juice**

2 tsp **granulated sugar**

1 tsp **sriracha sauce** or hot pepper sauce

¼ cup **vegetable oil** or peanut oil

2 **eggs,** lightly beaten

8 oz (225 g) **frozen large shrimp** (size 31 to 35), thawed, peeled and deveined

10 oz (280 g) **boneless skinless chicken breasts,** thinly sliced

4 **shallots** (or 1 onion), thinly sliced

4 cloves **garlic,** minced

1 **sweet red pepper,** thinly sliced

2 tsp minced **fresh ginger**

6 oz (170 g) **medium tofu,** drained and cubed

3 cups **bean sprouts**

3 **green onions,** sliced

½ cup **fresh cilantro leaves**

¼ cup chopped toasted **unsalted peanuts**

Lime wedges

Thai Aromatic Thai basil is wonderful in this simple stir-fry, but Italian basil works just fine. It's not a fiery-hot dish, so add more chilies if you like heat. Serve with rice and an Asian green vegetable, such as Chinese broccoli or bok choy.

Stir-Fried Chicken With Cashews and Thai Basil

1 lb (450 g) **boneless skinless chicken thighs** or breasts, cut in 1-inch (2.5 cm) cubes

2 tsp grated **fresh ginger**

¼ tsp each **salt** and **pepper**

2 tsp **cornstarch**

2 tbsp **vegetable oil**

1 cup **raw cashews**

¼ cup thinly sliced **shallots** or onions

3 cloves **garlic,** minced

1 tsp chopped **hot pepper** (preferably Thai bird's-eye pepper)

1 tbsp **fish sauce**

2 tsp **granulated sugar**

2 tsp **lime juice**

1 cup loosely packed **fresh Thai basil leaves**

In bowl, toss together chicken, ginger, salt and pepper. Mix in cornstarch and 1 tbsp water; set aside.

In skillet or wok, heat oil over high heat; stir-fry cashews until golden, about 1 minute. With slotted spoon, remove and set aside.

Add shallots, garlic and hot pepper to pan; stir-fry until golden, about 2 minutes. Add chicken mixture; stir-fry for 4 minutes.

Stir in fish sauce, sugar and lime juice; cook until juices run clear when chicken is pierced, about 1 minute. Return cashews to pan along with Thai basil.

Makes 4 servings. PER SERVING: about 431 cal, 28 g pro, 29 g total fat (5 g sat. fat), 18 g carb, 1 g fibre, 94 mg chol, 598 mg sodium. % RDI: 5% calcium, 25% iron, 3% vit A, 10% vit C, 20% folate.

TIP | IF RAW CASHEWS ARE UNAVAILABLE, USE ROASTED CASHEWS AND OMIT THE SKILLET-TOASTING. ADD TO PAN ONE MINUTE BEFORE ADDING SUGAR AND LIME JUICE.

Korean Beef usually comes to mind when you think of Korean cuisine, but chicken that's soaked in a garlicky, slightly spicy marinade then broiled is another favourite home-style dish. The quick pickles mimic the flavours of traditional kimchi but have a touch less fire.

Garlic Chicken With Cucumber Pickles

CUCUMBER PICKLES: In small bowl, toss cucumber with salt; let stand for 15 minutes. Drain well. Add vinegar, sugar, oil, garlic and hot pepper flakes; toss to combine.

Meanwhile, trim any fat from chicken; cut chicken into bite-size pieces. In bowl, whisk together soy sauce, oil, sugar, ginger, sesame seeds, pepper and garlic. Add chicken and green onions; marinate at room temperature for 15 minutes, stirring occasionally.

Transfer chicken to foil-lined baking sheet; broil, stirring occasionally, until juices run clear when chicken is pierced, onions are slightly charred and almost no liquid remains, about 10 minutes. Serve with cucumber pickles.

Makes 4 servings. PER SERVING: about 251 cal, 27 g pro, 12 g total fat (3 g sat. fat), 10 g carb, 2 g fibre, 95 mg chol, 424 mg sodium, % RDI; 4% calcium, 14% iron, 7% vit A, 10% vit C, 11% folate.

8 **boneless skinless chicken thighs**

¼ cup **sodium-reduced soy sauce**

2 tbsp **sesame oil**

4 tsp **granulated sugar**

2 tsp minced **fresh ginger**

2 tsp **sesame seeds**

½ tsp **pepper**

4 cloves **garlic,** thinly sliced

4 **green onions,** cut in 2-inch (5 cm) lengths

CUCUMBER PICKLES:

1 **English cucumber,** thinly sliced

½ tsp **salt**

1 tbsp **unseasoned rice vinegar**

1 tsp **granulated sugar**

1 tsp **sesame oil**

2 cloves **garlic,** minced

½ tsp **hot pepper flakes**

Korean Ultra-popular bulgogi is easy to make at home with everyday ingredients. Traditionally, it is barbecued over a charcoal or wood fire, but nowadays it's often made on a tabletop grill or cast-iron skillet. It's a fun dish to eat, thanks to the lettuce wraps and choose-your-own condiments.

Bulgogi

1 tbsp **sesame oil**

Half **onion,** thinly sliced

1 large **green finger hot pepper** or Korean green hot pepper, seeded and sliced

Pinch **salt**

1 head **leaf lettuce,** leaves separated

2 tbsp **gochujang** (Korean hot pepper paste) or other Asian hot sauce

2 or 3 cloves **garlic,** thinly sliced

2 or 3 **green onions,** sliced

MARINATED STEAK:

1 lb (450 g) **boneless rib eye grilling steak,** or strip loin or sirloin grilling steak

1 tbsp packed **brown sugar**

1 tbsp **sake,** Chinese rice wine or dry sherry

2 **green onions** (white and light green parts only), minced

3 cloves **garlic,** pressed or minced

2 tbsp **soy sauce**

1 tbsp **sesame oil**

2 tsp toasted **sesame seeds**

MARINATED STEAK: Slice steak thinly across the grain. Stir together steak, brown sugar and sake until sugar is dissolved; let stand for 10 minutes. Mix in green onions, garlic, soy sauce, oil and sesame seeds; marinate in refrigerator for 20 minutes. *(Make-ahead: Refrigerate for up to 24 hours.)*

In heavy-bottomed skillet, heat oil over medium-high heat; sauté onion, hot pepper and salt until onion is lightly browned and tender-crisp, about 3 minutes. Transfer to plate.

Increase heat to high; in batches, sear steak slices, turning once and reducing heat if steak is browning too quickly, until browned, about 2 minutes. Return all steak and onion mixture to pan; toss to combine.

Serve immediately. To eat, place steak in lettuce leaf; top with gochujang, garlic and green onions to taste.

Makes 3 to 4 servings. PER EACH OF 4 SERVINGS: about 362 cal, 27 g pro, 22 g total fat (7 g sat. fat), 14 g carb, 2 g fibre, 59 mg chol, 799 mg sodium, 660 mg potassium. % RDI: 6% calcium, 32% iron, 69% vit A, 37% vit C, 23% folate.

TIP | GREEN FINGER HOT PEPPERS AND KOREAN GREEN HOT PEPPERS ARE FAIRLY MILD – PERFECT FOR THIS NOT-VERY-SPICY DISH. IF YOU LIKE A LITTLE MORE HEAT, YOU CAN USE A JALAPEÑO OR OTHER GREEN HOT PEPPER, BUT IT'S NOT THE TRADITIONAL CHOICE.

Indian Garam masala, a highly fragrant seasoning, is made from a variety of spices – and everyone has a unique blend, it seems. Indian grocery stores and many supermarkets carry it, but homemade (see page 19) is always freshest.

Spiced Chicken and Lentils

Sprinkle chicken with ¼ tsp of the salt and pepper. In Dutch oven, heat 2 tsp of the oil over medium-high heat; brown chicken for 3 to 4 minutes. Remove from pan; set aside.

In food processor, finely chop onions, garlic, hot pepper and ginger.

Heat remaining oil in pan; cook remaining salt, garam masala and cumin, stirring, until browned, about 1 minute. Stir in onion mixture; cook, stirring, until browned, about 6 minutes.

Add lentils and carrots, stirring to coat. Stir in 3 cups water and chicken; bring to boil. Reduce heat to medium; cook, stirring occasionally, until lentils are tender, about 25 minutes.

Makes 4 servings. PER SERVING: about 467 cal, 31 g pro, 14 g total fat (2 g sat. fat), 57 g carb, 12 g fibre, 48 mg chol, 658 mg sodium, 1,182 mg potassium. % RDI: 8% calcium, 60% iron, 83% vit A, 22% vit C, 182% folate.

4 **boneless skinless chicken thighs,** cut in quarters

1 tsp **salt**

¼ tsp **pepper**

3 tbsp **vegetable oil**

2 cups chopped **onions**

3 cloves **garlic,** chopped

1 **red hot pepper** or green hot pepper, chopped

2 tbsp chopped **fresh ginger**

1 tsp **garam masala** (recipe, page 19)

½ tsp **ground cumin**

1½ cups **dried green lentils** or dried brown lentils

2 large **carrots,** cut in chunks

Indian This southern-style curry starts with a fragrant masala (dried spice mixture), which is then mixed with fresh aromatics to form the sauce base. Quick-fried curry leaves, ginger and mustard seeds boost flavour just before serving.

Coconut Curried Eggplant

6 **green cardamom pods**

4 tsp **coriander seeds**

1 tbsp **fennel seeds**

2 tsp **cumin seeds**

1 tsp **black peppercorns**

½ tsp **fenugreek seeds**

3 **whole cloves**

2 **eggplants** (1½ lb/675 g total)

3 tbsp **vegetable oil**

1 **onion,** finely chopped

3 cloves **garlic,** minced

1 **green finger hot pepper,** seeded and sliced

1½ tsp **turmeric**

1 tsp each **granulated sugar** and **salt**

¼ tsp **cayenne pepper**

1 can (400 mL) **coconut milk**

20 **fresh curry leaves** (optional; see page 134)

2 tsp minced **fresh ginger**

1½ tsp **black mustard seeds**

2 tsp **lime juice**

Lightly crush cardamom pods; reserve seeds and discard pods. In small skillet, toast cardamom seeds, coriander seeds, fennel seeds, cumin seeds, peppercorns, fenugreek seeds and cloves over medium heat, stirring, until fragrant and slightly darkened, 3 to 4 minutes. Transfer to bowl; let cool. In spice grinder or clean coffee grinder, or using mortar and pestle, grind until powder; set aside.

Cut eggplants in half lengthwise, then into wedges; cut each wedge into 1½-inch (4 cm) chunks. Set aside.

In shallow Dutch oven, heat 2 tbsp of the oil over medium heat; cook onion, stirring often, until lightly browned, about 8 minutes. Add spice mixture, garlic, hot pepper, turmeric, sugar, salt and cayenne pepper; cook, stirring, for 2 minutes.

Add coconut milk; bring to boil. Add eggplant; cover, reduce heat and simmer until tender, about 15 minutes.

In skillet, heat remaining oil over medium heat; fry curry leaves (if using), ginger and mustard seeds until seeds pop, about 1 minute. Pour over eggplant mixture; cook, stirring, for 2 minutes. Stir in lime juice.

Makes 6 servings. PER SERVING: about 247 cal, 3 g pro, 22 g total fat (13 g sat. fat), 15 g carb, 4 g fibre, 0 mg chol, 398 mg sodium. % RDI: 5% calcium, 29% iron, 3% vit A, 13% vit C, 13% folate.

TIP | CAYENNE, OR GROUND DRIED CHILIES, AND FRESH HOT PEPPERS ARE OFTEN USED TOGETHER IN INDIAN CUISINE. THEY ADD HEAT IN BALANCE WITH EACH OTHER: DRIED ADD SUBTLE, RICH HEAT WHILE FRESH LEND A GREENER, FRESH PIQUANCY. FOR A SPICIER DISH, EITHER OR BOTH CAN BE INCREASED, TO TASTE.

Pakistani Balti curries like this are cooked quickly in a wok or wok-style pan. They're wildly popular in Britain, which is home to the largest community of people of Pakistani heritage outside of Pakistan.

Beef Stir-Fry Curry

In food processor, purée together hot peppers, chopped cilantro, garlic, onion and ginger until paste forms.

In wok, heat oil over medium heat; stir-fry pepper paste and curry powder, drizzling in 6 tbsp water, 1 tbsp at a time, as paste begins to stick to pan, until no water remains, about 4 minutes.

Add beef; stir-fry over high heat until seared, about 2 minutes. Add tomatoes, yogurt and salt; stir-fry until tomatoes are softened, about 2 minutes. Stir in lemon juice and garam masala; cook for 30 seconds. Garnish with cilantro sprigs.

Makes 4 servings. PER SERVING: about 369 cal, 27 g pro, 25 g total fat (8 g sat. fat), 10 g carb, 3 g fibre, 60 mg chol, 658 mg sodium, 704 mg potassium. % RDI: 7% calcium, 29% iron, 8% vit A, 25% vit C, 12% folate.

TIP | FRYING THE CHILIES AND AROMATICS FOR THIS DISH CAN MAKE YOUR EYES STING A LITTLE, SO TURN ON THE EXHAUST FAN OR OPEN A WINDOW.

4 **green hot peppers,** halved lengthwise and seeded

4 sprigs **fresh cilantro** (stems and leaves), coarsely chopped

2 cloves **garlic,** smashed

1 small **onion,** chopped

1 tbsp chopped **fresh ginger**

3 tbsp **peanut oil** or vegetable oil

2 tbsp **curry powder**

1 lb (450 g) **beef grilling steak** (such as rib eye or top sirloin), thinly sliced across the grain

4 **plum tomatoes,** cut in thin wedges

⅓ cup **plain yogurt**

1 tsp **salt**

1 tbsp **lemon juice**

1 tsp **garam masala** (recipe, page 19)

Fresh cilantro sprigs

Chinese Pork lends its rich flavour to many Chinese stir-fries, and in this one it complements grassy fresh asparagus. Steamed rice or noodles make a tasty side.

Pork and Asparagus Stir-Fry

Combine pork, half of the wine, the soy sauce, cornstarch and ginger; stir to coat. Cut each asparagus stalk into 4 pieces.

In wok, heat oil over high heat; stir-fry green onions until fragrant, about 30 seconds. Add pork mixture; stir-fry until no longer pink inside, about 1 minute.

Add asparagus and mushrooms; stir-fry for 1 minute. Stir in broth, sugar and remaining wine; stir-fry until asparagus is tender-crisp, 1 to 2 minutes.

Makes 4 servings. PER SERVING: about 173 cal, 16 g pro, 9 g total fat (1 g sat. fat), 8 g carb, 3 g fibre, 26 mg chol, 336 mg sodium, 438 mg potassium. % RDI: 3% calcium, 10% iron, 9% vit A, 13% vit C, 58% folate.

8 oz (225 g) **pork loin centre chops,** julienned

2 tbsp **Chinese rice wine** or dry sherry

1 tbsp **soy sauce**

2 tsp **cornstarch**

1 tsp grated **fresh ginger**

1 lb (450 g) **asparagus,** trimmed

2 tbsp **vegetable oil**

3 **green onions,** cut in 1½-inch (4 cm) lengths

1 cup sliced **shiitake mushroom caps**

½ cup **sodium-reduced chicken broth**

1 tsp **granulated sugar**

Chinese The tension between the fiery chili paste and the sweet elements in the sauce gives this retro Chinese restaurant favourite a pleasant balance.

Sweet and Spicy Cashew Chicken

½ cup **sodium-reduced chicken broth**

3 tbsp **oyster sauce**

1 tbsp **granulated sugar**

1 tbsp **cornstarch**

1 tbsp **vinegar**

2 tbsp **vegetable oil**

1 lb (450 g) **boneless skinless chicken breasts,** cut in chunks

¼ tsp each **salt** and **pepper**

2 **sweet red peppers,** chopped

2 **onions,** chopped

1 tsp **Thai chili paste** or sambal oelek

½ cup roasted **unsalted cashews**

3 **green onions,** chopped

Whisk together chicken broth, oyster sauce, sugar, cornstarch and vinegar; set aside.

In wok, heat half of the oil over medium-high heat; stir-fry chicken, salt and pepper until golden, about 4 minutes. Transfer to plate.

Add remaining oil to wok; stir-fry red peppers, onions and chili paste for 3 minutes. Return chicken and any accumulated juices to wok; stir-fry until chicken is no longer pink inside, about 1 minute.

Add broth mixture; stir-fry for 1 minute. Add cashews and green onions; stir-fry for 1 minute.

Makes 4 servings. PER SERVING: about 352 cal, 30 g pro, 17 g total fat (2 g sat. fat), 22 g carb, 3 g fibre, 66 mg chol, 675 mg sodium, 643 mg potassium. % RDI: 4% calcium, 15% iron, 23% vit A, 168% vit C, 15% folate.

Chinese This meal has it all: chicken, vegetables and starch, all in one bowl. Find flat, thin dried Chinese wheat noodles in Chinese grocery stores or some supermarkets. Or replace them with dried linguine or fettuccine and cook for eight to 10 minutes.

Chicken Lo Mein

10 **dried shiitake mushrooms**

12 oz (340 g) **dried Chinese wheat noodles**

1 lb (450 g) **boneless skinless chicken breasts**

2 tbsp **vegetable oil**

2 cups **snow peas,** trimmed

1 **sweet red pepper,** thinly sliced

2 **green onions,** chopped

3 cloves **garlic,** minced

2 tsp minced **fresh ginger**

½ cup **chicken broth**

2 tbsp **oyster sauce**

2 tbsp **soy sauce**

2 tsp **cornstarch**

1 can (14 oz/398 mL) **whole baby corn,** drained

In bowl, cover mushrooms with 1 cup warm water; soak until softened, about 15 minutes. Reserving ½ cup of the soaking liquid, drain mushrooms. Cut off stems and discard; slice caps. Set aside.

Meanwhile, in large pot of boiling salted water, cook noodles until tender but firm, about 2 minutes. Drain and set aside.

Meanwhile, thinly slice chicken. In wok or large deep skillet, heat half of the oil over high heat; stir-fry chicken, in batches, until no longer pink inside, about 2 minutes. With slotted spoon, transfer to bowl.

Add remaining oil to wok. Reduce heat to medium-high; stir-fry snow peas, red pepper, green onions, garlic and ginger until tender-crisp, about 3 minutes.

Whisk together broth, oyster sauce, soy sauce and cornstarch. To wok, add chicken along with any accumulated juices, corn, noodles, mushrooms and reserved soaking liquid; cook, stirring, until sauce is thickened and glossy, 2 to 3 minutes.

Makes 4 to 6 servings. PER EACH OF 6 SERVINGS: about 369 cal, 26 g pro, 8 g total fat (1 g sat. fat), 50 g carb, 2 g fibre, 44 mg chol, 1,475 mg sodium. % RDI: 4% calcium, 15% iron, 8% vit A, 85% vit C, 10% folate.

Chinese Whole fish steamed with green onions and ginger is typical fare at Chinese banquets, but this simplified version makes an easy meal for two.

Steamed Salmon and Mushrooms

Place salmon fillets, skin side down, on small heatproof plate. Sprinkle with salt and pepper; drizzle with sherry (if using). Set aside.

In small skillet, heat oil over medium heat; fry ginger until fragrant, about 1 minute. Add mushrooms and 1 tsp of the soy sauce; fry until softened, about 3 minutes. Scrape over salmon. Arrange red pepper, prosciutto (if using), and green onion over salmon.

Meanwhile, place rack or steamer in wok or shallow pan; pour in enough water to come 1 inch (2.5 cm) below rack. Cover and bring to boil; reduce heat to medium-high. Place plate on rack; cover and steam until salmon flakes easily when tested, about 12 minutes. Remove from steamer.

Pour liquid from plate into small skillet; cover fish and keep warm. Whisk together broth, cornstarch and remaining soy sauce. Whisk into skillet; bring to boil. Cook, stirring, until slightly thickened, about 2 minutes. Pour over salmon. Garnish with cilantro (if using).

Makes 2 servings. PER SERVING: about 327 cal, 27 g pro, 22 g total fat (3 g sat. fat), 5 g carb, 1 g fibre, 74 mg chol, 348 mg sodium. % RDI: 3% calcium, 6% iron, 13% vit A, 92% vit C, 24% folate.

2 **salmon fillets** or halibut, trout or tilapia fillets

Pinch each **salt** and **pepper**

1 tsp **dry sherry** (optional)

1 tbsp **vegetable oil**

2 tsp minced **fresh ginger**

½ cup sliced **shiitake mushroom caps**

2 tsp **light soy sauce**

Half **sweet red pepper,** very thinly sliced

2 thin slices **prosciutto** or ham (optional)

1 **green onion,** thinly sliced

3 tbsp **chicken broth**

½ tsp **cornstarch**

Fresh cilantro sprigs (optional)

Chinese The story goes that Ma Po (a nickname meaning "pock-marked madame") was the owner of a Szechuan restaurant who invented this famous dish. Szechuan pepper, made from ground dried prickly ash berries, is essential for authenticity, but the dish is still delicious without it.

Ma Po Tofu

Cut tofu into ¾-inch (2 cm) cubes; drain on paper towel–lined plate.

In wok, heat peanut oil over medium-high heat; stir-fry pork and chili paste until pork is browned, about 2 minutes. Stir in minced green onion, garlic, hot peppers and black beans; stir-fry for 1 minute.

Stir in broth, soy sauce, wine (if using), and Szechuan pepper (is using). Add tofu; bring to boil. Reduce heat to medium; cover and simmer for 3 minutes.

Mix cornstarch with 2 tsp water; stir into wok gently to avoid breaking up tofu. Simmer for 30 seconds. Remove from heat; stir in sesame oil. Sprinkle with sliced green onion.

Makes 4 servings. PER SERVING: about 257 cal, 24 g pro, 22 g total fat (4 g sat. fat), 5 g carb, 1 g fibre, 18 mg chol, 702 mg sodium, 264 mg potassium, % RDI: 9% calcium, 26% iron, 3% vit A, 3% vit C, 11% folate.

TIPS

• SOFT, NOT SILKEN, TOFU IS A MUST FOR THIS DISH. IF YOU CAN'T FIND IT, USE REGULAR (NOT FIRM) TOFU. CHINESE COOKS USUALLY BLANCH TOFU BEFORE ADDING IT TO A DISH. IF YOU LIKE, BLANCH THE TOFU IN BOILING WATER FOR TWO MINUTES. DRAIN WELL.

• CHINESE RECIPES, PARTICULARLY IN SZECHUAN PROVINCE, CALL FOR A VARIETY OF BEAN-BASED SAUCES. CHINESE GROCERY STORES CARRY THE CHILI BROAD BEAN PASTE OR HOT BEAN PASTE YOU NEED FOR THIS DISH. IF YOU CAN'T FIND IT, USE 1 TBSP BLACK BEAN AND GARLIC SAUCE MIXED WITH 1 TBSP ASIAN CHILI SAUCE.

1 pkg (425 g) **soft tofu,** drained

2 tbsp **peanut oil** or vegetable oil

4 oz (115 g) **ground pork** or ground beef

1½ tbsp **chili broad bean paste** or hot bean paste

1 **green onion,** minced

3 cloves **garlic,** minced

2 tsp chopped **preserved (salt-pickled) hot peppers** or ½ tsp hot pepper flakes

1½ tsp **fermented black beans** or black bean and garlic sauce

¾ cup **sodium-reduced chicken broth** or water

2 tsp **soy sauce**

2 tsp **Chinese rice wine** or dry sherry (optional)

¼ tsp **Szechuan pepper** (optional)

1 tsp **cornstarch**

1 tsp **sesame oil** or chili oil

2 tbsp thinly sliced **green onion** (dark green part only)

Mole Turkey Wings (page 224) and
Tricolour Rice (page 143)

{entertaining mains}

Italian Squid, or calamari in Italian, can be easier to find in the freezer section, but the frozen tastes just as good as fresh. A quick five-minute simmer in the sauce is plenty to cook the squid without making it tough. Sprinkle with chopped fresh parsley and black pepper for a little added colour.

Calamari in Tomato White Wine Sauce

Holding squid tube, pull off head and tentacles; set aside. Rinse tubes under cold water, rubbing off purplish skin. Pull out and discard quill (long clear plastic-like skeleton) from centre of tubes.

On cutting board, pull off and discard fins from tubes. Cut off and discard eyes and head from tentacles, keeping tentacles attached on ring on top. Squeeze hard beak from centre of tentacles and discard. Cut tubes crosswise into ½-inch (1 cm) wide rings; pat dry.

In saucepan, heat oil over medium heat; cook onion and garlic, stirring occasionally, until softened, about 3 minutes. Add wine and hot pepper flakes; cook for 1 minute.

Add tomatoes; bring to boil. Reduce heat and simmer for 5 minutes. Add squid; simmer until tender, about 5 minutes. Sprinkle with salt.

Makes 4 servings. PER SERVING: about 160 cal, 13 g pro, 8 g total fat (1 g sat. fat), 8 g carb, 1 g fibre, 174 mg chol, 294 mg sodium, 402 mg potassium. % RDI: 5% calcium, 11% iron, 2% vit A, 25% vit C, 5% folate.

TIP | THIS RECIPE EASILY DOUBLES FOR A LARGER GROUP.

1 lb (450 g) **fresh squid** or thawed frozen squid

2 tbsp **olive oil**

Half **onion,** thinly sliced

1 clove **garlic,** thinly sliced

½ cup **dry white wine**

¼ tsp **hot pepper flakes**

1½ cups chopped seeded drained **canned plum tomatoes**

¼ tsp **salt**

Italian Down-to-earth and delicious, this comforting dish braises away to tenderness while you sit back and enjoy the company of your guests. Serve with Polenta (below) and a green vegetable.

Osso Buco

6 thick (1½-inch/4 cm) pieces **veal hind shank** (about 3½ lb/1.5 kg)

2 tbsp **all-purpose flour**

½ tsp each **salt** and **pepper**

2 tbsp **olive oil** (approx)

1 cup chopped **onion**

1 cup chopped **carrot**

⅔ cup chopped **celery**

2 cloves **garlic,** minced

½ tsp **dried thyme**

½ tsp **dried sage**

½ tsp **dried rosemary**

¾ cup **dry white wine**

1½ cups drained **canned tomatoes,** coarsely chopped

½ cup **beef broth**

2 **bay leaves**

GREMOLATA:
¼ cup chopped **fresh parsley**

1 tbsp grated **lemon zest**

1 clove **garlic,** minced

Cut six 24-inch (60 cm) lengths of kitchen string; wrap each twice around edge of a shank and *tie* firmly. On plate, combine flour and half each of the salt and pepper; press shanks into flour mixture, turning to coat. Reserve any remaining flour mixture.

In large Dutch oven, heat oil over medium-high heat; *brown* shanks, in batches and adding up to 1 tbsp more oil if necessary. Transfer to plate.

Drain fat from pan; fry onion, carrot, celery, garlic, thyme, sage and rosemary over medium heat, stirring often, for 10 minutes. Sprinkle with any reserved flour mixture; cook, stirring, for 1 minute. Add wine, stirring and scraping up brown bits from bottom of pan. Bring to boil; boil until reduced by half, about 2 minutes.

Stir in tomatoes, broth, bay leaves and remaining salt and pepper. Nestle in shanks; bring to boil. Cover and cook in 350°F (180°C) oven, basting every 30 minutes, for 1½ hours. Turn shanks and cook, uncovered and basting twice, until tender, about 30 minutes.

Transfer shanks to serving platter; cut off string. Keep warm. Place pan over medium-high heat; *boil* gently, stirring, until thickened, about 5 minutes. Discard bay leaves. Pour over shanks.

GREMOLATA: Meanwhile, stir together parsley, lemon zest and garlic; sprinkle over shanks.

Makes 6 servings. PER SERVING: about 364 cal, 42 g pro, 16 g total fat (5 g sat. fat), 11 g carb, 2 g fibre, 171 mg chol, 576 mg sodium. % RDI: 9% calcium, 25% iron, 36% vit A, 25% vit C, 21% folate.

Polenta

In saucepan, bring 6 cups water and ¾ tsp salt to boil. Gradually whisk in 1½ cups cornmeal; cook, stirring often, until thick enough to mound on spoon, 20 to 25 minutes. **Makes 6 servings.**

~ *tie* ~   ~ *brown* ~   ~ *boil* ~

Italian The combination of pillowy gnocchi and rich and creamy sauce is truly decadent. Serve with shaved Parmesan cheese and a sprinkling of pepper.

Gnocchi in Cremini Cream Sauce

Potato Gnocchi (recipe, opposite)

2 tbsp chopped **fresh chives**

CREMINI CREAM SAUCE:

2 tbsp **butter**

3 **shallots,** minced

3 cups thinly sliced **cremini mushrooms** (12 oz/340 g)

¼ tsp each **salt** and **pepper**

⅓ cup **dry white wine**

1½ cups **whipping cream**

¾ cup grated **Parmesan cheese**

CREMINI CREAM SAUCE: In large skillet, melt butter over medium-high heat; sauté shallots until softened, 2 to 3 minutes. Add mushrooms, salt and pepper; sauté until wilted, about 5 minutes.

Add wine; cook until almost no liquid remains. Add cream and Parmesan cheese; reduce heat and simmer, stirring often, until slightly thickened and reduced to about 2½ cups, about 7 minutes.

Add gnocchi; toss gently to coat and heat through. Sprinkle with chives.

Makes 6 to 8 servings. PER EACH OF 8 SERVINGS: about 468 cal, 12 g pro, 23 g total fat (13 g sat. fat), 55 g carb, 4 g fibre, 99 mg chol, 1,164 mg sodium. % RDI: 14% calcium, 21% iron, 20% vit A, 23% vit C, 45% folate.

Italian Homemade gnocchi are easier to make than you might think, and their silkiness is absolutely unparalleled. A food mill or ricer is essential to get the proper texture; a food mill is a little more expensive, but it's a versatile tool for puréeing.

Potato Gnocchi

In large saucepan of boiling water, cover and cook potatoes until tender, about 30 minutes.

Drain potatoes and let cool enough to handle. Peel and place in large bowl. Refrigerate potatoes until cold, about 30 minutes.

Through medium disc of food mill or using ricer, press potatoes into bowl to make 8 cups unpacked. Mix in egg yolk and 1 tsp of the salt.

With wooden spoon, stir in 2 cups of the flour. Turn out onto unfloured work surface. Knead to form soft, slightly sticky, spongy dough. Divide into 8 pieces.

Roll each piece into 20-inch (50 cm) rope about ¾ inch (2 cm) thick. Cut each rope into ½-inch (1 cm) lengths. On work surface, toss with ¼ cup of the remaining flour.

Dip fork into remaining flour. Holding fork with tines facing down and using fingertips of other hand, lightly roll each piece down tines of fork to create ridges. Dust baking sheet with remaining flour. Place gnocchi on pan. *(Make-ahead: Freeze for 2 hours or until firm; using metal spatula, scrape into freezer bags and freeze for up to 2 weeks.)*

Bring large pot of water to boil; add remaining salt. Cook half of the gnocchi, stirring gently, until gnocchi float to top, about 3 minutes. With slotted spoon, transfer to warmed serving bowl. Repeat with remaining gnocchi.

Makes 6 to 8 servings. PER EACH OF 8 SERVINGS: about 234 cal, 6 g pro, 1 g total fat (trace sat. fat), 50 g carb, 3 g fibre, 25 mg chol, 903 mg sodium. % RDI: 1% calcium, 15% iron, 1% vit A, 23% vit C, 40% folate.

6 **Yukon Gold potatoes** (2½ lb/ 1.125 kg), unpeeled

1 **egg yolk**

1 tbsp **salt**

2⅓ cups **all-purpose flour**

Italian Baked lasagna is a special treat throughout Italy, with many regional variations. In this northern-style dish, there is no melting cheese; that's more Neapolitan or southern. Spinach pasta sheets are traditional, but we like the fresh egg pasta sheets available at most grocery stores.

Lasagna al Forno

RAGÙ SAUCE: Soak mushrooms in 1 cup warm water until softened, about 20 minutes. Reserving liquid, drain; finely chop mushrooms. In heavy-bottomed Dutch oven, heat oil over medium heat; cover and cook onion, celery, carrots and garlic, stirring, until softened, 5 minutes.

Uncover; increase heat to medium-high. Sauté veal, pork, prosciutto, pepper and mushrooms, stirring, until meat begins to brown, 4 minutes. Increase heat to high; sauté until meat is no longer pink, 5 minutes. Reduce heat to medium-high; stir in tomato paste, parsley and bay leaf. Fry, stirring, until paste is slightly darkened, 2 to 3 minutes. Stir in wine and salt; cook until wine is evaporated. Stir in reserved mushroom liquid, tomatoes and ½ cup water. Bring to boil; reduce heat to low and simmer, covered and stirring occasionally, for 2 hours.

PARMESAN BÉCHAMEL SAUCE: In saucepan, melt butter over medium heat; fry flour, salt, nutmeg and pepper, stirring, for 2 minutes. Whisk in milk; bring to boil, whisking constantly. Reduce heat; simmer for 5 minutes. Remove from heat; stir in cheese. Cover; set aside.

In pot of boiling salted water, boil pasta sheets for 3 minutes. Drain and rinse under cold water; drain well. Lay, without touching, on tea towel.

Spread about ¼ cup ragù sauce in 13- x 9-inch (3 L) baking dish. Cover with layer of pasta sheets. Spread one-third of the remaining ragù sauce over pasta; spread with one-quarter of béchamel sauce; smooth top. Repeat layers twice. Top with remaining béchamel sauce; sprinkle with Parmesan cheese. Cover with foil; bake in 375°F (190°C) oven until bubbly, 35 to 40 minutes. Uncover and bake until top is lightly browned, 20 to 25 minutes. Let stand for 30 minutes before serving.

Makes 8 to 12 servings. PER EACH OF 12 SERVINGS: about 353 cal, 20 g pro, 17 g total fat (8 g sat. fat), 29 g carb, 2 g fibre, 89 mg chol, 892 mg sodium, 608 mg potassium. % RDI: 17% calcium, 19% iron, 21% vit A, 10% vit C, 29% folate.

TIP | EVEN IF THE PACKAGE SAYS NOT TO PRECOOK, BOIL THE PASTA SHEETS TO ACHIEVE THE PROPER TEXTURE.

1 pkg (360 g) **fresh lasagna sheets**

3 tbsp grated **Parmesan cheese**

RAGÙ SAUCE:

½ oz (15 g) **dried porcini mushrooms**

2 tbsp **olive oil**

1 **onion,** finely chopped

½ cup each finely diced **celery** and **carrots**

2 cloves **garlic,** minced

12 oz (340 g) **ground veal** or beef

8 oz (225 g) **lean ground pork**

3 oz (85 g) **prosciutto** or pancetta, diced

Generous pinch **black pepper**

1 can (5½ oz/156 mL) **tomato paste**

⅓ cup finely chopped **fresh parsley**

1 **bay leaf**

¾ cup **dry white wine** or red wine

1 tsp **salt**

1½ cups **bottled strained tomatoes** (passata) or crushed tomatoes

PARMESAN BÉCHAMEL SAUCE:

5 tbsp **butter**

5 tbsp **all-purpose flour**

1 tsp **salt**

Generous pinch **nutmeg**

Pinch **white pepper**

4 cups **2% milk** or homogenized milk

½ cup grated **Parmesan cheese**

Italian Inspired by the classic Sicilian combination of bread crumbs, pine nuts and currants plus caramelized onions, this dazzling dish is sure to impress.

Sicilian Stuffed Pork Tenderloin

1½ lb (675 g) **pork tenderloins**

2 tbsp **Dijon mustard**

2 tbsp **liquid honey**

1 tbsp **extra-virgin olive oil**

¼ tsp each **salt** and **pepper**

STUFFING:

2 tbsp **butter**

3 **onions,** thinly sliced

¼ cup **dried currants**

1 tbsp **balsamic vinegar**

¼ tsp each **salt** and **pepper**

⅓ cup **fresh bread crumbs**

¼ cup toasted **pine nuts**

3 tbsp chopped **fresh parsley**

1 tsp grated **orange zest**

1 tbsp **orange juice**

STUFFING: In skillet, melt butter over medium-low heat; fry onions, stirring occasionally, until deep golden, about 20 minutes. Stir in currants, vinegar, salt and pepper; cook for 5 minutes. Remove from heat; stir in bread crumbs, pine nuts, parsley, orange zest and orange juice.

Starting at thick end of each tenderloin, insert handle of wooden spoon lengthwise through centre, almost but not all the way through, to make pocket. Fill each with stuffing, using handle to gently push stuffing evenly into pocket. Refrigerate for 30 minutes. *(Make-ahead: Refrigerate for up to 24 hours.)*

Place on greased baking sheet. Stir together mustard, honey, oil, salt and pepper; brush over pork. Roast in 400°F (200°C) oven until juices run clear when pork is pierced and just a hint of pink remains inside, about 40 minutes. Transfer to cutting board; tent with foil and let stand for 10 minutes before slicing.

Makes 4 to 6 servings. PER EACH OF 6 SERVINGS: about 298 cal, 30 g pro, 13 g total fat (4 g sat. fat), 15 g carb, 2 g fibre, 73 mg chol, 363 mg sodium. % RDI: 3% calcium, 18% iron, 5% vit A, 22% vit C, 10% folate.

Turkish Lamb is a common ingredient in Turkish cuisine, and it's easy to find in most major grocery stores here. The bulgur in the filling makes the small amount of meat go farther.

Turkish-Style Stuffed Eggplant

In saucepan, bring ¾ cup water to boil; stir in bulgur. Reduce heat to low; cover and cook until no liquid remains, about 10 minutes. Fluff with fork; set aside.

Meanwhile, pressing lightly, roll eggplants over work surface to loosen flesh; cut in half lengthwise. With spoon, scoop out flesh, leaving ½-inch (1 cm) thick shells. Sprinkle shells with 1 tbsp of the lemon juice and ½ tsp of the salt; set aside. Chop flesh.

In skillet, heat 1 tbsp of the oil over medium-high heat; sauté lamb, garlic and ¼ tsp of the remaining salt until lamb is no longer pink. Drain off fat; fry tomato paste until no liquid remains, about 3 minutes. Stir in bulgur, breaking up with spoon; transfer to large bowl.

Heat remaining oil over medium-high heat; sauté chopped eggplant, onion, cumin, cinnamon, cayenne pepper and remaining salt until vegetables are softened and golden, about 5 minutes. Add to lamb mixture. Stir in parsley, mint and remaining lemon juice.

Fill eggplant shells with lamb mixture; place in casserole dish just large enough to hold them snugly. Spread tomato slices over top. Cover with lightly greased foil. Bake in 400°F (200°C) oven for 1 hour.

Makes 4 to 6 servings. PER EACH OF 6 SERVINGS: about 355 cal, 16 g pro, 22 g total fat (8 g sat. fat), 28 g carb, 6 g fibre, 53 mg chol, 633 mg sodium, 616 mg potassium. % RDI: 5% calcium, 19% iron, 6% vit A, 18% vit C, 21% folate.

TIP | SLICE A SMALL PIECE OFF THE BOTTOM OF EACH EGGPLANT HALF TO MAKE IT SIT FLAT IN THE BAKING DISH.

⅓ cup **bulgur**

2 **eggplants** (1 lb/450 g each)

2 tbsp **lemon juice**

1½ tsp **salt**

2 tbsp **olive oil**

1 lb (450 g) **ground lamb** or ground beef

4 cloves **garlic,** minced

2 tbsp **tomato paste**

2 cups diced **Spanish onion**

1 tsp **ground cumin**

½ tsp **cinnamon**

¼ tsp **cayenne pepper**

¼ cup chopped **fresh parsley**

1 tsp **dried mint**

2 small **tomatoes,** sliced

Spanish Paella is fiesta food that's traditionally cooked in a wide, shallow two-handled pan over a hot fire. This stove-top version with rice, sausage and lots of seafood has something for everyone – truly perfect for a party.

Party Paella

1½ cups **sodium-reduced chicken broth**

1½ cups **hot water**

½ tsp **saffron threads**

8 oz (225 g) **cured chorizo sausage**

1 tbsp **extra-virgin olive oil**

1 cup thinly sliced **roasted red pepper**

1 **onion,** chopped

2 cloves **garlic,** minced

1 tsp each **salt** and **pepper**

2 cups **short-grain rice**

1 cup **white wine**

2 ripe **tomatoes,** finely chopped

1 cup cut (1-inch/2.5 cm lengths) **green beans**

8 oz (225 g) **mussels** or clams

8 oz (225 g) cleaned **squid**

8 oz (225 g) **raw large shrimp** (size 31 to 35), peeled and deveined

2 **green onions,** thinly sliced

8 **lemon wedges**

Stir together broth, hot water and saffron; set aside. Cut chorizo into ½-inch (1 cm) thick slices. In 16-cup (4 L) paella pan or large deep skillet, heat oil over high heat; fry chorizo, turning, until browned, about 3 minutes. Using slotted spoon, transfer to bowl; set aside.

Add half of the red pepper, the onion, garlic, salt and pepper to pan; cook over medium heat, stirring often, until onion is softened, about 4 minutes. Stir in rice. Add saffron mixture, wine and tomatoes. Return chorizo to pan; bring to boil. Reduce heat to medium-low; cover with foil and simmer, stirring often, until rice is almost tender, about 15 minutes. Stir in green beans.

Scrub mussels; remove any beards. Discard any that do not close when tapped. Cut squid into ½-inch (1 cm) rings. Nestle mussels, squid and shrimp into rice; arrange remaining red pepper on top. Cover with foil; simmer until almost no liquid remains, rice is tender, shrimp are pink and mussels are open, about 20 minutes. Discard any mussels that do not open. Garnish with green onions and lemon wedges.

Makes 8 servings. PER SERVING: about 414 cal, 21 g pro, 14 g total fat (5 g sat. fat), 48 g carb, 2 g fibre, 126 mg chol, 855 mg sodium. % RDI: 4% calcium, 17% iron, 11% vit A, 70% vit C, 11% folate.

TIP | YOU CAN MAKE PAELLA FOR ANY SIZE CROWD. PLAN ON ¼ CUP UNCOOKED RICE AND A TOTAL OF 8 OZ (225 G) CHICKEN, MEAT AND SEAFOOD PER PERSON.

Variation
CHICKEN PAELLA: Replace mussels, squid and shrimp with 1½ lb (675 g) boneless skinless chicken thighs, trimmed and halved. Increase oil to 2 tbsp. Brown chicken, then chorizo as directed; transfer to bowl. Continue with recipe, returning chicken to pan along with chorizo.

French This robust peasant dish was made to stave off the cold of bone-chilling winters. The base is beans with bacon, but the pièce de résistance, nestled among the sausage and pork, is the confit of duck – seasoned duck roasted in duck fat until meltingly tender.

Cassoulet

With kitchen shears, remove duck backbone (see photo, below) and wing tips; reserve for making stock. Trim excess fat and skin; reserve. Cut duck into 8 pieces and place in bowl; toss with salt, peppercorns and thyme. Cover and refrigerate for 24 hours.

Meanwhile, chop reserved duck skin and fat; place in skillet and cook over low heat until skin is browned and fat is clear, 1 hour. Strain into bowl; discard skin. Let cool; cover and refrigerate until solid. *(Make-ahead: Refrigerate for up to 24 hours.)*

In pot, cover beans with cold water; bring to boil. Boil for 2 minutes. Remove from heat; let stand for 1 hour. Drain; return to pot. Add bacon, broth, 2 tbsp of the parsley, cloves and bay leaves; bring to boil. Reduce heat, cover and simmer just until tender, 30 to 40 minutes. Reserving cooking liquid, drain; discard bay leaves. Let cool; cover and refrigerate.

Meanwhile, rub most of the seasonings off duck. In large Dutch oven, melt reserved duck fat over low heat; add duck pieces and melted duck fat. Roast in 300°F (150°C) oven until tender, about 1½ hours. Remove duck from pan, reserving 1 tbsp fat; refrigerate remaining fat for more confit or cassoulets. Brown duck under broiler.

In large clean Dutch oven, heat 1 tbsp of the reserved duck fat over medium-high heat; brown pork and sausage, in batches. Drain off fat; fry onions and garlic over medium heat for 5 minutes. Return pork and sausage to pan along with reserved cooking liquid and tomatoes; simmer, covered, until meat is very tender, 1½ hours.

Spread half of the bean mixture in 24-cup (6 L) Dutch oven or roasting pan. With slotted spoon, layer pork mixture, duck, then remaining beans. Pour pork cooking liquid over top. Bake in 350°F (180°C) oven for 1 hour. Mix bread crumbs, butter and remaining parsley; sprinkle over beans. Bake until topping is golden and crisp, about 1 hour.

Makes 8 to 10 servings. PER EACH OF 10 SERVINGS: about 563 cal, 41 g pro, 29 g total fat (11 g sat. fat), 35 g carb, 5 g fibre, 113 mg chol, 1,213 mg sodium. % RDI: 13% calcium, 41% iron, 11% vit A, 20% vit C, 60% folate.

1 **whole duck** (5 lb/2.25 kg)

2 tbsp **pickling salt**

1 tsp cracked **black peppercorns**

¼ tsp **dried thyme**

2 cups **dried Great Northern beans** or navy (pea) beans

4 oz (115 g) **slab bacon,** diced

4 cups **chicken broth**

⅓ cup chopped **fresh parsley**

Pinch **ground cloves**

3 **bay leaves**

1½ lb (675 g) **duck fat** or lard, melted

1 lb (450 g) **boneless pork,** cubed

12 oz (340 g) **garlic sausage,** sliced

3 **onions,** chopped

4 cloves **garlic,** minced

1 can (28 oz/796 mL) **diced tomatoes**

3 cups **fresh bread crumbs**

¼ cup **butter,** melted

French This regional style of cooking, called à la normande, often features a heavenly sauce made from apples, Calvados (apple brandy), cream, butter and the pan juices from the roasted hens.

Normandy-Style Roast Guinea Hens

1½ tsp **salt**

½ tsp **pepper**

2 **guinea hens** (about 4¼ lb/ 1.9 kg total)

2 **bay leaves**

6 sprigs **fresh thyme** (or 1 tsp dried thyme)

2 **apples** (unpeeled and uncored), halved and thinly sliced

1 **onion,** thinly sliced

⅓ cup **butter**

¼ cup **Calvados** or brandy

½ cup **sodium-reduced chicken broth**

⅓ cup **whipping cream**

Mix salt with pepper; sprinkle about one-third inside hens. Divide bay leaves and thyme between cavities. Mix apples with onion; place handful inside each hen, setting remaining mixture aside. Skewer openings closed; tie legs together and tuck wings under back.

In large ovenproof skillet, melt butter over medium heat; brown hens all over, about 12 minutes. Transfer to plate.

Add remaining apple mixture to pan; top with hens, breast side up. Sprinkle with remaining salt mixture. Roast in 375°F (190°C) oven, basting every 10 minutes, until digital thermometer inserted in thickest part of thigh registers 185°F (85°C), 1 to 1¼ hours. Untie; add contents of cavities to skillet. Transfer hens to serving platter; keep warm.

Place skillet over medium-high heat; cook until almost no liquid remains. Add Calvados; holding at arm's length, ignite liquid. Let flames die.

Stir in broth; cook until reduced by half. Stir in cream; bring to boil. Strain through sieve, pressing solids to extract liquid; discard solids. Serve sauce with hens.

Makes 4 to 6 servings. PER EACH OF 6 SERVINGS: about 620 cal, 67 g pro, 33 g total fat (14 g sat. fat), 8 g carb, 0 g fibre, 253 mg chol, 890 mg sodium. % RDI: 5% calcium, 18% iron, 19% vit A, 7% vit C, 6% folate.

French Bright green flecks of peppery watercress dot this elegant springtime dish. It makes a pretty addition to a luncheon menu; just make sure everyone is ready to eat when it comes out perfectly puffed from the oven.

Watercress Soufflé

Grease 8- x 3¾-inch (2.5 L) soufflé dish with 1 tsp of the butter; sprinkle evenly with Parmesan cheese. Set aside.

In saucepan, melt remaining butter over medium heat. Stir in flour, salt and pepper; cook, stirring, for 1 minute. Whisk in milk; cook, whisking, until thickened, about 5 minutes. Pour into large bowl; whisk in egg yolks, watercress and mustard.

In separate bowl, beat egg whites until stiff peaks form. Fold one-third into egg yolk mixture; fold in remaining whites. Pour into prepared dish.

Bake in 400°F (200°C) oven until puffed, dark golden and firm to the touch, about 30 minutes. Serve immediately.

Makes 4 to 6 servings. PER EACH OF 6 SERVINGS: about 193 cal, 11 g pro, 14 g total fat (7 g sat. fat), 6 g carb, trace fibre, 268 mg chol, 371 mg sodium. % RDI: 11% calcium, 7% iron, 21% vit A, 7% vit C, 20% folate.

3 tbsp **butter**

2 tbsp finely grated **Parmesan cheese**

3 tbsp **all-purpose flour**

½ tsp **salt**

¼ tsp **pepper**

1 cup **milk**

8 **eggs,** separated

2 cups **watercress leaves,** finely chopped

½ tsp **Dijon mustard**

French This rustic French peasant-style dish celebrates the humble cabbage by turning it into an edible work of art. Bring the entire cabbage to the table to cut into wedges and serve with the delicious reduced sauce.

Stuffed Savoy Cabbage

1 **savoy cabbage** (3 lb/1.35 kg)

1½ cups **fresh bread crumbs**

¼ cup **milk**

1 tbsp **vegetable oil**

1 large **onion,** finely chopped

1 **egg**

2 tbsp **tomato paste**

1 clove **garlic,** minced

2 tsp chopped **fresh thyme**
    (or ¾ tsp dried thyme)

¾ tsp **salt**

½ tsp each **pepper, ground allspice** and **nutmeg**

1 lb (450 g) **lean ground veal** or lean ground beef

1 cup minced **lean ham** (about 6 oz/170 g)

½ cup chopped **fresh parsley**

2½ cups **chicken broth** or vegetable broth

1 rib **celery,** cut in 3 pieces

3 sprigs **fresh parsley**

3 sprigs **fresh thyme**

1 **bay leaf**

1 bunch small **carrots,** peeled

1 tbsp **all-purpose flour**

1 tbsp **butter,** softened

In large pot of boiling salted water, cover and cook cabbage until skewer inserts easily into centre, about 10 minutes. Chill under cold water and drain upside down; pat off all water with towels.

Mix bread crumbs with milk; set aside. In small skillet, heat oil over medium-high heat; sauté onion until golden, about 9 minutes. Mix into bread crumb mixture.

In large bowl, whisk together egg, tomato paste, garlic, chopped thyme, salt, pepper, allspice and nutmeg; *mix* in bread crumb mixture, veal, ham and all but 1 tbsp of the chopped parsley.

Place cabbage on 7-inch (18 cm) square of double-thickness cheesecloth. Gently separate leaves almost to centre, keeping intact at base. Starting at centre, *stuff* meat mixture between and about two-thirds of the way up leaves. Pull up outer leaves to return cabbage to original shape. Tightly fold up cheesecloth around cabbage; tie securely with string.

In large saucepan, bring broth and 2 cups water to boil. Add cabbage, celery, parsley sprigs, thyme sprigs and bay leaf; cover and *simmer* over medium heat for 40 minutes. Add carrots; cook until cabbage is tender when tested with skewer, about 20 minutes. Remove cabbage, letting liquid drain back into pan. Place on platter; with slotted spoon, arrange carrots around cabbage. Keep warm.

Increase heat to high; boil until liquid is reduced to (or add water to make) about 1½ cups. Mix flour with butter; whisk into pan. Reduce heat and simmer, stirring, until slightly thickened, about 3 minutes. Strain into sauceboat. Stir in remaining chopped parsley. Cut cabbage into wedges; serve with sauce.

Makes 8 servings. PER SERVING: about 242 cal, 22 g pro, 8 g total fat (3 g sat. fat), 21 g carb, 7 g fibre, 80 mg chol, 1,344 mg sodium. % RDI: 10% calcium, 18% iron, 116% vit A, 60% vit C, 50% folate.

~ mix ~   ~ stuff ~   ~ simmer ~

Portuguese The Douro region of Portugal is famous for its tasty black pork, which is usually served with roasted or fried potatoes. This recipe, studded with Port-soaked prunes, is the perfect mix of sweet, savoury and rich.

Roast Pork Loin

8 **pitted prunes,** halved

¼ cup **ruby Port** or tawny Port

2 cloves **garlic,** minced

1¼ tsp **salt**

3 lb (1.35 kg) **boneless pork loin centre roast**

¾ tsp **sweet paprika**

¼ cup **extra-virgin olive oil**

Mix prunes, Port, garlic and ½ tsp of the salt; let stand for 1 hour.

Cut slits in pork evenly all over; insert prune half with clinging garlic into each slit. Place in roasting pan. Sprinkle with paprika and remaining salt. Mix prune juices with oil; spoon 3 tbsp over pork.

Roast in 325°F (160°C) oven, basting often with remaining oil mixture and later with pan juices, until juices run clear when pork is pierced and just a hint of pink remains inside, or digital thermometer registers 160°F (71°C), 1 to 1½ hours.

Reserving pan juices, transfer pork to serving platter; tent with foil and let stand for 10 minutes before slicing thinly. Mix carving juices with pan juices; spoon some over slices and serve remainder alongside pork.

Makes 8 servings. PER SERVING: about 380 cal, 38 g pro, 21 g total fat (7 g sat. fat), 7 g carb, 1 g fibre, 92 mg chol, 443 mg sodium, 653 mg potassium. % RDI: 1% calcium, 9% iron, 2% vit A, 3% vit C, 3% folate.

Portuguese Many Portuguese dishes have been inspired by flavours from former colonies; in this case, Mozambique and Angola in Africa. The exotic combination of peanut, coconut and hot pepper is irresistible. Serve it with rice and a cucumber salad to cool the fire.

Portuguese African Chicken

Season chicken with ¼ tsp each of the salt and pepper; set aside.

In large skillet, heat half of the oil over medium-high heat; sauté onion, garlic and hot pepper until softened, about 4 minutes.

Stir in tomato paste, paprika, 2 tbsp water, ginger and remaining salt and pepper; cook, stirring, for 1 minute. Stir in coconut milk and peanut butter; let cool slightly. Transfer to food processor; purée until smooth.

Wipe out skillet. Add remaining oil; heat over medium-high heat. Brown chicken, in batches, about 5 minutes. Transfer to roasting pan; cover with 1 cup of the sauce. Roast in 425°F (220°C) oven for 30 minutes, basting twice.

Mix remaining sauce with cilantro; pour over chicken. Cook until juices run clear when chicken is pierced, about 12 minutes.

Makes 6 to 8 servings. PER EACH OF 8 SERVINGS: about 514 cal, 41 g pro, 36 g total fat (12 g sat. fat), 6 g carb, 1 g fibre, 149 mg chol, 399 mg sodium. % RDI: 4% calcium, 25% iron, 19% vit A, 15% vit C, 8% folate.

4 lb (1.8 kg) **chicken pieces**

¾ tsp each **salt** and **pepper**

¼ cup **vegetable oil**

1 **onion,** chopped

4 cloves **garlic,** chopped

2 tbsp minced **red hot pepper** or jalapeño pepper

3 tbsp **tomato paste**

2 tbsp **sweet paprika**

⅓ tsp **ground ginger**

1 cup **coconut milk**

3 tbsp **peanut butter**

¼ cup chopped **fresh cilantro** or parsley

Greek This hearty stew mingles common Greek flavours, such as oregano, lemon, cinnamon, artichokes and feta cheese, and turns lamb shoulder into company fare. Best of all, you can make it ahead for a relaxed night with friends.

Greek Lamb Stew With Artichokes

3 lb (1.35 kg) **boneless lamb shoulder**

1 tbsp **extra-virgin olive oil**

3 **onions,** sliced

6 cloves **garlic,** minced

1 tbsp **dried oregano**

1 tbsp grated **lemon zest**

¼ tsp **salt**

Pinch **ground allspice**

Pinch **cinnamon**

2 tbsp **all-purpose flour**

2 cups **beef broth**

¼ cup **tomato paste**

1 can (14 oz/398 mL) **artichoke hearts,** drained and quartered

½ cup crumbled **feta cheese**

2 tbsp chopped **fresh parsley**

Trim fat from lamb; cut into 1-inch (2.5 cm) cubes. In shallow Dutch oven, heat oil over medium-high heat; brown lamb, in batches. Transfer to plate.

Drain any fat from pan; cook onions, garlic, oregano, lemon zest, salt, allspice and cinnamon over medium heat, stirring occasionally, until onions are softened, about 5 minutes.

Sprinkle with flour; cook, stirring, for 1 minute. Add broth and tomato paste; bring to boil, stirring and scraping up any brown bits from bottom of pan.

Return lamb and any accumulated juices to pan; cover and simmer until lamb is tender, about 45 minutes. Add artichokes; cook until heated through, about 15 minutes. *(Make-ahead: Let cool for 30 minutes. Transfer to airtight container; refrigerate, uncovered, until cold. Cover and refrigerate for up to 2 days or freeze for up to 2 weeks.)*

Serve sprinkled with feta cheese and parsley.

Makes 6 to 8 servings. PER EACH OF 8 SERVINGS: about 242 cal, 25 g pro, 11 g total fat (4 g sat. fat), 11 g carb, 3 g fibre, 77 mg chol, 535 mg sodium. % RDI: 8% calcium, 21% iron, 4% vit A, 18% vit C, 21% folate.

English As long as you have the deep fryer and beer batter ready for the fish, why not make onion rings too? Any beer will work for this batter, but a crisp pilsner or India pale ale complements the fish nicely. Serve with tartar sauce.

Beer-Battered Fish and Onion Rings

In bowl, whisk together flour, salt and cayenne; whisk in beer until smooth. Let stand for 15 minutes. Meanwhile, peel and cut onion into ½-inch (1 cm) thick slices; separate into rings.

In deep fryer or deep heavy pot, pour in enough oil to come at least 2 inches (5 cm) up side. Heat until deep-fry thermometer registers 375°F (190°C). With fork, dip onion rings into batter, 4 or 5 at a time; add to deep-fryer and cook, turning halfway through, until golden, about 1 minute. With slotted spoon, transfer to paper towel–lined baking sheet; keep warm in 250°F (120°C) oven for up to 1 hour.

Meanwhile, cut fish fillets into serving-size pieces. Dip into batter; fry in oil, turning halfway through, until golden and fish flakes easily when tested, 5 to 7 minutes. With slotted spoon, add to baking sheet to drain. Sprinkle with more salt, if desired. Serve with lemon wedges.

Makes 4 servings. PER SERVING: about 493 cal, 27 g pro, 20 g total fat (2 g sat. fat), 46 g carb, 3 g fibre, 65 mg chol, 944 mg sodium. % RDI: 6% calcium, 23% iron, 2% vit A, 5% vit C, 31% folate.

TIP | FOR AN EXTRA TASTE OF THE OCEAN, USE SEA SALT.

1½ cups **all-purpose flour**
1½ tsp **salt** (approx)
¼ tsp **cayenne pepper**
1 bottle (341 mL) **beer**
1 small **Spanish onion**
Vegetable oil for frying
1 lb (450 g) **haddock fillets** or cod fillets
Lemon wedges

Scottish Enjoy these hearty meat pies hot, or refrigerate them to enjoy cold for lunch the next day. They travel well, which makes them ideal for potlucks.

Traditional Scotch Pies

4 **eggs**

HOT MILK PASTRY:

1¼ cups **milk**

⅔ cup **lard**

3½ cups **all-purpose flour**

¾ tsp **salt**

FILLING:

1 tsp **vegetable oil**

1 **onion,** minced

2 lb (900 g) **lean ground lamb,** beef or veal

3 cloves **garlic,** chopped

1½ tsp **pepper**

1 tsp **salt**

1 tsp **dried savory**

1 tsp **dried sage**

½ tsp **allspice**

HOT MILK PASTRY: In saucepan, heat milk with lard over medium heat until almost boiling. In food processor, blend flour with salt. Add milk mixture; pulse until pastry forms ball. Shape into disc; cover and let rest on floured surface for 20 minutes. *(Make-ahead: Wrap and refrigerate for up to 2 days. Let come to room temperature before using.)*

Meanwhile, in saucepan, cover 3 of the eggs with enough cold water to come at least 1 inch (2.5 cm) above eggs. Cover and bring to boil over high heat. Remove from heat; let stand for 15 minutes. Drain and chill in cold water. Peel and cut each egg in half lengthwise.

FILLING: Meanwhile, in small skillet, heat oil over medium heat; fry onion, stirring, until golden, about 15 minutes. Transfer to bowl; let cool. Mix in lamb, garlic, pepper, salt, savory, sage and allspice.

Divide pastry into 6 pieces; shape into balls. Cut off one-third of each; set aside for tops. On floured surface, roll out each of the remaining balls into 8-inch (20 cm) circle; press into six 5-inch (12 cm) foil pie plates. Divide meat mixture into 12 portions; press 1 into each pie shell. Place 1 egg half, cut side down, in centre of each. Press remaining meat portions over top to cover. Beat remaining egg with 1 tbsp water. Roll out remaining pastry to 5-inch (12 cm) circles; cut ½-inch (1 cm) round hole in centre of each. Brush top edge of bottom pastry with egg wash. Place pastry circle on top; trim and crimp edges to seal.

Brush top with egg wash. Bake in bottom third of 325°F (160°C) oven until meat thermometer inserted in centre registers 160°F (71°C), about 1 hour. Let stand for 15 minutes before serving. *(Make-ahead: Let cool for 30 minutes; refrigerate until cold. Wrap individually and refrigerate for up to 24 hours. Or overwrap in heavy-duty foil and freeze for up to 2 weeks; thaw in refrigerator. Unwrap and reheat in 375°F/190°C oven until hot, about 20 minutes.)*

Makes 6 servings. PER SERVING: about 903 cal, 41 g pro, 54 g total fat (22 g sat. fat), 60 g carb, 3 g fibre, 255 mg chol, 824 mg sodium. % RDI: 11% calcium, 46% iron, 8% vit A, 3% vit C, 59% folate.

~ roll ~　　　　*~ cut ~*　　　　*~ seal ~*

Ukrainian This is probably the most time-honoured filling for perogies. The buttery golden onion on top is wonderful, but add a sprinkle of crumbled crisp bacon and a dollop of sour cream for the ultimate indulgence.

Potato Cheddar Perogies

FILLING: In large pot of boiling salted water, cook potatoes until tender, about 15 minutes; drain and transfer to large bowl. Mash well. In saucepan, melt butter over medium heat; cook onion until golden and tender, about 5 minutes. Add to potatoes; stir in Cheddar cheese, salt and pepper.

Working with 1 portion of dough at a time and keeping remainder covered, *roll* out on lightly floured surface to scant ¼-inch (5 mm) thickness. Using 3-inch (8 cm) round cutter, *cut* into rounds.

Place 1 tsp filling on each round. Lightly moisten edge of half of the round with water; fold over filling and pinch edges together to *seal*. Place on flour-dusted cloth; cover with tea towel. Repeat with remaining dough and filling, rerolling scraps, to make 36 perogies.

In large pot of boiling salted water, cook perogies, in batches and stirring gently, until floating and tender, about 5 minutes. With slotted spoon, transfer to colander to drain.

In skillet, melt butter over medium heat; cook onion until golden, about 8 minutes. Add perogies; cook until golden.

Makes about 36 pieces. PER PIECE: about 75 cal, 2 g pro, 3 g total fat (1 g sat. fat), 11 g carb, 1 g fibre, 10 mg chol, 142 mg sodium, 55 mg potassium. % RDI: 1% calcium, 4% iron, 2% vit A, 2% vit C, 110% folate.

Savoury Perogy Dough

In bowl, whisk 3 cups all-purpose flour with 1 tsp salt. Whisk together 1 egg, ¾ cup water and 2 tbsp vegetable oil; stir into flour mixture, adding up to 2 tbsp more water if needed to make soft but not sticky dough. Turn out onto lightly floured surface; knead until smooth, about 10 times. Halve dough; cover with plastic wrap or damp towel and let rest for 20 minutes. **Makes enough for about 36 perogies.**

Savoury Perogy Dough
(recipe, below left)

2 tbsp **butter**

1 **onion,** sliced

FILLING:
1 lb (450 g) **russet potatoes,** peeled and cubed

2 tbsp **butter**

⅓ cup finely chopped **onion**

½ cup shredded **Cheddar cheese**

¼ tsp each **salt** and **pepper**

Ukrainian Once you've had your fill of Potato Cheddar Perogies (page 217), try your hand at these full-flavoured beauties. They really don't need any adornments, so you can serve them plain, but they're even more delicious topped with sautéed onions.

Mushroom Sauerkraut Perogies

2 tbsp **butter**

1 cup diced **onion**

2 cups finely chopped **button mushrooms**

2 cups chopped drained **sauerkraut**

¼ tsp each **salt** and **pepper**

Savoury Perogy Dough (recipe, page 217)

In skillet, melt butter over medium heat; cook onion until softened, about 5 minutes. Add mushrooms; cook until no liquid remains, about 4 minutes. Add sauerkraut, salt and pepper; cook until no liquid remains, about 4 minutes.

Working with 1 portion of dough at a time and keeping remainder covered, roll out on lightly floured surface to scant ¼-inch (5 mm) thickness. Using 3-inch (8 cm) round cutter, cut into rounds.

Place 1 tsp filling on each round. Lightly moisten edge of half of the round with water; fold over filling and pinch edges together to seal. Place on flour-dusted cloth; cover with tea towel. Repeat with remaining dough and filling, rerolling scraps, to make 36 perogies.

In large pot of boiling salted water, cook perogies, in batches and stirring gently, until floating and tender, about 5 minutes. With slotted spoon, transfer to colander to drain.

Makes about 36 pieces. PER PIECE: about 57 cal, 2 g pro, 2 g total fat (1 g sat. fat), 9 g carb, 1 g fibre, 7 mg chol, 180 mg sodium, 40 mg potassium. % RDI: 1% calcium, 5% iron, 1% vit A, 3% vit C, 12% folate.

Caribbean Firm green plantains, or cooking bananas, are starchy like potatoes and won't fall apart when stewed. In combination with the sweet potatoes, they give this mildly spiced dish a touch of sweetness. Serve the stew over steamed rice.

Curried Plantain Beef Stew

In shallow Dutch oven, heat 1 tbsp of the oil over medium-high heat; brown beef, in batches. Transfer to plate.

Drain off fat from pan. Add remaining oil; fry onions, garlic, salt and pepper over medium heat until onion is softened, about 5 minutes. Add curry paste; cook, stirring, for 1 minute. Add tomatoes; bring to boil, breaking up tomatoes with spoon and scraping up brown bits from bottom of pan. Reduce heat to medium; stir in coconut milk.

Return beef and any accumulated juices to pan; cover and simmer until beef is tender, about 1½ hours. Add sweet potatoes and plantains; simmer, covered, for 20 minutes. Uncover and simmer, stirring occasionally, until thickened and potatoes and plantains are tender, about 15 minutes. Sprinkle with cilantro.

Makes 6 to 8 servings. PER EACH OF 8 SERVINGS: about 410 cal, 28 g pro, 16 g total fat (6 g sat. fat), 39 g carb, 3 g fibre, 56 mg chol, 343 mg sodium. % RDI: 5% calcium, 25% iron, 136% vit A, 47% vit C, 15% folate.

2 tbsp **vegetable oil**

2 lb (900 g) **stewing beef cubes**

2 **onions,** chopped

4 cloves **garlic,** minced

½ tsp **salt**

¼ tsp **pepper**

2 tbsp **curry paste**

1 can (19 oz/540 mL) **tomatoes**

1 can (400 mL) **light coconut milk**

2 **sweet potatoes** (1½ lb/675 g total), peeled and cut in chunks

2 **plantains** (1 lb/450 g total), peeled and sliced

¼ cup chopped **fresh cilantro**

Australian Native Australian pepperberries look and taste like peppercorns but with a mineral citrus finish. They're hard to find here, but the rub below is an excellent taste-alike.

Pepperberry Butterflied Leg of Lamb

3 tbsp **Pepperberry Spice Blend** (recipe, below right)

2 tbsp **dry red wine**

1 tbsp **vegetable oil**

1 **butterflied boneless leg of lamb** (3 lb/1.35 kg)

Quick Plum Chutney (recipe, below right)

In large bowl, combine spice blend, wine and oil; add lamb, rubbing to coat all over. Cover and refrigerate for 2 hours. *(Make-ahead: Refrigerate for up to 8 hours.)*

Grill lamb, covered, on greased grill over medium-high heat, turning once, until meat thermometer registers 160°F (71°C) for medium, about 40 minutes. Transfer to cutting board and tent with foil; let stand for 10 minutes before slicing thinly across the grain. Serve with chutney.

Makes 6 servings. PER SERVING: about 367 cal, 40 g pro, 13 g total fat (5 g sat. fat), 22 g carb, 2 g fibre, 141 mg chol, 459 mg sodium. % RDI: 2% calcium, 26% iron, 7% vit A, 12% vit C, 1% folate.

Pepperberry Spice Blend
Combine 1 tbsp chili powder, 1½ tsp each pepper and grated lemon zest, 1 tsp each packed brown sugar and salt, and ½ tsp dried oregano.
Makes about 3 tbsp.

Quick Plum Chutney
Pit 1¼ lb (565 g) plums (about 5); cut into 1-inch (2.5 cm) chunks to make about 3 cups. In saucepan, combine ¼ cup each granulated sugar and cider vinegar, 2 whole star anise (or ¼ tsp aniseed), and pinch pepper. Bring to boil over medium heat; stir in plums. Reduce heat, cover and simmer for 5 minutes; let cool. *(Make-ahead: Refrigerate in airtight container for up to 2 days; bring to room temperature to serve.)*
Makes 2 cups.

*Pepperberry Butterflied Leg of Lamb and
Quick Plum Chutney (opposite) with
Pawpaw and Avocado Salad (page 122)*

Eastern European Stuffed cabbage leaves are a favourite across Europe. There are endless variations, but in eastern Europe, the stuffing is generally meat, sometimes mixed with rice or other grains. Our recipe is inspired by Polish, Czech, Slovakian and Hungarian recipes.

Cabbage Rolls

Core cabbage. In large pot of boiling water, blanch cabbage, covered, until leaves are softened, 10 to 15 minutes. Working from core end, carefully pull pliable outer leaves off with tongs; return cabbage to boiling water for 2 to 3 minutes when leaves become difficult to remove. Remove 14 to 20 leaves total; drain on tea towels.

In skillet over medium heat, fry bacon until crisp; transfer to paper towel–lined plate to drain. Set aside 1 tbsp bacon fat; drain off all but 2 tbsp of the remaining fat from pan. Chop bacon; place in large bowl.

Add onions and carrots to pan; fry until onions are golden, about 15 minutes. Stir into bowl along with beef, pork, ½ cup of the strained tomatoes, egg, parsley, garlic, 1½ tsp of the salt, marjoram and pepper.

Pat each cabbage leaf dry; cut off any tough ribs. For each roll, spoon 2 to 3 tbsp filling onto leaf; tuck in sides and roll up. Place, seam side down, in greased 13- x 9-inch (3 L) or larger baking dish. If desired, shred a few of the leftover cabbage leaves; scatter thin layer over top.

In bowl or large glass measure, whisk tomato paste, reserved bacon fat and ¼ cup warm water; whisk in remaining strained tomatoes, sugar, lemon juice, vinegar and remaining salt. Spread over cabbage rolls. Cover with foil; bake on rimmed baking sheet in 350°F (180°C) oven for 1¼ hours. Uncover; bake until cabbage is soft and translucent and filling is firm, about 45 minutes more. Serve with sour cream.

Makes 7 to 10 servings. PER EACH OF 10 SERVINGS: about 280 cal, 17 g pro, 17 g total fat (6 g sat. fat), 14 g carb, 2 g fibre, 71 mg chol, 817 mg sodium, 560 mg potassium. % RDI: 5% calcium, 22% iron, 25% vit A, 33% vit C, 15% folate.

1 large head **cabbage**

8 oz (225 g) **bacon**

2 **onions,** finely chopped

1 cup finely diced **carrots**

1 lb (450 g) **lean ground beef**

8 oz (225 g) **ground pork** or ground beef

1 bottle (680 mL) **strained tomatoes** (passata)

1 **egg,** beaten

½ cup finely chopped **fresh parsley**

2 cloves **garlic,** pressed or minced

2 tsp **salt**

1½ tsp **dried marjoram**

1¼ tsp **pepper**

3 tbsp **tomato paste**

2 tbsp **granulated sugar**

2 tbsp **lemon juice**

2 tsp **cider vinegar**

Sour cream, at room temperature

TIP | LIFTING HOT CABBAGE OUT OF BOILING WATER CAN BE A LITTLE TRICKY. TRY PUSHING THE HANDLE OF A WOODEN SPOON INTO THE CENTRE WHERE THE CORE WAS, THEN RAISING THE CABBAGE UP OUT OF THE WATER.

Mexican Rich and nutty with hits of spice and dark chocolate, this simplified version of the Mexican sauce called mole (pronounced MO-lay) uses easily available ingredients. Turkey wings are often sold already split with tips removed. Serve these with Tricolour Rice (page 143).

Mole Turkey Wings

2 tbsp **vegetable oil**

2 **onions,** chopped

3 cloves **garlic,** sliced

1 tbsp **chili powder**

1 tsp **ancho chili powder** or chili powder

1 tsp **ground coriander**

1 tsp **salt**

½ tsp **pepper**

¼ tsp **cinnamon**

¼ tsp **aniseed** (optional)

Pinch **ground cloves**

1½ cups **canned diced tomatoes with juice**

1 cup **sodium-reduced chicken broth**

2 tbsp **raisins**

2 tbsp **almond butter** or peanut butter

1 oz (30 g) **unsweetened chocolate,** chopped

3 lb (1.35 kg) trimmed split **turkey wings** (about 12 pieces)

2 tsp **sesame seeds**

In large heavy skillet or wide shallow Dutch oven, heat oil over medium-high heat; sauté onions and garlic until softened, about 5 minutes. Add chili powder, ancho chili powder, coriander, half each of the salt and pepper, the cinnamon, aniseed (if using), and cloves; cook, stirring, for 1 minute.

Add tomatoes and juice, broth, ½ cup water, raisins, almond butter and chocolate. Reduce heat, cover and simmer, stirring occasionally, for 20 minutes. Let cool slightly. Transfer to blender or food processor; purée. Strain through fine sieve, pressing solids. *(Make-ahead: Refrigerate in airtight container for up to 3 days or freeze for up to 2 months.)*

Meanwhile, season turkey wings with remaining salt and pepper; arrange on rack on foil-lined rimmed baking sheet. Broil 6 to 8 inches (15 to 20 cm) from heat, turning once, until golden, about 16 minutes. *(Make-ahead: Let cool. Refrigerate in airtight container for up to 24 hours.)*

Return sauce to skillet. Add wings, turning to coat; cover and simmer, stirring occasionally, until tender, about 45 minutes. Serve sprinkled with sesame seeds.

Makes 6 servings. PER SERVING: about 424 cal, 33 g pro, 28 g total fat (7 g sat. fat), 10 g carb, trace fibre, 92 mg chol, 647 mg sodium. % RDI: 8% calcium, 24% iron, 5% vit A, 17% vit C, 10% folate.

Variation
MOLE CHICKEN WINGS: Replace turkey wings with chicken wings (split and tips removed). Omit water. Simmer wings in mole sauce for only 20 minutes.

Moroccan Lamb is often served on Eid-ul-Fitr, the celebration marking the end of the Ramadan fast. This lovely platter of lamb, rice and seasonings makes a regal presentation.

Roast Leg of Lamb With Apricots, Almonds and Pine Nuts

On cutting board and using fork, or using mortar and pestle, crush garlic with salt until fine paste; transfer to bowl. Add parsley, allspice, cardamom, cinnamon, cloves and pepper. Blend in butter.

Trim excess fat from lamb, leaving ¼-inch (5 mm) thick layer, if desired. Cut 15 slits all over lamb; rub spice mixture over surface, working into slits. Place on rack in roasting pan. Cover and refrigerate for 2 hours. *(Make-ahead: Refrigerate for up to 24 hours.)*

Meanwhile, in small bowl, cover apricots with boiling water; cover and let stand until plump, about 1 hour. Drain, reserving liquid in large measuring cup; add enough water to make 4 cups. Set aside.

Roast lamb in 350°F (180°C) oven for 1 hour. Add apricots to pan; roast until meat thermometer inserted in centre of lamb registers 140°F (60°C) for rare or 150°F (65°C) for medium-rare, about 15 minutes. Using slotted spoon, transfer apricots to cutting board. Transfer lamb to cutting board, reserving juices in pan; tent with foil. Let stand for 20 minutes before carving.

BASMATI RICE: Meanwhile, in saucepan, heat oil over medium heat; cook onion until softened, about 2 minutes. Pour one-third of the reserved apricot soaking liquid into roasting pan; bring to boil, stirring and scraping up brown bits from bottom of pan. Pour pan juices and remaining apricot soaking liquid over onion. Stir in rice and salt; bring to boil. Reduce heat to low; cover and simmer until tender and liquid is absorbed, about 20 minutes. Fluff with fork.

Scoop rice onto warmed platter; arrange apricots, almonds and pine nuts on rice. Top with lamb.

Makes 8 servings. PER SERVING: about 567 cal, 37 g pro, 24 g total fat (9 g sat. fat), 51 g carb, 4 g fibre, 124 mg chol, 663 mg sodium. % RDI: 6% calcium, 34% iron, 14% vit A, 5% vit C, 5% folate.

4 cloves **garlic**

1 tsp **salt**

2 tbsp minced **fresh parsley**

2 tsp **ground allspice**

2 tsp **ground cardamom**

2 tsp **cinnamon**

2 tsp **ground cloves**

1 tsp **pepper**

2 tbsp **butter**, softened

1 **leg of lamb** (4 lb/1.8 kg)

1 cup **dried apricots**

1 cup **boiling water**

¼ cup **slivered almonds**

¼ cup **pine nuts**, toasted

BASMATI RICE:
1 tbsp **extra-virgin olive oil**

1 **onion,** finely chopped

2 cups **basmati rice**

1 tsp **salt**

Cuban Mojo criollo is the marinade of citrus juice spiked with garlic and cumin that you see all over Cuba. Typically, it calls for sour orange juice from Seville oranges, but here lime and lemon juice are easier to find. Use a roast with the backbone removed or ask the butcher to remove it for you.

Pork Roast With Mojo Criollo

1 **pork rib roast rack** (about 8 ribs, or 4 lb/1.8 kg)

2 cloves **garlic,** slivered

½ cup **orange juice**

¼ cup each **lime juice** and **lemon juice**

2 tbsp **extra-virgin olive oil**

1 tsp **dried oregano**

1 tsp **ground cumin**

1 tsp **pepper**

¾ cup **sodium-reduced chicken broth** (approx)

Cut several slits around pork; insert garlic into slits. Place roast in large resealable plastic bag. In glass measure, whisk together orange juice, lime juice, lemon juice, oil, oregano, cumin and pepper; pour over pork and seal bag. Place in large bowl and refrigerate, turning occasionally, for 8 hours. *(Make-ahead: Refrigerate for up to 24 hours.)*

Place roast and marinade in roasting pan; cover and roast in 325°F (160°C) oven for 1 hour. Uncover and roast, basting several times, until meat thermometer registers 160°F (71°C), about 1 hour. Broil until golden, about 3 minutes. Transfer to cutting board and tent with foil; let stand for 10 minutes before slicing between ribs.

Meanwhile, skim fat from pan juices; add enough of the broth to make about 1¼ cups, adding more for less-tangy sauce, if desired. Keep warm until serving with roast.

Makes about 8 servings. PER SERVING: about 352 cal, 34 g pro, 22 g total fat (6 g sat. fat), 3 g carb, trace fibre, 89 mg chol, 151 mg sodium. % RDI: 4% calcium, 13% iron, 12% vit C, 4% folate.

Pork Roast With Mojo Criollo (opposite), Tostones (page 127) and Yuca With Red Onion (page 126)

Argentinian Tangy chimichurri sauces are a must with grilled meats in Argentina. Quail is especially delicious with Chimichurri Rojo (below), whereas the chicken variation is best with fresh-tasting Chimichurri Verde (page 167). Basting with an oil mixture keeps barbecued poultry moist.

Grilled Marinated Quail

¼ cup **lime juice**

¼ cup **extra-virgin olive oil**

2 tbsp minced **fresh parsley**

2 tbsp minced **fresh oregano**

3 cloves **garlic,** minced

3 **bay leaves,** torn

¼ tsp **salt**

¼ tsp coarsely ground **pepper**

¼ tsp **dried thyme**

6 **whole quails**

In large glass bowl, combine 3 tbsp each of the lime juice and oil; add parsley, oregano, garlic, bay leaves, salt, pepper and thyme.

Using kitchen shears, cut each quail down each side of backbone; remove backbone (save for stockpot). Turn quails breast side up; press to flatten. Add to marinade, turning to coat. Cover and refrigerate for 4 hours.

Stir remaining lime juice with remaining oil. Grill quail, covered and skin side down, on greased grill over medium-high heat, turning once and basting occasionally with lime juice mixture, until skin is crisp and juices run clear when thigh is pierced, 12 to 15 minutes.

Makes 4 to 6 servings. PER EACH OF 6 SERVINGS: about 267 cal, 20 g pro, 20 g total fat (4 g sat. fat), 2 g carb, 1 g fibre, 66 mg chol, 140 mg sodium, 198 mg potassium. % RDI: 3% calcium, 29% iron, 7% vit A, 7% vit C, 4% folate.

Variation
GRILLED MARINATED CHICKEN BREASTS: Replace quail with 4 boneless skinless chicken breasts. Sprinkle with additional salt and pepper before grilling, if desired.

Chimichurri Rojo
Whisk together ½ cup sherry vinegar or red wine vinegar; ¼ cup extra-virgin olive oil; 3 tbsp minced fresh parsley; 3 cloves garlic, minced; 4 tsp sweet paprika; 1 tsp ground cumin; ½ tsp each salt and pepper; and ¼ to ½ tsp cayenne pepper. **Makes ¾ cup.**

Indian Cashew trees grow abundantly across India, and the nuts are used many ways in cooking. Here, they thicken and flavour a delicately spiced, rich, creamy sauce that's typical of northern Indian cuisine.

Chicken Korma

Toast cashews on rimmed baking sheet in 350°F (180°C) oven until golden, about 8 minutes. Let cool.

Meanwhile, lightly crush cardamom pods; reserve seeds and discard pods. In large dry skillet, toast cardamom seeds, cloves, peppercorns and cumin seeds over medium heat, stirring, until slightly darkened, about 1 minute. Transfer to bowl; let cool.

In spice grinder or clean coffee grinder, or using mortar and pestle, grind cooled spices with 1 cup of the cashews; set aside.

Remove skin from chicken; trim off any excess fat. In skillet, heat oil over medium-high heat; brown chicken, in batches, for 5 to 10 minutes. Transfer to plate. Add onions, garlic and ginger to pan; cook over medium heat, stirring occasionally, until softened, about 5 minutes. Stir in reserved spice mixture, cinnamon, turmeric, cayenne pepper and salt; stir in broth.

Return chicken and any accumulated juices to pan; bring to boil. Reduce heat, cover and simmer until juices run clear when chicken is pierced, about 40 minutes.

Blend in cream, garam masala and lemon juice; cook until heated through. *(Make-ahead: Let cool for 30 minutes; refrigerate until cold. Cover and refrigerate for up to 24 hours. Reheat to serve.)* Garnish with remaining cashews.

Makes 6 servings. PER SERVING: about 446 cal, 28 g pro, 31 g total fat (10 g sat. fat), 15 g carb, 1 g fibre, 129 mg chol, 436 mg sodium. % RDI: 6% calcium, 26% iron, 11% vit A, 10% vit C, 15% folate.

1¼ cups **raw cashews**

6 **green cardamom pods**

6 **whole cloves**

¾ tsp **black peppercorns**

¾ tsp **cumin seeds**

12 **chicken thighs** (4 lb/1.8 kg)

1 tbsp **vegetable oil**

2 **onions,** chopped

4 cloves **garlic,** minced

1 tbsp minced **fresh ginger**

½ tsp **cinnamon**

½ tsp **turmeric**

½ tsp **cayenne pepper**

½ tsp **salt**

1 cup **chicken broth**

⅔ cup **whipping cream**

1 tsp **garam masala** (recipe, page 19)

1 tsp **lemon juice**

Indian The name of this dish literally means "spinach cheese." A classic northern Indian dish, it's so popular here that it's sold in the frozen food section. But homemade is always best – especially the creamy paneer cheese.

Saag Paneer

2 bunches **fresh spinach,** trimmed

2 tbsp **vegetable oil**

¾ tsp **cumin seeds**

1 **onion,** finely chopped

1 tbsp **butter**

3 cloves **garlic,** minced

2 tsp finely grated or minced **fresh ginger**

¼ cup finely chopped **fresh cilantro**

2 tsp **ground Indian hot pepper** (or ½ tsp cayenne pepper)

¾ tsp **salt**

½ tsp **ground coriander**

½ tsp **turmeric**

Pinch **cinnamon**

3 **plum tomatoes,** peeled and finely chopped

⅓ cup **Balkan-style plain yogurt**

2 tsp **lemon juice**

½ tsp **garam masala** (recipe, page 19)

8 oz (225 g) **Homemade Paneer** (recipe, right) or store-bought paneer, cubed

In large pot of boiling salted water, blanch spinach until just wilted; drain, chill under cold water and drain again. In food processor, purée spinach with ¼ cup water; set aside.

In large deep skillet, heat oil over medium-high heat; cook cumin seeds until slightly darkened, about 10 seconds. Add onion and butter; cook until onion is golden, about 8 minutes.

Reduce heat to medium. Stir in garlic and ginger; cook for 1 minute. Stir in cilantro, hot pepper, salt, coriander, turmeric and cinnamon; cook, stirring, until very fragrant, about 30 seconds. Add tomatoes; cook, stirring, until tomatoes break down, about 3 minutes.

Stir in puréed spinach; cover and cook, stirring occasionally and adding up to 2 tbsp water if mixture is no longer saucy, until steaming hot, about 3 minutes.

Stir in yogurt, lemon juice and garam masala; bring to simmer. Reduce heat to low; add paneer. Cover and cook until heated through, about 2 minutes.

Makes 4 to 6 servings. PER EACH OF 6 SERVINGS: about 162 cal, 7 g pro, 11 g total fat (4 g sat. fat), 11 g carb, 4 g fibre, 20 mg chol, 688 mg sodium, 715 mg potassium. % RDI: 25% calcium, 31% iron, 122% vit A, 30% vit C, 77% folate.

Homemade Paneer

In large saucepan, bring 12 cups homogenized milk to boil; remove from heat. Add 1 cup lemon juice; stir until milk curdles and separates into spongy white chunks (curds) and greenish milky water (whey). Stir in ¼ tsp salt. Set strainer over bowl; line with double-thickness cheesecloth. Strain milk mixture. Let stand until most of the liquid has drained off. Fold cheesecloth over top; weigh down with plate and full 28-oz (796 mL) can. Refrigerate for 8 hours or up to 24 hours. Remove cheesecloth. *(Make-ahead: Refrigerate in airtight container for up to 5 days.)* **Makes about 1 lb (450 g).**

Malaysian An equal weight of lamb and sweet caramelized onions makes a deeply satisfying dish. If you like curry milder, use only eight dried red hot peppers. Serve this with blanched or sautéed Chinese broccoli or spinach and, of course, rice.

Rich Lamb Curry

In large Dutch oven, heat half of the oil over medium heat; cook onions, stirring often, until golden, about 40 minutes. Transfer to bowl.

Meanwhile, break hot peppers in half; shake out and discard seeds. In dry skillet, toast hot peppers over medium heat, shaking pan constantly, until darkened and fragrant, about 3 minutes. In clean coffee grinder, grind to fine powder.

In food processor, purée together ground hot peppers, roasted red pepper, shallots, garlic, curry powder, ginger, galangal, shrimp paste, turmeric and ⅓ cup water until smooth.

In same Dutch oven, combine hot pepper mixture, remaining oil and bay leaves; cook, stirring constantly, until fragrant and slightly darkened, about 4 minutes. Add lamb; cook over medium-high heat, stirring, for 5 minutes. Stir in reserved onions, 1⅓ cups of the coconut milk, salt and ¾ cup water; bring to boil.

Reduce heat, cover and simmer, stirring occasionally, until lamb is almost tender, 50 to 60 minutes. Stir in potatoes; cover and simmer, stirring occasionally, until lamb and potatoes are tender, about 20 minutes.

Meanwhile, mix tamarind pulp with ¼ cup water; strain through sieve into bowl, pressing solids to extract liquid. Discard solids; stir liquid into pan along with remaining coconut milk. Cook until steaming, about 5 minutes. Discard bay leaves.

Makes 6 to 8 servings. PER EACH OF 8 SERVINGS: about 410 cal, 25 g pro, 22 g total fat (11 g sat. fat), 32 g carb, 4 g fibre, 76 mg chol, 494 mg sodium. % RDI: 7% calcium, 39% iron, 5% vit A, 47% vit C, 15% folate.

¼ cup **vegetable oil**

6 **onions,** sliced

15 **dried red hot peppers**

1 **roasted red pepper,** peeled, cored and seeded

4 **shallots** (or 1 red onion), coarsely chopped

6 cloves **garlic**

2 tbsp **Malay-Style Curry Powder** (recipe, page 19)

2 tbsp minced **fresh ginger**

2 tbsp minced **galangal** or fresh ginger

1 tbsp **shrimp paste**

2 tsp **turmeric**

3 **bay leaves**

2 lb (900 g) **boneless leg of lamb** or lamb shoulder, trimmed and cubed

1 can (400 mL) **coconut milk**

1½ tsp **salt**

4 **potatoes,** peeled and cubed

2 tbsp **tamarind pulp**

THE SOUTHEAST ASIAN PANTRY

The cuisines of Southeast Asia – including those of Thailand, Vietnam, Malaysia and Indonesia – are quite different, but they use many of the same tropical ingredients. Here are some of the staples you'll need to make the dishes in this book.

DRIED SPICES AND SAUCES

- Chili sauces (sriracha sauce and chili garlic sauces, such as sambal oelek*)
- Coriander seeds (whole and ground)
- Cumin seeds
- Fennel seeds
- Fish sauce
- Hoisin sauce
- Malay-style curry powder* (for homemade, see page 19)
- Soy sauce
- Sweet soy sauce* (called kecap manis in Indonesia; for recipe, see page 49)
- Turmeric

PANTRY STAPLES

- Canned coconut milk
- Cashews (roasted and raw)
- Dried red hot peppers
- Laksa noodles* (use wide rice stick noodles if unavailable)
- Palm sugar* (use light brown sugar if unavailable)
- Peanut oil
- Peanuts (roasted and raw)
- Rice noodles (various sizes, from thin vermicelli to wide rice stick noodles)
- Rice paper wrappers
- Rice vinegar
- Sesame oil
- Shrimp paste* (Malaysian comes in dry blocks and Thai comes in tubs; in a pinch, use jarred Chinese shrimp paste)
- Tamarind* (blocks of pulp, with or without seeds, and concentrate)

FRESH STAPLES

- Fresh cilantro
- Fresh ginger
- Fresh grated coconut (frozen* works well; use unsweetened desiccated coconut in a pinch)
- Fresh hot peppers (red finger hot peppers and Thai bird's-eye peppers)
- Fresh mint
- Fresh Thai basil
- Galangal* (substitute fresh ginger if not available)
- Green onions
- Lemongrass* (dried adds little flavour; if unavailable, substitute 1 strip lemon zest for each stalk)
- Limes
- Mangoes
- Shallots

* Might be easier to find at Asian grocery stores than at supermarkets

Malaysian If you like a nice bit of heat, then this is your dish. For a milder version, use just 10 dried red hot peppers and substitute one sweet red pepper for the fresh red finger hot peppers. Serve with plenty of white rice and a cucumber-and-onion salad to quench the fire.

Beef Rendang

Cut beef into 2-inch (5 cm) cubes. Cut lemongrass into paper-thin slices. Set aside separately.

Break dried hot peppers in half; shake out and discard seeds. In clean coffee grinder or spice grinder, grind to slightly coarse powder. Mix ground hot peppers with 3 tbsp water. Mix curry powder with 2 tbsp water. Set aside separately.

In small dry skillet, toast coconut over medium-low heat, stirring, until golden, about 12 minutes. In clean coffee grinder, grind to coarse powder; set aside.

In food processor, purée together shallots, fresh hot peppers, almonds, garlic, ginger, galangal, shrimp paste and 2 tbsp water to make smooth paste. In deep skillet, heat oil over medium heat; fry dried hot pepper paste, stirring, until oil turns red, about 3 minutes. Add curry powder paste and shallot paste; fry, stirring, until fragrant, 4 to 5 minutes.

Add ¼ cup of the coconut milk, the beef, lemongrass, ground toasted coconut, sugar, soy sauce and salt. Sauté over medium-high heat, scraping bottom to prevent scorching, until very fragrant and oil begins to separate, 12 to 15 minutes.

Add remaining coconut milk; reduce heat to low. Cover and simmer, stirring often, until meat is tender, about 1¾ hours.

Uncover; cook over medium-high heat, stirring constantly, until sauce is very thick, dry and clinging to meat, 2 to 3 minutes.

Makes 8 servings. PER SERVING: about 421 cal, 26 g pro, 31 g total fat (14 g sat. fat), 12 g carb, 2 g fibre, 57 mg chol, 517 mg sodium. % RDI: 7% calcium, 42% iron, 4% vit A, 13% vit C, 9% folate.

2 lb (900 g) trimmed **boneless beef short-rib pot roast** or boneless beef blade pot roast

3 stalks tender **lemongrass,** trimmed

30 **dried red hot peppers**

2 tbsp **Malay-Style Curry Powder** (recipe, page 19)

½ cup grated **fresh coconut** or unsweetened desiccated coconut

4 **shallots** (or 1 onion), coarsely chopped

4 **fresh red finger hot peppers,** seeded and coarsely chopped

¼ cup **blanched almonds,** toasted

3 cloves **garlic**

2 tbsp minced **fresh ginger**

2 tbsp minced **galangal** or fresh ginger

2 tsp **shrimp paste**

¼ cup **vegetable oil**

1¼ cups **coconut milk**

1 tbsp packed **palm sugar** or light brown sugar

1 tbsp **soy sauce**

1 tsp **salt**

Vietnamese Fresh fish and saucy noodle dishes, seasoned with aromatic spices and fresh herbs, are hallmarks of Vietnamese cuisine. Serve a simple salad alongside this beautiful dish, which is easily doubled for a larger group.

Hanoi-Style Vermicelli Noodles With Fish

2 **shallots,** finely chopped

2 cloves **garlic,** finely chopped

2 tbsp chopped **fresh dill**

1 tbsp **fish sauce**

1 tbsp **vinegar**

1 tbsp **vegetable oil**

1½ tsp minced **fresh ginger**

¾ tsp **turmeric**

½ tsp **pepper**

1 lb (450 g) **tilapia fillets**

8 oz (225 g) **rice vermicelli**

2 cups **bean sprouts**

1 cup packed **fresh cilantro leaves**

½ cup coarsely chopped **unsalted peanuts**

NOODLE SAUCE:

2 tbsp **granulated sugar**

¼ cup finely shredded **carrot**

2 tbsp **fish sauce**

2 tbsp **lime juice**

2 tsp **vinegar**

1 or 2 **Thai bird's-eye peppers,** minced

PICKLED SHALLOTS:

3 **shallots,** thinly sliced in rings

1 tbsp **vinegar**

¼ tsp **granulated sugar**

Using mortar and pestle, mash shallots with garlic to make paste (or very finely chop with knife). Stir in dill, fish sauce, vinegar, 1 tbsp water, oil, ginger, turmeric and pepper; spread all over fish. Cover and refrigerate for 1 hour.

NOODLE SAUCE: Meanwhile, whisk sugar with ⅔ cup hot water until dissolved; let cool. Stir in carrot, fish sauce, lime juice, vinegar and hot pepper; set aside.

PICKLED SHALLOTS: Meanwhile, combine shallots, vinegar and sugar; set aside.

Broil fish on greased broiler pan until browned and fish flakes easily when tested with fork, 8 to 10 minutes. Cut into 4 portions.

Meanwhile, in large pot of boiling water, cook vermicelli according to package instructions, about 2 minutes. Drain and rinse under cold running water. Drain well; shake. Set aside to air-dry.

Divide vermicelli among 4 large bowls. Top with bean sprouts, cilantro, fish and pickled shallots; sprinkle with peanuts. Serve with noodle sauce, adding as desired and tossing to coat.

Makes 4 servings. PER SERVING: about 513 cal, 32 g pro, 15 g total fat (2 g sat. fat), 66 g carb, 5 g fibre, 50 mg chol, 1,145 mg sodium, 695 mg potassium. % RDI: 6% calcium, 16% iron, 14% vit A, 22% vit C, 35% folate.

Japanese If you want a comforting, comfortable meal to share with a couple of friends, this is it. Called mizutaki in Japanese, the communal pot simmers on a portable burner as guests help themselves to chicken and vegetables. After those are gone, noodles go into the broth to finish the meal.

Chicken Hot Pot

BROTH: Cut up chicken; remove and discard skin. Bone chicken, reserving bones; cut into bite-size pieces. Cover and set meat aside in refrigerator. In Dutch oven, bring carcass, wings, bones, seaweed (if using), rice, sake, salt, sugar and 8 cups water to boil; discard seaweed. Cover and simmer, skimming off foam, until reduced to about 5 cups, about 1 hour. Strain through cheesecloth into serving pot. *(Make-ahead: Strain into airtight container; let cool. Refrigerate for up to 24 hours.)*

Pat tofu dry; cut tofu and cabbage into bite-size cubes. Remove stems from shiitake mushrooms; cut shallow X in each cap if desired. Peel carrots; slice carrots and leeks diagonally into ⅓-inch (8 mm) thick slices.

Arrange tofu, cabbage, shiitake mushrooms, carrots, leeks and enoki mushrooms on platter. Sprinkle with green onion.

DIPPING SAUCE: Divide ponzu among 4 small bowls; mix in daikon.

Heat chicken broth on stove top just until simmering; add chicken meat and return to simmer. Place pot on burner on table. Simmer for 10 minutes.

Add about one-quarter of the tofu and vegetables at a time to hot pot; simmer until desired doneness. Remove chicken, tofu and vegetables from broth; dip into sauce to eat.

Add noodles to remaining broth; cook until heated through. Ladle into bowls.

Makes 4 servings. PER SERVING: about 375 cal, 14 g pro, 4 g total fat (trace sat. fat), 70 g carb, 5 g fibre, 0 mg chol, 169 mg sodium, 476 mg potassium. % RDI: 12% calcium, 21% iron, 67% vit A, 15% vit C, 41% folate.

8 oz (225 g) **soft tofu**

Half small **napa cabbage**

8 **shiitake mushrooms**

2 **carrots**

2 small **leeks**

1 bunch **enoki mushrooms**

1 **green onion,** thinly sliced

1 pkg (14 oz/400 g) **parboiled udon noodles** or ramen noodles

BROTH:

1 **whole chicken** (3 lb/1.35 kg)

1 piece **dried kelp** (konbu), optional

4 tsp **Japanese short-grain rice**

1 tbsp **sake**

1 tsp **salt**

1 tsp **granulated sugar**

DIPPING SAUCE:

½ cup **ponzu sauce**

3 tbsp finely grated **daikon radish**

TIP | DON'T HAVE A TABLETOP BURNER? COOK THE MEAL ON THE STOVE. KEEP THE POT WARM ON A HOT PLATE OR DISH UP INDIVIDUAL BOWLS.

Linzertorte (page 258)

{desserts}

Italian Scented with lemon, orange and cinnamon, this rich cheese-based tart is best cut into thin slices. Serve with espresso to balance the sweetness.

Sweet Ricotta Crostata

3 cups **ricotta cheese** (1½ lb/ 675 g)

⅓ cup **granulated sugar**

1 tbsp grated **orange zest**

1 tbsp grated **lemon zest**

¼ cup **lemon juice**

2 **eggs**

½ tsp **cinnamon**

1 **egg yolk**

PASTRY:

3 cups **all-purpose flour**

¼ cup **granulated sugar**

1 tsp **baking powder**

½ tsp **salt**

½ cup cold **unsalted butter,** cubed

3 **eggs,** lightly beaten

PASTRY: In large bowl, whisk together flour, sugar, baking powder and salt. Using pastry blender or 2 knives, cut in butter until in fine crumbs with a few larger pieces. Add eggs; toss with fork until dough starts to clump together, adding 1 tbsp cold water if too dry. Press into disc; wrap and refrigerate until chilled, about 30 minutes.

Whisk together ricotta, sugar, orange zest, lemon zest, lemon juice, eggs and cinnamon.

Cut off one-third of the dough; set aside. On lightly floured surface, roll out remaining dough into 13-inch (33 cm) circle. Fit into 10-inch (25 cm) round tart pan with removable bottom. Scrape in ricotta mixture, smoothing top. Trim dough to leave ½-inch (1 cm) overhang.

On lightly floured surface, roll out reserved dough into 12-inch (30 cm) square. Cut into twelve 1-inch (2.5 cm) strips. Weave strips, about ½ inch (1 cm) apart, over filling to form lattice top. Trim strips even with edge of overhang.

Whisk egg yolk with 1 tsp water; brush some under each strip where it meets bottom pastry edge. Press to seal. Turn overhang inside and flute edge.

Brush remaining egg yolk mixture all over top of tart. Bake in 350°F (180°C) oven until pastry is golden, about 55 minutes. Let cool on rack. *(Make-ahead: Cover and refrigerate for up to 24 hours.)*

Makes 24 servings. PER SERVING: about 178 cal, 6 g pro, 9 g total fat (5 g sat. fat), 18 g carb, 1 g fibre, 72 mg chol, 95 mg sodium, 67 mg potassium. % RDI: 7% calcium, 7% iron, 9% vit A, 3% vit C, 18% folate.

Italian Panna cotta, which means "cooked cream," is silky and decadently rich. And there's nothing better than a gorgeous make-ahead dessert that waits patiently in the refrigerator to show off its spectacular flavours.

Two-Tone Chocolate Espresso Panna Cotta

CHOCOLATE LAYER: In small saucepan, sprinkle gelatin over milk; let stand for 5 minutes. Warm over low heat until dissolved; remove from heat.

Place chocolate in heatproof bowl. In separate saucepan, bring cream, sugar and coffee granules just to boil, stirring to dissolve sugar; pour over chocolate and stir until melted. Stir in gelatin mixture. Pour into eight 1-cup wine or martini glasses, or bowls. Refrigerate until firm, about 2 hours.

VANILLA LAYER: In small saucepan, sprinkle gelatin over milk; let stand for 5 minutes. Warm over low heat until dissolved; remove from heat.

In separate saucepan, heat cream with sugar until dissolved and bubbles form around edge. Stir in gelatin mixture; stir in vanilla. Pour over chocolate layer. Refrigerate until firm, about 2 hours. *(Make-ahead: Cover and refrigerate for up to 2 days.)*

With skewer or tweezers, arrange a few Curly Marble Shards upright in centre of each serving.

Makes 8 servings. PER SERVING: about 609 cal, 10 g pro, 45 g total fat (27 g sat. fat), 49 g carb, 2 g fibre, 127 mg chol, 105 mg sodium. % RDI: 21% calcium, 6% iron, 35% vit A, 2% vit C, 5% folate.

Curly Marble Shards

In bowl over saucepan of hot (not boiling) water, melt 2 oz (55 g) bittersweet or semisweet chocolate, chopped. In separate bowl over same saucepan, melt 1 oz (30 g) white chocolate, chopped. Spread bittersweet chocolate as thinly as possible on the back of a baking sheet. Drizzle with white chocolate; swirl with tip of knife. Refrigerate until firm, about 15 minutes. Let stand at room temperature to soften slightly, about 1 minute. Using edge of metal lifter, firmly scrape chocolate away from you into curly shards. Arrange on waxed paper–lined baking sheet; refrigerate until firm, 20 minutes. *(Make-ahead: Cover with plastic wrap; refrigerate for up to 2 days.)*

Curly Marble Shards (recipe, below left)

CHOCOLATE LAYER:
2 pkg (7 g each) **unflavoured gelatin**

2 cups **milk**

6 oz (170 g) **milk chocolate,** chopped

2 cups **whipping cream**

⅔ cup **granulated sugar**

2 tsp **instant coffee granules**

VANILLA LAYER:
1 pkg (7 g) **unflavoured gelatin**

1 cup **milk**

1 cup **whipping cream**

⅓ cup **granulated sugar**

1 tsp **vanilla**

Italian Gelato is smooth, never overly sweet and unbelievably creamy. This recipe calls for slightly overripe bananas – flecked with black, but not completely black – because they have the richest flavour. Garnish the treat with chopped hazelnuts.

Gelato di Banana al Rum

4 slightly overripe **bananas**
   (about 1¾ lb/790 g)
1 cup **milk**
1 cup **whipping cream**
4 **egg yolks**
¼ cup **granulated sugar**
2 tbsp **rum**

Peel bananas; cut in thirds. In heavy-bottomed saucepan, bring bananas, milk and whipping cream to boil over medium-high heat; reduce heat and simmer until bananas are very soft, about 5 minutes. Let cool for 10 minutes. In food processor, whirl banana mixture until smooth.

In large bowl, whisk egg yolks with sugar until pale yellow and frothy; slowly whisk in banana mixture. Return to pan; cook over medium-low heat, stirring constantly, until banana mixture is thick enough to coat back of spoon, about 5 minutes. Strain into bowl, pressing solids through sieve with spatula. Place plastic wrap directly on surface; refrigerate until cold, about 1½ hours. Stir in rum.

Freeze banana mixture in ice-cream maker according to manufacturer's instructions. *(Make-ahead: Freeze for up to 1 week. Let soften in refrigerator until scoopable.)*

Makes 6 to 8 servings. PER EACH OF 8 SERVINGS: about 231 cal, 4 g pro, 14 g total fat (8 g sat. fat), 23 g carb, 0 g fibre, 142 mg chol, 30 mg sodium. % RDI: 7% calcium, 4% iron, 16% vit A, 7% vit C, 10% folate.

TIPS

• IF YOU LOVE RUM, ADD AN ADDITIONAL 2 TBSP; IF YOU DON'T, REPLACE THE RUM WITH 1 TBSP VANILLA.

• IF YOU DON'T HAVE AN ICE-CREAM MAKER, POUR MIXTURE INTO 9-INCH (2.5 L) SQUARE CAKE PAN; FREEZE UNTIL ALMOST SOLID, ABOUT ONE AND A HALF HOURS. BREAK INTO CHUNKS; IN FOOD PROCESSOR, PURÉE UNTIL SMOOTH. SCRAPE INTO AIRTIGHT CONTAINER; FREEZE UNTIL FIRM, AT LEAST FOUR HOURS.

Greek One of Greece's most iconic desserts, this sweet nut-and-honey pastry is known all over the world. This baklava is coiled in a pan and cut into slices rather than the typical diamond-shaped pieces.

Honey Nut Baklava Roll

FILLING: Stir together walnuts, apricots, almonds, pistachios, bread crumbs, sugar, cinnamon and cloves; set aside.

SYRUP: In saucepan, bring 1 cup water, sugar, honey, lemon zest and cinnamon to boil, stirring. Reduce heat and boil gently until syrupy, about 12 minutes. Stir in lemon juice; simmer for 1 minute. Let cool.

In small saucepan, melt butter over low heat. Skim off foam; pour clear melted butter into bowl, leaving milky liquid in pan.

Place 1 sheet of the phyllo on work surface, covering remainder with damp towel to prevent drying out. Brush sheet with butter. Top with second sheet; brush with butter. Spread generous ½ cup of the filling along 1 long edge; roll up and fit around edge of greased 9-inch (2.5 L) springform pan. Repeat with remaining pastry, butter and filling until pan is full, coiling rolls around edge of pan, then in spiral toward centre, and pressing firmly to form compact rounds. Brush with butter. Place on 12-inch (30 cm) pizza pan.

Bake in 350°F (180°C) oven until phyllo is golden and crisp, about 40 minutes. Remove from oven; pour syrup over coil. Let cool on pan on rack, pouring any syrup that leaks onto pan over coil. *(Make-ahead: Cover and store at room temperature for up to 24 hours.)*

Makes 16 servings. PER SERVING: about 311 cal, 4 g pro, 19 g total fat (7 g sat. fat), 33 g carb, 2 g fibre, 27 mg chol, 168 mg sodium. % RDI: 3% calcium, 10% iron, 12% vit A, 2% vit C, 12% folate.

¾ cup **butter**
10 sheets **phyllo pastry**

FILLING:
1½ cups chopped **walnut halves**
⅔ cup slivered **dried apricots**
⅓ cup chopped **almonds**
⅓ cup chopped **pistachios**
¼ cup **fresh bread crumbs,** toasted
2 tbsp **granulated sugar**
1 tsp **cinnamon**
Pinch **ground cloves**

SYRUP:
⅔ cup **granulated sugar**
½ cup **liquid honey**
1 strip **lemon zest**
1 **cinnamon stick**
1 tbsp **lemon juice**

Indian Cultures across the globe enjoy their particular takes on this universal dessert. This version of rice pudding is inspired by creamy cardamom-infused, pistachio-topped Indian kheer. For an exotic edge, add just a few drops of rose water or orange blossom water.

Cardamom Rice Pudding

2 tbsp **butter**

½ cup **short-grain rice**

¼ tsp **ground cardamom**

¼ tsp **cinnamon**

2½ cups **homogenized milk**

2 tbsp **granulated sugar**

¼ cup toasted **pistachios**

2 tsp **liquid honey**

In saucepan, melt butter over medium heat; stir in rice, cardamom and cinnamon until coated.

Stir in milk and sugar; bring to boil. Reduce heat, cover and simmer, stirring often, until most of the liquid is absorbed and rice is tender, 25 to 30 minutes. *(Make-ahead: Let cool for 30 minutes; refrigerate in airtight container for up to 24 hours.)*

Serve warm sprinkled with pistachios and drizzled with honey.

Makes 4 servings. PER SERVING: about 314 cal, 8 g pro, 14 g total fat (7 g sat. fat), 39 g carb, 1 g fibre, 36 mg chol, 116 mg sodium. % RDI: 18% calcium, 4% iron, 9% vit A, 2% vit C, 5% folate.

INDIAN DESSERTS & CHAI

Indian meals are most often followed by a sweetened cup of chai or fresh fruit. What we think of as desserts are often served as afternoon snacks. Here are some homemade Indian-inspired sweets you can make with easy-to-find ingredients.

• Sprinkle toasted pistachios and a pinch of cardamom over vanilla ice cream.

• Purée cubed mango; spice with cinnamon, cloves and/or cardamom. Fold purée into whipped cream to make a mango fool.

• Turn your favourite fruit into a refreshing sorbet to cool off after a highly spiced meal.

• Dried fruits, including dates, mangoes, pineapples and papayas, are the ultimate convenient desserts. Serve them with cookies and tea.

CHAI

Chai simply means "tea" in Hindi. People often use the term generically to refer to masala chai, the spiced tea that is served in various forms across the Indian Subcontinent.

The most common flavourings for masala chai are cardamom, cloves, cinnamon, black pepper and ginger, in varying proportions. The spices are lightly crushed, then infused in a boiling mixture of water and milk before tea leaves are added. The mixture then steeps for a few minutes to blend the flavours.

You can buy premade chai mixtures, but it's just as easy to make your own version at home. Serve chai in small tea cups either with snacks or after dinner as a digestive.

HOMEMADE MASALA CHAI

• Lightly crush one 1½-inch (4 cm) cinnamon stick, 4 cardamom pods, 5 black peppercorns and 3 cloves. In saucepan, combine spices, 3½ cups water and 1½ cups milk; bring to boil.

• Add 3 tbsp Darjeeling or black tea leaves (or 5 tea bags). Turn off heat; cover and let steep for 5 minutes. Strain and add sugar to taste. **Makes about 6 servings.**

Indian Fresh ginger, dried spices and tea make this exotic ice cream a refreshing finale to a spicy meal. Light black teas, such as Darjeeling, infuse the smoothest flavour.

Chai Ice Cream

In saucepan, heat together milk, cream, ginger, cinnamon, cloves, cardamom, aniseed and bay leaf over medium heat until tiny bubbles form around edge. Remove from heat. Add tea leaves; cover and let steep for 10 minutes. Strain through fine sieve into glass measure.

In bowl, whisk together egg yolks, sugar and salt; slowly whisk in tea mixture. Return to pan; cook over medium-low heat, stirring constantly, until mixture is slightly thickened and just coats back of spoon, about 8 minutes. Strain into 9-inch (2.5 L) square cake pan. Place plastic wrap directly on surface; refrigerate until cold, about 1½ hours.

Transfer to freezer; freeze until almost solid, about 1½ hours. Break into chunks; in food processor, purée until smooth. Scrape into airtight container; freeze until firm, about 4 hours. *(Make-ahead: Freeze for up to 1 week.)*

Makes 8 servings. PER SERVING: about 171 cal, 5 g pro, 9 g total fat (5 g sat. fat), 17 g carb, 0 g fibre, 170 mg chol, 50 mg sodium. % RDI: 11% calcium, 4% iron, 13% vit A, 12% folate.

1½ cups **milk**

1½ cups **10% cream**

1 slice **fresh ginger**

Half **cinnamon stick,** broken

4 **cloves**

4 **green cardamom pods**

¼ tsp **aniseed** or fennel seeds

1 **bay leaf**

¼ cup **black tea leaves**

6 **egg yolks**

½ cup **granulated sugar**

Pinch **salt**

TIP | IF YOU PREFER, YOU CAN FREEZE THE MIXTURE IN AN ICE-CREAM MAKER. FOLLOW THE MANUFACTURER'S INSTRUCTIONS FOR BEST RESULTS.

~ stir ~

~ beat ~

~ brush ~

French Surprisingly easy to make, this classic dessert will definitely impress. You can make just the puffs ahead, or make and fill them with ice cream, ready to pull from the freezer at a moment's notice.

Profiteroles

In heavy saucepan, bring water, butter and salt just to boil; remove from heat. Add flour all at once; *stir* vigorously with wooden spoon until mixture comes away from side of pan in smooth ball. Reduce heat to medium-low; cook, stirring constantly, until coating begins to form on bottom of pan, 1 to 2 minutes. Transfer to large bowl; stir for 30 seconds.

Make well in centre of flour mixture. Using electric mixer, beat in eggs, one-quarter at a time and beating well after each addition. *Beat* until smooth, shiny and pastry holds its shape in bowl. Spoon pastry into pastry bag fitted with ½-inch (1 cm) plain tip, or use spoon. Pipe into twenty-four 2-inch (5 cm) wide by 1-inch (2.5 cm) high mounds onto 2 parchment paper–lined baking sheets.

GLAZE: Beat egg with water; lightly *brush* over mounds, flattening tips and making sure glaze doesn't drip onto paper.

Bake in top and bottom thirds of 425°F (220°C) oven for 20 minutes. Reduce heat to 375°F (190°C); switch and rotate pans. Bake until golden and crisp, 15 minutes. Turn off oven; let stand in oven for 10 minutes to dry. Transfer to rack; let cool. *(Make-ahead: Store in airtight container for up to 24 hours. Recrisp in 350°F/180°C oven for 5 minutes.)*

CHOCOLATE SAUCE: In saucepan, bring cream to boil; pour over chocolate in heatproof bowl. Whisk until melted.

RASPBERRY COULIS: Press raspberries through fine sieve into bowl; whisk in sugar. *(Make-ahead: Refrigerate sauce and coulis in airtight containers for up to 3 days. Rewarm chocolate sauce to liquefy.)*

Cut puffs in half horizontally. Spoon ¼ cup of the ice cream into bottom half of each; replace top. *(Make-ahead: Wrap individually in foil and freeze for up to 3 days.)* Drizzle raspberry coulis onto plates. Arrange 2 profiteroles on each plate; spoon chocolate sauce over top.

Makes 12 servings. PER SERVING: about 419 cal, 8 g pro, 26 g total fat (15 g sat. fat), 39 g carb, 1 g fibre, 146 mg chol, 138 mg sodium. % RDI: 11% calcium, 11% iron, 22% vit A, 13% vit C, 23% folate.

1 cup **water**
½ cup **butter**
Pinch **salt**
1¼ cups **all-purpose flour**
4 **eggs,** beaten
6 cups **vanilla ice cream**

GLAZE:
1 **egg**
1 tbsp **water**

CHOCOLATE SAUCE:
¾ cup **whipping cream**
6 oz (170 g) **semisweet chocolate,** chopped

RASPBERRY COULIS:
3 cups thawed **frozen raspberries**
3 tbsp **icing sugar**

French Gorgeous and rustic, this upside-down apple pie is a hit when entertaining. Be cautious of the hot filling as you invert the tarte.

Classic Tarte Tatin

1 cup **all-purpose flour**

1 tbsp **granulated sugar**

Pinch **salt**

½ cup cold **butter,** cubed

1 **egg yolk**

2 tbsp **ice water**

FILLING:

3¼ lb (1.5 kg) **Crispin apples** (8 to 10 apples)

⅓ cup **butter,** softened

1 cup **granulated sugar**

In large bowl, stir together flour, sugar and salt. With pastry blender or 2 knives, cut in butter until in coarse crumbs. Whisk egg yolk with ice water; drizzle over flour mixture and toss with fork until dough clumps together. With floured hands, form into ball; press into 1-inch (2.5 cm) thick disc. Wrap and refrigerate for 30 minutes.

FILLING: Meanwhile, peel, quarter and core apples. Spread butter over 8- to 9-inch (20 to 23 cm) wide cast-iron skillet that is at least 2½ inches (6 cm) deep. Sprinkle evenly with sugar. Set apple wedges upright in sugar, arranging tightly to fill skillet.

Cook over medium heat, uncovered and basting occasionally, until syrup is thickened and apples are light caramel brown, 30 to 40 minutes. If tips of apples are not tender, bake in skillet in 375°F (190°C) oven until tender, about 10 minutes. Let cool in refrigerator until no longer steaming, about 10 minutes.

On lightly floured surface, roll out pastry into circle slightly larger than top of skillet. Trim edge if necessary. Roll loosely around rolling pin; unroll over apples, tucking between pan and apples. Cut 4 steam vents in centre. Bake in 425°F (220°C) oven for 10 minutes. Reduce heat to 375°F (190°C); bake until crust is golden, 15 to 20 minutes. Let cool for 3 to 4 minutes.

Invert heatproof platter over tarte. Wearing oven mitts, turn skillet upside down onto platter. With spatula, remove any apples stuck to skillet and arrange on tarte. Spoon syrup over top. Let cool slightly before cutting into wedges to serve.

Makes 6 to 8 servings. PER EACH OF 8 SERVINGS: about 406 cal, 3 g pro, 20 g total fat (12 g sat. fat), 57 g carb, 2 g fibre, 76 mg chol, 137 mg sodium, 155 mg potassium. % RDI: 2% calcium, 6% iron, 18% vit A, 7% vit C, 16% folate.

French This time-tested pear dessert was created in honour of the operetta *La Belle Hélène*. Here, spices replace the traditional vanilla. Don't throw out any leftover poaching syrup; use it to sweeten and spice up hot chocolate and coffee.

Spiced Poire Hélène

In saucepan, bring 4 cups water, sugar, hot peppers, cinnamon, star anise, peppercorns and ginger to boil; reduce heat and simmer for 5 minutes.

Peel, halve and core pears; add to saucepan. Press piece of parchment paper onto pears; simmer until tender but firm, 10 to 15 minutes. Remove from heat and let cool in syrup; cover and refrigerate overnight. Remove ⅓ cup poaching syrup and reserve for sauce.

SPICED CHOCOLATE SAUCE: Place chocolate in heatproof bowl. Bring reserved poaching syrup and cream to boil; pour over chocolate, whisking until melted. *(Make-ahead: Refrigerate chocolate sauce and pears with syrup in separate airtight containers for up to 24 hours.)*

Scoop ½ cup of the ice cream into each of 6 dessert dishes. Top each with a pear half; drizzle with chocolate sauce.

Makes 6 servings. PER SERVING: about 409 cal, 4 g pro, 17 g total fat (10 g sat. fat), 63 g carb, 4 g fibre, 42 mg chol, 58 mg sodium, 225 mg potassium. % RDI: 10% calcium, 6% iron, 11% vit A, 5% vit C, 4% folate.

2½ cups **granulated sugar**

4 **dried hot peppers**

2 **cinnamon sticks,** broken

2 **whole star anise**

½ tsp **black peppercorns**

1 piece (1 inch/2.5 cm) **fresh ginger,** sliced

3 ripe **Bosc pears**

3 cups **vanilla ice cream**

SPICED CHOCOLATE SAUCE:

1 bar (3½ oz/100 g) **quality bittersweet chocolate,** finely chopped

¼ cup **whipping cream**

Austrian This homey cake is simple and fairly low in calories (as cakes go). Spelt, an ancient low-gluten variety of wheat, grows in alpine regions, so it's popular in baked goods in Switzerland, Austria and northern Italy. Look for it at bulk or health food stores.

Apple Spelt Cake

1⅔ cups **cake-and-pastry flour**

1 cup **whole spelt flour** or whole wheat flour

½ tsp **baking powder**

½ tsp **baking soda**

¼ tsp **salt**

3 **eggs**

⅔ cup **granulated sugar**

⅓ cup **butter,** melted

¼ cup **vegetable oil**

1 tsp **vanilla**

Icing sugar

APPLE FILLING:

8 large **tart apples**

2 tbsp **butter**

¼ cup **granulated sugar**

¼ cup packed **brown sugar**

1½ tsp **cinnamon**

Grated zest of 1 **lemon**

APPLE FILLING: Peel, quarter, core and slice apples. In skillet, melt half of the butter over medium heat; cook half of the apples, stirring often, until tender-crisp, about 7 minutes. Repeat with remaining butter and apples. Scrape into bowl; mix in granulated sugar, brown sugar, cinnamon and lemon zest. Let cool.

Whisk together cake-and-pastry flour, spelt flour, baking powder, baking soda and salt. In large bowl, beat eggs with granulated sugar until pale and thickened, 2 to 3 minutes. Mix in butter, oil and vanilla; stir in flour mixture until smooth.

Line bottom of 9-inch (2.5 L) springform pan with parchment or waxed paper; grease sides. Spread two-thirds of the cake batter in pan. Layer apple filling evenly over batter. Top with spoonfuls of remaining batter; do not smooth top.

Bake in 325°F (160°C) oven until golden and cake tester inserted in centre comes out clean, about 50 minutes. Let cool in pan on rack. Remove from pan; peel off paper. Dust top with icing sugar.

Makes 8 to 12 servings. PER EACH OF 12 SERVINGS: about 361 cal, 4 g pro, 14 g total fat (5 g sat. fat), 59 g carb, 5 g fibre, 69 mg chol, 197 mg sodium. % RDI: 3% calcium, 14% iron, 9% vit A, 8% vit C, 12% folate.

TIP | IF YOUR APPLES ARE SWEET, YOU CAN REDUCE THE SUGAR IN THE APPLE FILLING.

Alsatian This bread-cake hybrid unites the culinary traditions of France and Germany. The rich flavours of a traditional French baba au rhum are baked in a kugelhopf pan or Bundt pan, then soaked in rum syrup to make one spectacular dessert.

Kugelhopf Baba au Rhum

In bowl, toss together apples, rum and currants; let stand for 30 minutes, stirring occasionally. Reserving rum, drain; set aside.

In small bowl, sprinkle yeast over warm water; let stand until frothy, about 10 minutes.

In stand mixer and using paddle attachment, mix flour with salt. Add yeast mixture, honey and eggs; mix on low speed until combined, about 2 minutes. Scrape down side of bowl. On low speed, drop in pieces of butter, beating until smooth, about 2 minutes. Fold in apple mixture.

Scrape into well-greased 10-inch (3 L) kugelhopf or Bundt pan, smoothing top. Cover with plastic wrap; let rise in warm place until doubled in bulk, about 2 hours.

Bake in bottom third of 375°F (190°C) oven, covering with foil if browning too quickly, until cake tester inserted in centre comes out clean, about 45 minutes. Let cool in pan for 5 minutes. With skewer, poke holes all over cake.

In saucepan, bring 1¼ cups water and sugar to boil, stirring to dissolve. Remove from heat; stir in reserved rum and vanilla. Brush ¼ cup over cake; invert onto rimmed plate. Pour remaining syrup over top; let stand until cool, about 45 minutes. Brush with jam. *(Make-ahead: Store in airtight container for up to 24 hours.)*

Makes 8 to 10 servings. PER EACH OF 10 SERVINGS: about 459 cal, 8 g pro, 17 g total fat (10 g sat. fat), 66 g carb, 2 g fibre, 130 mg chol, 156 mg sodium. % RDI: 3% calcium, 17% iron, 16% vit A, 3% vit C, 49% folate.

2 cups diced peeled cored **apples**

⅔ cup **dark rum**

½ cup **dried currants**

2 tsp **active dry yeast**

⅓ cup **warm water**

2¾ cups **all-purpose flour**

½ tsp **salt**

¼ cup **liquid honey**

5 **eggs**

¾ cup **unsalted butter,** softened

⅔ cup **granulated sugar**

1 tsp **vanilla**

½ cup **apricot jam,** melted and strained

Austrian The first linzertorte recipe was published in 1653, making this the oldest documented cake in Europe. Popular fillings include red or black currant preserves, plum preserves or seedless raspberry jam. The pastry is a bit delicate, but don't fret if it cracks – just pinch together to seal.

Linzertorte

1 cup **hazelnuts**

½ cup **whole natural almonds**

1½ cups **all-purpose flour**

¾ cup **granulated sugar**

¼ cup packed **brown sugar**

1 tsp grated **lemon zest**

½ tsp **cinnamon**

¼ tsp **salt**

¼ tsp **nutmeg**

¼ tsp **ground ginger**

Pinch **ground cloves**

¾ cup cold **unsalted butter,** cubed

1 **egg**

1 **egg,** separated

4 tsp **lemon juice**

1¼ cups **red currant preserves,** black currant or plum preserves, or seedless raspberry jam (or strained seeded raspberry jam)

2 tsp **whipping cream**

⅓ cup **sliced almonds**

Icing sugar

Toast hazelnuts and whole almonds on separate baking sheets in 325°F (160°C) oven until lightly browned, 10 minutes for almonds; 15 minutes for hazelnuts. Rub hazelnuts in tea towel to remove skins; let nuts cool. In food processor, grind flour, hazelnuts and whole almonds until fine. Whirl in granulated sugar, brown sugar, lemon zest, cinnamon, salt, nutmeg, ginger and cloves. Pulse in butter until crumbly. Pulse in egg, egg yolk and half of the lemon juice until dough almost holds together. Form into 2 discs; cover and refrigerate for 30 minutes or up to 2 days.

Butter 9-inch (23 cm) tart pan with removable bottom. Press 1 disc of the dough into pan, pressing 1 inch (2.5 cm) up side and ensuring even thickness. Refrigerate until firm, 30 minutes. (Or chill in freezer for 10 to 15 minutes.) With fork, prick pastry all over. Whisk egg white until foamy; brush some over pastry. Bake in 350°F (180°C) oven until lightly set, about 15 minutes. Let cool in pan on rack.

Meanwhile, let remaining disc stand at room temperature for 10 minutes. On lightly floured waxed or parchment paper, roll out to ¼-inch (5 mm) thickness. With fluted pastry wheel, cut into ½-inch (1 cm) wide strips.

Mix preserves with remaining lemon juice; spread over base. Weave pastry strips over top to make lattice, refrigerating dough if too soft. Trim ends even with pan edge. Whisk remaining egg white with cream until foamy; brush some over pastry. Sprinkle sliced almonds around edge; brush lightly with egg white mixture, discarding remainder. Bake in 350°F (180°C) oven until filling is bubbly and pastry is golden, 45 to 50 minutes. Let cool in pan on rack; dust with icing sugar.

Makes 10 to 12 servings. PER EACH OF 12 SERVINGS: about 568 cal, 8 g pro, 24 g total fat (9 g sat. fat), 84 g carb, 4 g fibre, 63 mg chol, 72 mg sodium, 240 mg potassium. % RDI: 6% calcium, 19% iron, 11% vit A, 7% vit C, 38% folate.

TIP | FOR A QUICKER OPTION, LAY STRIPS IN CRISSCROSS PATTERN INSTEAD OF WEAVING THEM.

German This moist, tender coffee cake scented with lemon and nutmeg is a farmhouse classic that's sturdy enough to carry to picnics or potlucks. It is irresistible with coffee or a glass of milk, especially when still warm from the oven.

Custard-Topped Berry Kuchen

In bowl, beat butter with granulated sugar until light; beat in eggs, 1 at a time. Beat in lemon zest and vanilla. Whisk together flour, baking powder, baking soda, salt and nutmeg; stir into butter mixture alternately with sour cream, making 3 additions of flour mixture and 2 of sour cream.

Sprinkle ⅔ cup of the raspberries and ⅓ cup of the blackberries in parchment paper–lined 9-inch (2.5 L) springform pan; spread batter over top. Scatter remaining berries over batter. Bake in 350°F (180°C) oven until toothpick inserted in centre comes out clean, about 1 hour.

TOPPING: In small bowl, stir together egg yolks, sour cream and sugar; pour evenly over warm cake. Bake until set, about 10 minutes. Let cool in pan on rack for 10 minutes. Remove side of pan; let cool for 10 minutes longer. *(Make-ahead: Let cool completely; wrap and refrigerate for up to 24 hours.)*

Sprinkle with icing sugar.

Makes 8 servings. PER SERVING: about 379 cal, 6 g pro, 19 g total fat (11 g sat. fat), 48 g carb, 3 g fibre, 139 mg chol, 319 mg sodium. % RDI: 8% calcium, 12% iron, 18% vit A, 15% vit C, 32% folate.

½ cup **butter,** softened
¾ cup **granulated sugar**
2 **eggs**
½ tsp grated **lemon zest**
½ tsp **vanilla**
1½ cups **all-purpose flour**
1½ tsp **baking powder**
½ tsp **baking soda**
¼ tsp **salt**
¼ tsp **grated nutmeg**
½ cup **sour cream**
2 cups **fresh raspberries**
1 cup **fresh blackberries**
1 tbsp **icing sugar**

TOPPING:
2 **egg yolks**
½ cup **sour cream**
2 tbsp **granulated sugar**

German This variation on the splendid German Schwarzwälder Kirschtorte goes one step further with a luscious chocolate mousse filling. You can find jars of sour cherries preserved in light syrup at delis and supermarkets.

Black Forest Mousse Cake

1 jar (28 oz/796 mL) **red sour cherries**

⅔ cup **granulated sugar**

1 tbsp **brandy** or kirsch

2½ cups **whipping cream**

1 tsp **vanilla**

CHOCOLATE MOUSSE:
6 oz (170 g) **semisweet chocolate,** chopped

2 cups **whipping cream**

2 tbsp **brandy** or kirsch

CAKE:
1 cup **butter,** softened

1½ cups **granulated sugar**

2 **eggs**

1 tsp **vanilla**

2 cups **all-purpose flour**

½ cup **cocoa powder**

1 tsp **baking powder**

1 tsp **baking soda**

¼ tsp **salt**

1½ cups **buttermilk**

CHOCOLATE CURLS:
4 oz (115 g) **semisweet chocolate,** chopped

CAKE: Grease sides of two 8-inch (1.2 L) round cake pans; line bottoms with waxed paper. In large bowl, beat butter with sugar until light; beat in eggs, 1 at a time, then vanilla. Sift together flour, cocoa, baking powder, baking soda and salt. Stir into butter mixture alternately with buttermilk, making 3 additions of flour mixture and 2 of buttermilk. Spoon into prepared pans, smoothing tops. Bake in 350°F (180°C) oven until cake tester inserted in centre comes out clean, 35 minutes. Let cool in pans on rack for 20 minutes. Remove from pans; let cool completely.

Meanwhile, in sieve over bowl, drain cherries, pressing lightly; reserve ⅓ cup of the juice. In saucepan, bring ⅓ cup of the sugar and juice to boil; boil until reduced to ½ cup, 5 minutes. Let cool; stir in brandy.

CHOCOLATE MOUSSE: Place chocolate in large heatproof bowl. In saucepan, bring cream and brandy just to boil; pour over chocolate, whisking until smooth. Refrigerate until thickened and chilled, about 1 hour. Beat until soft peaks form. Cover and set aside.

CHOCOLATE CURLS: In heatproof bowl over saucepan of hot (not boiling) water, melt chocolate. Pour into foil-lined 5¾- x 3¼-inch (625 mL) loaf pan. Refrigerate until set, about 2 hours. Unmould; let stand for 10 minutes. Using sharp vegetable peeler across narrow side, peel off curls; set aside on waxed paper–lined baking sheet.

Slice each cake layer in half horizontally. Brush each cut side with 2 tbsp of the cherry syrup; let stand for 5 minutes. Meanwhile, whip cream, remaining sugar and vanilla. Spoon one-quarter into large piping bag fitted with ¾-inch (2 cm) star tip. Place 1 cake layer on flat cake plate; spread with 1 cup of the mousse. Top with ¾ cup of the cherries. Repeat layers twice; top with remaining cake layer. Spread remaining whipped cream over top and side; pipe rosettes on top. Decorate with remaining cherries; gently press chocolate curls onto side. *(Make-ahead: Loosely cover with plastic wrap and refrigerate for up to 1 day.)*

Makes 16 servings. PER SERVING: about 625 cal, 6 g pro, 41 g total fat (25 g sat. fat), 63 g carb, 3 g fibre, 146 mg chol, 301 mg sodium. % RDI: 9% calcium, 15% iron, 38% vit A, 2% vit C, 15% folate.

English Similar to molasses, treacle is a beloved sweetener in Britain (see page 264 for more on these and other sweet syrups used in cooking). Treacle's lighter counterpart, golden syrup, is vital to a number of toothsome English cakes and tarts, including this deliciously sticky creation.

Treacle Tart

PÂTE SUCRÉE: In food processor, pulse together flour, sugar and salt; pulse in butter until in coarse crumbs with some larger pieces. Pulse in egg and egg yolk just until dough comes together. Press into disc; wrap and refrigerate until chilled, about 30 minutes.

On lightly floured surface, roll out pastry into 12-inch (30 cm) circle; fit in 9-inch (23 cm) round tart pan with removable bottom, pressing to inside edge and leaving overhang. Fold in overhang, pressing to rim.

With fork, prick bottom all over; refrigerate for 20 minutes. Line with foil; fill with pie weights or dried beans. Bake in bottom third of 400°F (200°C) oven for 20 minutes. Remove weights and foil; bake until centre is golden, about 5 minutes.

Meanwhile, remove lid of golden syrup. Place jar in small saucepan of gently simmering water and heat just until syrup is easily pourable.

In bowl, whisk together cream, egg and salt; stir in bread crumbs, lemon zest and lemon juice. Stir in golden syrup, butter and molasses. Pour into baked crust. Bake in 325°F (160°C) oven until centre is puffed and browned, 40 to 45 minutes. Let cool in pan on rack.

Makes 10 to 12 servings. PER EACH OF 12 SERVINGS: about 329 cal, 4 g pro, 16 g total fat (9 g sat. fat), 45 g carb, 1 g fibre, 89 mg chol, 196 mg sodium, 110 mg potassium. % RDI: 3% calcium, 9% iron, 14% vit A, 5% vit C, 22% folate.

1 jar **Lyle's Golden Syrup**

½ cup **whipping cream**

1 **egg**

¼ tsp **salt**

2½ cups **fresh bread crumbs**

2 tsp grated **lemon zest**

¼ cup **lemon juice**

3 tbsp **unsalted butter,** melted

2 tbsp **fancy molasses**

PÂTE SUCRÉE:

1½ cups **all-purpose flour**

3 tbsp **granulated sugar**

¼ tsp **salt**

½ cup **unsalted butter,** cubed

1 **egg**

1 **egg yolk**

English This uncomplicated cake, with the rich flavour of English toffee, stays amazingly moist for up to three days. Serve with just a dollop of whipped cream if you like.

Sticky Toffee Cake With Decadent Toffee Sauce

1 pkg (12 oz/375 g) **dried pitted dates** (about 2⅓ cups)

2½ cups **water**

1⅓ cups **granulated sugar**

½ cup **unsalted butter,** softened

1½ tsp grated **lemon zest**

½ tsp **salt**

4 **eggs**

1½ tsp **vanilla**

2¾ cups **all-purpose flour**

2 tsp **baking powder**

2 tsp **baking soda**

TOFFEE SAUCE:
¾ cup **unsalted butter**

1 cup **granulated sugar**

¾ cup **whipping cream**

2 tbsp **lemon juice**

Pinch **salt**

2 tbsp **brandy**

In saucepan, bring dates and water to boil; let cool. Mash until smooth; set aside.

In large bowl, beat together sugar, butter, lemon zest and salt until light; beat in eggs, 1 at a time. Beat in vanilla. Whisk together flour, baking powder and baking soda; stir into butter mixture. Stir in dates.

Scrape into greased 10-inch (4 L) tube pan or 10-inch (3 L) Bundt pan. Bake in bottom third of 350°F (180°C) oven until cake tester inserted in centre comes out clean, about 55 minutes. Let cool in pan on rack for 15 minutes; invert cake onto plate.

TOFFEE SAUCE: Meanwhile, in saucepan, melt butter over medium heat; whisk in sugar until dissolved. Cook, whisking, until caramel coloured, about 5 minutes. Averting face, whisk in cream, lemon juice and salt; bring to boil. Cook until thickened, 3 to 5 minutes. Whisk in brandy. Pour ¾ cup over warm cake; let stand to absorb.

To serve, slice cake; drizzle with remaining warm sauce.

Makes 12 to 16 servings. PER EACH OF 16 SERVINGS: about 437 cal, 5 g pro, 20 g total fat (12 g sat. fat), 62 g carb, 2 g fibre, 99 mg chol, 290 mg sodium, 196 mg potassium. % RDI: 4% calcium, 10% iron, 18% vit A, 2% vit C, 24% folate.

SWEET SYRUPS

Sweeteners take many forms around the globe. Sweet syrups are versatile ingredients in baking, dressings, marinades and more. Here are a few you'll need to create the recipes in this book.

MOLASSES

The types of molasses made in Canada are different than the ones that are available in the United States. Canada has fancy, cooking and blackstrap molasses; the U.S. has light, dark and blackstrap.

• **Fancy molasses** is the pure juice of sugar cane that has been condensed and purified. There are no additives or preservatives. It is used in baked goods, main dishes and straight from the container. It has the lightest flavour.

• **Cooking molasses** is a combination of fancy molasses and blackstrap molasses. It is used in dishes where a more pronounced molasses flavour is desired.

• **Blackstrap molasses** is the byproduct of sugar refining. This molasses is very dark, with a robust, bitter flavour. It is most often used in baked goods. It is also considered a health food, because it contains the minerals, vitamins and trace elements lost in the refining process of the other grades.

TREACLE AND GOLDEN SYRUP

Treacle is a syrup made during the refining of sugar cane. It's particularly popular in the United Kingdom. There are two types: **Dark treacle** is similar to molasses; **light treacle** is lighter in flavour than the dark. Light treacle is also called **golden syrup.**

POMEGRANATE MOLASSES

Not related to sugar cane molasses, **pomegranate molasses** is made by reducing pomegranate juice to a dark, thick syrup. Its sweet-sour taste is wonderful in dips and on grilled meats. Look for it in Middle Eastern markets.

English Named after the pretty town of Bakewell in Derbyshire, these almond-and-jam tarts are allegedly a local creation. No one can agree on their true origin, but they do agree that they're a scrumptious way to end a meal.

Mini Bakewell Tarts

On lightly floured surface, roll out dough to ⅛-inch (3 mm) thickness. Using 2½-inch (6 cm) fluted round cutter, cut out 24 circles.

Fit circles into 24 mini muffin cups. Line with foil or parchment paper; fill with pie weights or dried beans. Bake in 400°F (200°C) oven for 15 minutes. Remove foil and weights; bake for 10 minutes.

In bowl, beat butter with sugar until fluffy. Beat in egg and egg yolk until smooth. Stir in ground almonds and vanilla. Refrigerate for 20 minutes.

Spoon ½ tsp jam into each tart shell. Divide ground almond mixture evenly among tarts. Sprinkle with sliced almonds.

Bake in 375°F (190°C) oven until puffed and golden, about 20 minutes. Remove from pan; let cool on rack.

Makes 24 tarts. PER TART: about 146 cal, 2 g pro, 10 g total fat (5 g sat. fat), 13 g carb, 1 g fibre, 34 mg chol, 27 mg sodium, 46 mg potassium. % RDI: 1% calcium, 4% iron, 6% vit A, 8% folate.

All-Purpose Sweet Pie Dough
In bowl, whisk together 2½ cups all-purpose flour, 1 tsp granulated sugar and ½ tsp salt. Using pastry blender or 2 knives, cut in ⅔ cup cold unsalted butter, cubed, and ⅓ cup cold lard, cubed, until in coarse crumbs with a few larger pieces. Drizzle with ⅓ cup cold water, tossing with fork until ragged dough forms and adding up to 1 tbsp more water if necessary. Divide in half; press into discs. Wrap each and refrigerate until chilled, about 30 minutes. *(Make-ahead: Freeze wrapped discs in resealable freezer bag for up to 2 months. Thaw in refrigerator.)*
Makes enough for 1 double-crust 9-inch (23 cm) pie.

Half batch **All-Purpose Sweet Pie Dough** (recipe, below left)

½ cup **unsalted butter,** softened

½ cup **granulated sugar**

1 **egg**

1 **egg yolk**

¾ cup **ground almonds**

½ tsp **vanilla** or grated lemon zest

⅓ cup **strawberry jam** or raspberry jam

⅓ cup **sliced almonds**

English Saffron is said to have arrived in England with the Phoenicians, who traded it for Cornish tin. In the past, when ingredients such as eggs were expensive, saffron was used to give rich yellow colour to this breadlike cake.

Cornish Saffron Cake

¾ cup warm **milk**

½ tsp **saffron threads,** crumbled

¼ cup **granulated sugar**

½ cup **warm water**

1 pkg **active dry yeast** (2¼ tsp)

4 cups **all-purpose flour**

¼ tsp **salt**

⅔ cup **unsalted butter,** cubed

1 **egg,** beaten

¾ cup **dried currants**

¼ cup **candied mixed peel**

GLAZE:
1 tbsp **milk**

Stir milk with saffron; let stand for 10 minutes or up to 20 minutes.

Dissolve 1 tsp of the sugar in warm water. Sprinkle in yeast; let stand until frothy, about 10 minutes.

In large bowl, whisk together flour, remaining sugar and salt. With pastry blender or 2 knives, cut in butter until in crumbs with a few larger pieces. With wooden spoon, stir in yeast mixture, saffron mixture and egg to form soft dough.

Turn out onto floured surface; knead until smooth and elastic, 8 minutes. Place in greased bowl, turning to grease all over. Cover with plastic wrap; let rise in warm draft-free place until doubled in bulk, 1 hour.

Punch down dough; knead in currants and mixed peel. Divide in half; knead each into ball. Cover with tea towel; let rest for 5 minutes.

Press each half into 12- x 8-inch (30 x 20 cm) rectangle. Starting at narrow end, roll up into cylinder; pinch along bottom to smooth and seal. Fit into 2 greased then parchment paper–lined 8- x 4-inch (1.5 L) loaf pans. Cover loosely; let rise until ½ inch (1 cm) above rim and dough does not spring back when lightly pressed, about 1 hour.

GLAZE: Brush tops with milk. Bake in centre of 350°F (180°C) oven until golden and cakes sound hollow when tapped on bottoms, about 45 minutes. Remove from pans; let cool on racks.

Makes 2 cakes, or 12 servings each. PER SERVING: about 156 cal, 3 g pro, 6 g total fat (3 g sat. fat), 24 g carb, 1 g fibre, 22 mg chol, 33 mg sodium. % RDI: 2% calcium, 9% iron, 5% vit A, 24% folate.

Variation
BREAD MACHINE CORNISH SAFFRON CAKE (DOUGH ONLY): Stir milk with saffron; let stand for 10 minutes. Into pan of bread machine, add (in order) water, saffron mixture, sugar, salt, egg, butter, flour and yeast. Choose dough setting. Turn out dough and knead in currants and mixed peel. Continue with recipe.

Guyanese Not for the faint of heart, this dark, rich cake is laden with fruit and soaked with rum in the Caribbean tradition. It's a decidedly grown-up indulgence.

Guide Cake

In food processor, pulse together raisins, currants, prunes and mixed peel until smooth thick paste forms. Transfer to large bowl or jar; stir in 2 cups of the rum. Cover and keep in cold dark place, stirring once daily and adding more rum as needed to keep top of fruit covered, for 3 days or up to 2 months.

In small heavy saucepan, melt ½ cup of the brown sugar over medium heat, stirring; boil for 1 minute. Pour into fruit mixture, stirring to break up solidified sugar.

In large bowl, beat butter with remaining sugar until smooth; beat in eggs, 1 at a time. Beat in almond extract. Whisk together flour, almonds, baking powder, cinnamon, cloves, nutmeg and salt; stir into butter mixture in 2 additions. Stir in raisin mixture and glacé cherries.

Scrape into 9-inch (2.5 L) springform pan lined with double-thickness parchment paper; smooth top. Bake on baking sheet in 300°F (150°C) oven until cake comes away from side of pan, about 3 hours, covering with foil during last hour if necessary to prevent overbrowning.

Using skewer, poke holes in top of cake; brush with remaining ½ cup of the rum. Let cool in pan for 24 hours. *(Make-ahead: Store in airtight container for up to 3 months.)*

Makes 20 servings. PER SERVING: about 362 cal, 4 g pro, 12 g total fat (6 g sat. fat), 64 g carb, 3 g fibre, 52 mg chol, 106 mg sodium, 424 mg potassium. % RDI: 6% calcium, 14% iron, 10% vit A, 2% vit C, 15% folate.

1¾ cups **raisins**

1¾ cups **dried currants**

1½ cups pitted **prunes**

½ cup **candied mixed peel**

2½ cups **rum** (approx)

1¾ cups packed **brown sugar**

1 cup **butter,** softened

3 **eggs**

½ tsp **almond extract**

2 cups **all-purpose flour**

½ cup chopped **almonds**

1 tsp **baking powder**

¼ tsp **cinnamon**

¼ tsp **ground cloves**

¼ tsp **nutmeg**

Pinch **salt**

½ cup chopped **red glacé cherries**

TIP | IF YOU'RE IN A RUSH FOR THIS CAKE, IT'S QUITE TASTY AFTER THE 24-HOUR COOLING PERIOD. BUT IF YOU CAN HOLD OFF, THE CAKE MELLOWS AND DEVELOPS AN EVEN RICHER FLAVOUR AS IT AGES.

Caribbean This dessert is a tribute to the many fruit desserts created in the islands of the Caribbean. Serve with whipped cream spiked with rum.

Tropical Fruit Pudding

2 **mangoes**

1 **golden pineapple**

2 tbsp **granulated sugar**

2 tbsp **dark rum**

2 tbsp **lime juice**

1 cup **pineapple juice**

1 tbsp **icing sugar**

CAKE TOPPING:
4 **eggs,** separated

1 cup **granulated sugar**

¾ cup **all-purpose flour**

2 tbsp **dark rum**

1 tbsp grated **lime zest**

¼ tsp **salt**

Cut off mango flesh from each side of pits. Cut grid pattern of ¾-inch (2 cm) squares in flesh down to but not through skin. Gently push skin to turn inside out; cut off flesh and place in greased 13- x 9-inch (3 L) baking dish. Cut off rind of pineapple; trim, quarter, core and cut pineapple into bite-size cubes. Add to mangoes along with granulated sugar, rum and lime juice; toss to combine. Set aside.

CAKE TOPPING: In bowl, beat egg whites until soft peaks form. Beat in ⅓ cup of the sugar, 1 tbsp at a time, until stiff glossy peaks form. In separate bowl, beat egg yolks with remaining sugar until pale; stir in flour, rum, lime zest and salt. Whisk in one-quarter of the whites; fold in remainder.

Scrape topping over fruit; spread evenly. Pour pineapple juice over top.

Bake in 350°F (180°C) oven until cake tester inserted in centre comes out clean, about 50 minutes. Let cool in pan on rack for 1 hour.

Dust with icing sugar. Serve warm.

Makes 8 servings. PER SERVING: about 279 cal, 5 g pro, 3 g total fat (1 g sat. fat), 60 g carb, 2 g fibre, 93 mg chol, 105 mg sodium. % RDI: 3% calcium, 9% iron, 20% vit A, 68% vit C, 18% folate.

Latin American Flan, a light baked egg custard topped with delicious caramel syrup, is a popular dessert in Latin America – especially Mexico – and in Spain, where it originated.

Caramel Citrus Flan

½ cup **granulated sugar**

CUSTARD:
4 cups **milk**
½ cup **granulated sugar**
Pinch **salt**
2 strips **orange zest**
2 strips **lime zest**
4 **eggs**
6 **egg yolks**
2 tsp **vanilla**

In small heavy saucepan, stir sugar with 2 tbsp water over medium heat until dissolved. Bring to boil over medium-high heat; boil vigorously, without stirring but brushing down side of pan often, until amber coloured, about 3 minutes. Immediately pour into flan mould or 6-cup (1.5 L) baking dish.

CUSTARD: In clean saucepan, heat milk until tiny bubbles form around edge. Add sugar and salt; simmer, stirring occasionally, until milk mixture is reduced to 3½ cups, about 15 minutes. Remove from heat. Add orange zest and lime zest; cover and let stand for 5 minutes.

In bowl, whisk eggs with egg yolks; gradually pour in milk mixture through cheesecloth-lined sieve, whisking constantly. Whisk in vanilla. Pour into caramel-coated mould.

Place mould in larger roasting pan; pour enough hot water into pan to come halfway up side of mould. Bake in 350°F (180°C) oven until firm and knife inserted in centre comes out clean, 45 to 60 minutes.

Let cool in water in roasting pan until at room temperature. Remove from water and refrigerate until chilled. *(Make-ahead: Cover and refrigerate for up to 24 hours.)*

Place mould in larger pan of hot water until syrup loosens. Run knife around edge of mould; invert onto serving platter.

Makes 8 servings. PER SERVING: about 240 cal, 9 g pro, 9 g total fat (3 g sat. fat), 31 g carb, trace fibre, 255 mg chol, 86 mg sodium. % RDI: 16% calcium, 6% iron, 16% vit A, 3% vit C, 16% folate.

South American   This sensational dessert features delicious dulce de leche, a South American sauce made by caramelizing evaporated milk. The Mexican version, called cajeta, is made with goat's milk rather than cow's milk. It's also a treat over ice cream.

Dulce de Leche Cream Cake

In large bowl, beat butter with sugar until light and fluffy; beat in eggs, 1 at a time. Beat in almond extract.

Whisk flour, baking powder, baking soda and salt; stir into butter mixture alternately with milk, making 3 additions of flour mixture and 2 of milk. Scrape into parchment paper–lined 8-inch (2 L) square cake pan.

Bake in 350°F (180°C) oven until cake tester inserted in centre comes out clean, about 40 minutes. Let cool in pan on rack. *(Make-ahead: Cover and store for up to 1 day.)* On cutting board, cut cake in half horizontally; without separating layers, cut into 9 pieces.

In bowl, whip cream; fold in ¼ cup of the dulce de leche.

Spoon 1 tbsp of the remaining dulce de leche onto centre of each serving plate; top with bottom slice of cake. Top each with 1 tbsp of the dulce de leche and 2 tbsp of the whipped cream mixture. Cover with top slice of cake; dollop 1 tbsp each of the dulce de leche and whipped cream mixture on top. Sprinkle with almonds.

Makes 9 servings. PER SERVING: about 632 cal, 13 g pro, 31 g total fat (17 g sat. fat), 78 g carb, 2 g fibre, 93 mg chol, 430 mg sodium. % RDI: 30% calcium, 11% iron, 32% vit A, 10% vit C, 17% folate.

Dulce de Leche

In large heavy saucepan, bring 2 cans (each 385 mL) 2% evaporated milk and 1¼ cups milk to boil. Whisk together ½ cup milk, 4 tsp cornstarch and ½ tsp baking soda. Add to pan; reduce heat to low and bring to simmer. Meanwhile, in large stockpot, stir 1½ cups granulated sugar with 1 cup water over medium heat until dissolved, brushing down side of saucepan with brush dipped in cold water. Bring to boil; boil, without stirring but brushing down side of pan often, until light golden, about 25 minutes. Remove from heat. Averting face, slowly strain milk mixture into caramel, whisking constantly. Simmer, stirring, until dark golden and thick, 1½ to 2 hours. Strain if necessary; let cool. *(Make-ahead: Refrigerate for up to 6 months.)* **Makes about 2 cups.**

½ cup **butter,** softened

1 cup **granulated sugar**

2 **eggs**

½ tsp **almond extract**

1½ cups **all-purpose flour**

1½ tsp **baking powder**

¼ tsp **baking soda**

¼ tsp **salt**

⅔ cup **milk**

1½ cups **whipping cream**

2 cups **dulce de leche** (recipe, below left)

¾ cup **sliced almonds,** toasted

Latin American These tender, shortbread-like sandwich cookies, filled with creamy dulce de leche, are popular in South and Central America. You can make the dulce de leche yourself or buy it in jars in your local supermarket.

Mini Alfajores

In bowl, rub superfine sugar with lemon zest between fingers until fragrant. Beat in butter until light and fluffy; beat in egg yolks, 1 at a time. Beat in vanilla.

Whisk together flour, cornstarch, baking powder, baking soda and salt; stir into butter mixture to make soft dough. Divide in half; wrap each and refrigerate for 1 hour.

On lightly floured surface or between waxed paper, roll out dough to scant ¼-inch (5 mm) thickness. Using 1½-inch (4 cm) round cutter, cut out circles to make 56 pieces, rerolling scraps.

Place, 1 inch (2.5 cm) apart, on parchment paper–lined baking sheets. Bake in 350°F (180°C) oven until golden, about 9 minutes. Let cool on pans on racks.

Spread bottoms of half of the cookies with ½ tsp dulce de leche each. Sandwich each with another cookie, top side up. Roll edges in coconut. Dust tops with icing sugar. Let stand until set, about 1 hour. *(Make-ahead: Store in airtight container for up to 24 hours.)*

Makes 28 cookies. PER COOKIE: about 88 cal, 1 g pro, 5 g total fat (3 g sat. fat), 11 g carb, trace fibre, 24 mg chol, 42 mg sodium, 13 mg potassium. % RDI: 1% calcium, 2% iron, 4% vit A, 6% folate.

⅓ cup **superfine sugar**

½ tsp grated **lemon zest**

½ cup **unsalted butter,** softened

2 **egg yolks**

½ tsp **vanilla**

1¼ cups **all-purpose flour**

¼ cup **cornstarch**

½ tsp **baking powder**

¼ tsp **baking soda**

¼ tsp **salt**

⅓ cup **dulce de leche** (recipe, page 271)

¼ cup **unsweetened desiccated coconut**

2 tbsp **icing sugar**

Brazilian These candy treats are said to be named after a brigadier general. They look like truffles but are made with sweetened condensed milk, which is a South American pantry staple.

Brigadeiros

3 tbsp **cocoa powder,** sifted

1 can (300 mL) **sweetened condensed milk**

1 tbsp **unsalted butter**

½ cup **chocolate sprinkles**

In small bowl, stir cocoa powder with ¼ cup of the condensed milk until smooth. Stir in remaining condensed milk.

In small saucepan, melt butter over medium heat. Using heatproof spatula, stir in milk mixture; cook, stirring constantly and scraping bottom of pan to prevent scorching, until thickened and glossy, and mixture holds wide trail after spatula is pulled through centre, 12 to 14 minutes. Immediately scrape into buttered shallow dish. Let cool enough to handle, about 20 minutes.

With well-buttered hands, roll by 1 tsp into balls. Immediately roll each in chocolate sprinkles. *(Make-ahead: Store between waxed paper in airtight container for up to 24 hours.)* Nestle into paper candy cup, if desired.

Makes 36 pieces. PER PIECE: about 46 cal, 1 g pro, 1 g total fat (1 g sat. fat), 8 g carb, trace fibre, 5 mg chol, 14 mg sodium, 52 mg potassium. % RDI: 3% calcium, 1% iron, 1% vit A.

Mexican Originally from Spain, these deep-fried lengths of choux-type pastry are coated in sugar and sold warm by street vendors. Mexican churros are firm and dry, but this at-home version is easier to pipe. Serve them with the traditional accompaniment, Mexican Hot Chocolate (below).

Churros

TOPPING: In shallow dish, mix sugar with cinnamon; set aside.

In saucepan, bring water, sugar and salt to boil over medium-high heat. Stir in flour all at once; cook, stirring, until dough forms ball and thin film forms on bottom of pan, 3 to 5 minutes.

Transfer to stand mixer with paddle attachment; beat for 30 seconds to cool slightly. On medium speed, beat in eggs, scraping down side, just until stiff dough forms, about 2 minutes. Beat in baking powder.

Spoon dough into piping bag fitted with ½-inch (1 cm) star tip. Pipe 6-inch (15 cm) lengths of dough onto lightly floured surface.

Meanwhile, in wide shallow saucepan, heat 2 inches (5 cm) oil until deep-fry thermometer registers 375°F (190°C). Fry churros, 3 at a time and turning once, until golden and puffed, 4 to 5 minutes. With tongs, transfer to paper towel–lined plate to drain. While still hot, roll in topping

Makes about 18 pieces. PER PIECE: about 134 cal, 2 g pro, 8 g total fat (1 g sat. fat), 13 g carb, trace fibre, 21 mg chol, 88 mg sodium. % RDI: 1% calcium, 4% iron, 1% vit A, 12% folate.

Mexican Hot Chocolate

In heatproof bowl over saucepan of hot (not boiling) water, melt 4 oz (115 g) unsweetened chocolate, chopped. In saucepan, combine 4 cups milk, ½ cup granulated sugar, ½ tsp cinnamon, pinch salt and melted chocolate; heat over medium-low heat, whisking, until smooth and hot, about 5 minutes. Stir in ½ tsp vanilla and dash almond extract. Whisk vigorously with whisk or immersion blender with whisk attachment until foamy. Serve immediately. **Makes 4 servings.**

1½ cups **water**

1 tbsp **granulated sugar**

½ tsp **salt**

1¾ cups **all-purpose flour**

2 **eggs,** lightly beaten

1 tsp **baking powder**

Oil for frying (canola, safflower or vegetable)

TOPPING:
½ cup **granulated sugar**

¼ tsp **cinnamon**

Japanese This soft golden cake, called kasutera or castella, is a specialty of Nagasaki, introduced by the Portuguese merchants who once traded there. Nowadays, it's often given as a gift, and the slices are often enjoyed with a cup of green tea.

Honey Sponge Cake

5 **eggs**

Pinch **salt**

Pinch **cream of tartar**

¼ cup **liquid honey**

½ cup **granulated sugar**

½ tsp grated **orange zest**

¾ cup **all-purpose flour**

¾ tsp **baking powder**

Icing sugar (optional)

Place eggs in warm water; let stand for 10 minutes.

In stand mixer on medium-high speed or in large bowl with hand mixer on high speed, beat eggs, salt and cream of tartar until foamy. Beat in honey. Gradually beat in sugar until thickened and pale yellow, about 10 minutes. Beat in orange zest.

Sift flour with baking powder over egg mixture; gently fold in. Scrape into parchment paper–lined 8-inch (2 L) square cake pan.

Bake in 350°F (180°C) oven until tester inserted in centre comes out clean, about 25 minutes. Let cool in pan on rack for 10 minutes. Remove from pan; peel off paper. Let cool on rack. (Cake will sink slightly in centre as it cools.)

Dust with icing sugar, if desired. *(Make-ahead: Wrap in plastic wrap and store for up to 24 hours.)*

Makes 8 servings. PER SERVING: about 168 cal, 5 g pro, 3 g total fat (1 g sat. fat), 31 g carb, trace fibre, 116 mg chol, 67 mg sodium, 58 mg potassium. % RDI: 3% calcium, 7% iron, 4% vit A, 18% folate.

{acknowledgments}

The team that created this book – whether they were Test Kitchen staff, editors, designers, stylists or photographers – dove into this project with relish, eager to represent a Canadian version of the international culinary experiences they remembered from their childhoods, native countries or travels. And their passion comes through on each mouthwatering page.

First, many thanks to The Canadian Living Test Kitchen staff – present and past – who used their considerable talents to create and test the recipes in this book. Alison Kent compiled a dauntingly long list of ethnic recipes from our repertoire, which food director Annabelle Waugh helped me pare down into this collection. Where there were gaps in the lineup, longtime contributor and chef Andrew Chase stepped in to help create delicious new dishes that showcase global flavours without sending you to a bunch of stores for hard-to-find ingredients.

Thanks next to our delightful design team, Chris Bond and Michael Erb, for their loving attention to all the details that make this book so beautiful. Chris's thoughtful interior design makes the pictures and the text sing in perfect harmony. I'm also grateful to Pat Flynn, who cheerfully assembled hundreds of photo and text files at the beginning of the project.

A full list of the talented photographers and stylists who created the images in this book is on page 287. Special thanks go to Felix Wedgwood, Nicole Young and Genevieve Wiseman, who shot, food-styled and propped (respectively) an array of new images specifically for this project. Their good humour and expertise made for a fun, fulfilling experience.

Keeping her eyes peeled for errors or inconsistencies of any kind was our talented copy editor, Jill Buchner. Thanks to her and to indexer Gillian Watts for their hard, meticulous work.

Another big thank-you goes to the editor and publishers behind this book. *Canadian Living* editor-in-chief Susan Antonacci, *Canadian Living* publisher Lynn Chambers and Transcontinental Books publisher Jean Paré all gave an enthusiastic green light to the project and supported us throughout the creation process.

Promoting and distributing this collection out in the real world is the team at Random House Canada, including Janet Joy Wilson, Duncan Shields and Adria Iwasutiak. Thanks to them for bringing this book to passionate cooks across Canada and the United States.

To all these people – and many others who weren't mentioned by name but contributed their time and expertise nonetheless – thank you. Gracias. Merci. Danke. Xie xie. Tak. Obrigada.

– *Christina Anson Mine, project editor*

RECIPES

All recipes developed by The Canadian Living Test Kitchen, except the following.
Andrew Chase: pages 24, 84, 85, 130, 131, 132, 162, 163, 168 (courtesy of *Homemakers* Magazine), 178, 189, 199, 223, 254 (courtesy of *Homemakers* Magazine) and 258.

PHOTOGRAPHY

Michael Alberstat: pages 82 and 243.
Christopher Campbell: pages 108 (steps) and 209 (steps).
Hasnain Dattu: page 203.
Yvonne Duivenvoorden: pages 2, 11, 12, 22, 32, 42, 45, 56, 59 (steps), 61, 71, 72, 98, 108 (main), 111, 114, 151, 159, 160, 173, 195 (main), 209 (main), 221, 227, 236, 244, 247, 250 (main), 256, 263, 269, 272, 275, 276 and 279.
Geoff George: page 5.
Jim Norton: pages 78 and 182.
Edward Pond: pages 36, 50, 92 (steps), 95, 137, 185, 195 (steps) and 250 (steps).
Jodi Pudge: pages 81, 89, 170, 174 and 235.
David Scott: pages 75 and 92 (main).
Ryan Szulc: page 216.
Felix Wedgwood: pages 4, 7, 8, 9, 15, 19, 25, 35, 39, 55, 59 (background), 64, 65, 105, 116, 117, 121, 124, 129, 134, 138, 141, 145, 146, 147, 165, 172, 188, 190, 191, 192, 198, 204, 205, 215, 222, 232, 238, 239, 248, 255, 264 and 288.

FOOD STYLING

Julie Aldis: pages 72 and 209 (main).
Donna Bartolini: pages 203, 227 and 269.
Andrew Chase: pages 137 and 216.
Heather Howe: pages 92 (steps), 95, 108 (steps), 195 (steps), 209 (steps) and 250 (steps).
Lucie Richard: pages 42, 50, 56, 59 (steps), 61, 92 (main), 108 (main), 111, 151, 159, 160, 173, 174, 195 (main) and 244.
Claire Stancer: pages 12, 71, 82, 243, 247, 250 (main), 256 and 276.
Claire Stubbs: pages 2, 11, 22, 32, 36, 45, 75, 78, 81, 89, 98, 105, 114, 170, 182, 185, 221, 235, 236, 263, 272, 275 and 279.
Nicole Young: pages 4, 8, 9, 15, 25, 39, 55, 64, 65, 116, 117, 121, 124, 129, 138, 141, 146, 147, 165, 172, 188, 190, 191, 192, 198, 204, 205, 215, 222, 238, 239 and 255.

PROP STYLING

Martine Blackhurst: page 105.
Laura Branson: pages 111, 159, 236 and 279.
Catherine Doherty: pages 50, 170, 174, 185, 195 (main), 235, 247 and 256.
Marc-Philippe Gagné: page 209 (main).
Madeleine Johari: page 216.
Chareen Parsons: pages 82 and 243.
Oksana Slavutych: pages 11, 12, 22, 32, 36, 42, 45, 56, 59 (steps), 61, 71, 72, 75, 81, 89, 92 (main), 98, 108 (main), 114, 160, 173, 203, 221, 227, 244, 250 (main), 263, 269 and 276.
Genevieve Wiseman: pages 2, 4, 8, 9, 15, 25, 39, 55, 64, 65, 78, 116, 117, 121, 124, 129, 138, 141, 146, 147, 151, 165, 172, 182, 188, 190, 191, 192, 198, 204, 205, 215, 222, 238, 239, 255, 272 and 275.

INTERNATIONAL MENUS

Here are just a few of the tasty menus you can make from the recipes in this book.

CARIBBEAN
Split Pea Fritters — 41
Salt Fish Cakes — 43
Island Grilled Chicken — 166
Cookup Rice — 142
Guide Cake — 267

CHINESE
Pork Dumplings — 58
Bok Choy, Mushroom
  and Tofu Soup — 76
Sweet and Spicy
  Cashew Chicken — 184
Steamed rice*
Sliced oranges and
  jasmine tea*

FRENCH
Alsatian-Style Fruit and
  Nut Bread — 104
Assorted cheeses*
Cassoulet — 205
Classic Tarte Tatin — 252

GREEK
Stuffed Vine Leaves — 20
Grilled Fish With
  Olive Oil — 161
Tomato and Feta Salad — 118
Roasted potatoes
  or rice*
Honey Nut Baklava Roll — 245

INDIAN
Spiced Lamb Samosas — 28
Spiced Chicken and
  Lentils — 179
Spinach with Ginger
  and Hot Pepper — 135
Basmati rice*
Chai Ice Cream — 249

ITALIAN
Tuscan Bean Soup — 66
Calabrese Potato
  Provolone Pizza — 153
Two-Tone Chocolate
  Espresso Panna Cotta — 241

JAPANESE
California Rolls — 54
Miso-Marinated
  Broiled Fish — 168
Steamed rice*
Honey Sponge Cake — 278

MOROCCAN
Harira — 73
Roast Leg of Lamb With
  Apricots, Almonds
  and Pine Nuts — 225
Fresh fruit, dates and
  mint tea*

PORTUGUESE
Clam Soup — 68
Roast Pork Loin — 210
Roasted potatoes*
Green salad*
Massa Sovada — 106

SOUTH AMERICAN
Empanadas — 48
Grilled Marinated
  Flank Steak — 167
Grilled Marinated Quail — 228
Green salad*
Dulce de Leche
  Cream Cake — 271

SPANISH
Rosemary Shrimp
  in Sherry — 16
Classic Gazpacho — 84
Party Paella — 202
Caramel Citrus Flan — 270

THAI
Squash and Coconut
  Soup With Shrimp — 83
Pad Thai — 175
Green Mango Salad — 123
Fresh fruit and
  jasmine tea*

Recipe not included

{menus}